A NEW CENTURY OF
HEROES

A NEW CENTURY OF HEROES

Edited by

ERIC P. ZAHREN

LYONS PRESS

Essex, Connecticut

Certain case information accompanies the names of
Carnegie Medal awardees appearing in this book:

C. H.   **CARNEGIE HEROES** are ordered numerically in the Hero Fund's archives. In accounts of rescues involving multiple awardees, the award numbers are listed in the order of the awardees' appearance in the narrative.

‡   This symbol alongside an award number signifies that the rescuer lost his or her life. Historically, one in five awardees was recognized posthumously.

FILE NO.   Every individual considered for the Carnegie Medal receives a file number upon nomination. Traditionally, only one in 10 nominees is selected for recognition.

An imprint of Globe Pequot, the trade division of
The Rowman & Littlefield Publishing Group, Inc.
4501 Forbes Blvd., Ste. 200
Lanham, MD 20706
www.rowman.com

Distributed by NATIONAL BOOK NETWORK

British Library Cataloguing in Publication Information available

Library of Congress Cataloging-in-Publication Data Available

ISBN 9781493070961 (cloth) | ISBN 9781493070978 (epub)

Printed in India

*Dedicated to the 10,000 individuals
awarded the Carnegie Medal, to the next 10,000 individuals
and beyond who will be honored in years to come,
and to the legacy of Andrew Carnegie,
whose idea and gift made possible
the recognition of selfless acts of heroism.*

CONTENTS

MARK LASKOW, CHAIR EMERITUS

If ever a story needed no introduction, it is the story of a Carnegie hero. The deeds of each hero electrify the reader at a gut level. Read these stories and you will appreciate, without any assistance from me, the moral strength and courage each rescuer demonstrated in the face of terrifying risks. These are great tales of great deeds by great heroes. But the heroes' acts don't just thrill us, they also serve a more serious function: They teach us about the nature of our relationship with our fellow human beings. What do we have in common with strangers outside our family, our ethnic group, our religion, or even our clubs and associations? What do we share with these people? What obligations do we owe them? The deeds of our heroes speak to these questions.

I think when Andrew Carnegie created the Hero Fund in 1904, he intended to both discover these great deeds and bring their stories to us. And just as he hoped, the Fund has brought well-deserved recognition and support to the Carnegie Medal awardees and generated admiration for their deeds. But I am convinced that Carnegie also intended more than that: He meant to inspire us and make *us* better for having learned the legacy of the Carnegie heroes.

The Hero Fund was part of a massive effort by Andrew Carnegie more than a century ago to build a series of organizations, in North America and Europe, that he intended to do nothing less than to make the world a better place. That was an ambitious goal, but he was an ambitious man. His building materials were money and ideas. He built well.

Today, of the 24 organizations he created and endowed, more than 20 remain alive and hard at work. Carnegie's money was important to the project, of course, but his ideas were even more important. His ideas were powerful enough that more than a century later they continue to attract professionals and volunteers alike to pursue them with all the zeal and imagination that Carnegie hoped for at the start of his great project.

I'd like to explain not only how the Hero Fund seems to differ from most of Carnegie's grand projects, but also how, on a deeper level, it is very much part of his broad effort to build a better society.

Andrew Carnegie was a man of big ideas, and a lot of them. Many of the organizations he created reflect that: the Carnegie Endowment for International Peace, the Carnegie United Kingdom Trust, the Carnegie Institution for Science, the Carnegie Council for Ethics in International Affairs, the Carnegie Trust for the Universities of Scotland, the Peace Palace at The Hague, Carnegie Mellon University, and of course, the Carnegie Corporation of New York. These organizations deal with the broadest and most significant problems that confront humanity, and their work can affect entire populations. Indeed, some of them shape our very view of what it means to be a human and our understanding of the universe in which we live. When Carnegie created his hero funds in North America and Europe, he was working at the other end of the spectrum: He designed them to focus on some of the most personal, intimate decisions an individual can face. That is, to decide in an instant whether to risk your own self to help another person in danger. Sometimes this kind of event occurs in physical isolation, in the wilderness, or along a vacant beach. Sometimes when an emergency arises there is a crowd around, but still, the pressure of the emergency and the peril to the victim leave little time for analysis, much less reflection or consultation. Our heroes, including each of the ones you will meet in this *New Century of Heroes*, have this in common. In that moment of peril, each said, "I will." And then each one acted, and each one put it all on the line.

The decisions of our heroes may have been solitary, but their decisions had wide consequences. First, of course, there were profound implications for their own families and for the families of the victims they sought to rescue. When a Carnegie hero dies in a rescue attempt, his whole family is deeply affected, as are the families of the victims who survive. Even unsuccessful rescues can have a deep impact. My Hero Fund colleague Sybil Veeder has observed that even unsuccessful rescues are meaningful to those involved. Carnegie Medal awardee JIMMY RHODES walked through a pool of fire to pull pilot Patrick Mahany from the wreckage of his crashed helicopter. Sadly, Mr. Mahany died from his injuries, but, nevertheless, Jimmy Rhodes accomplished this: When Patrick Mahany died, he knew he wasn't alone, that a stranger so valued him as a human being that the stranger walked through fire to try to bring him back to his family. Jimmy Rhodes accomplished a lot that day.

It is also clear to me that these heroic acts have a broader importance for us all, for our culture, and for our civilization.

America, and similarly Canada, are interesting countries in that they are not bound by ties of common ancestry. Instead, we are bound together by a set of ideas and values set forth in our founding documents. In the 1858 Lincoln–Douglas debates, Lincoln noted that, because of immigration, at the time of the debate about half of the population was no longer "descended by blood from our ancestors." The newcomers couldn't feel bound to the whole through blood lineage, but they could find a binding tie in the words of the founders in the Declaration of Independence: "We hold these truths to be self-evident, that all men are created equal." Lincoln believed that through these words recent immigrants could claim to be "blood of the blood, flesh of the flesh" with the founders. Those are Lincoln's words, and they are powerful.

The actions of our Carnegie heroes are equally powerful. They are living proof of that central principle that binds us. Think about what happens when a potential rescuer sees danger threatening another human being. In that instant of peril, the rescuer recognizes that they and the victim in danger share an equal right to life. And then the rescuer acts, steps forward, and shares that peril. One in five of our awardees has died in the attempt, a high price to pay for strangers. And they are mostly strangers, who are no part of the rescuer's own family or "tribe." Their actions were the ultimate demonstration that all men and women, family, friends, and strangers alike, are equally entitled to life, liberty, and the pursuit of happiness. Noble words are important, but these heroic deeds transcend words.

One of our relative strengths in the world today is that we have been as good as any country at welcoming strangers to our culture and values, even when many of the newcomers keep ties to their old cultures as well. Lately, though, our ability to assimilate newcomers has come under pressure on two fronts. First, our immigrants are more diverse. Lincoln spoke in his debate of German, Irish, French, and Scandinavian immigrants: That's what diversity looked like in 1858. Today we are receiving many people from the Middle East, Africa, and South Asia, representing a greater dichotomy between cultures. Those cultural differences might make it harder to unite as one body, but what helps pave the way is the manner in which ordinary Americans help each other across ethnic, religious, and social lines.

Americans of great and ordinary wealth give prodigiously to help others: The Carnegie Corporation of New York, the Ford Foundation, or, in grass roots philanthropy, the United Negro College Fund or the Jimmy Fund at Dana-Farber Cancer Institute. These newcomers can also see the individual actions of our heroes. They see an **A.R. Johnson** rescue Wen Ting Huang from assault by an assailant wielding an eight-inch meat cleaver. They see a **Wesley James Autrey** shield Cameron Hollopeter beneath an onrushing New York City subway train. They see a **Timothy E. Mosher** rescue Mana Mashoon from a knife attack.

This pattern goes all the way back to the Harwick Mine disaster that specifically inspired Carnegie to create the Hero Fund. A mining engineer, Selwyn Taylor, and coal miner Daniel Lyle, the rescuers who inspired Carnegie, were sons of the British Isles, but they died trying to rescue Hungarians, Poles, Italians, Swedes, and others.

These acts by our Carnegie heroes help us understand a debate that simmers in our society. What is more important, the common humanity that binds us or the characteristics that separate us? Normally only academics or politicians get tangled up in a debate like this. Ordinary people have little trouble going straight to the right answer. The answer to the question does have practical implications, though. Suppose you were the victim of some calamity—a car wreck, fire, assault, or water accident—and found yourself in mortal peril, very much in need of a rescuer willing to risk their life for you. How sad for you if the pool of potential rescuers was limited to a particular subgroup of people who only look like you! Happily, our Carnegie heroes followed the other path, and not just with words but with action. They recognized the common humanity they shared with a stranger not of their clan or tribe. They risked their very selves acting on that belief. I submit that these actions, far from the TV talk shows or faculty lounges, are the best evidence of our relationship with each other.

Andrew Carnegie, of course, was way ahead of us on all this. When he created the Hero Fund, he laid on us the direction that "The Hero Fund is to become the recognized agency, watching, applauding, and supporting where support is needed, heroic action wherever displayed and by whomever displayed—White or Black, Male or Female—or at least this is my hope." The Hero Fund acted accordingly and not long after its founding awarded the Carnegie Medal to a Black rescuer, realities of the challenges of both Carnegie's and our own world in 1907. Carnegie's instructions were consistent with his broader philanthropy, such as his major support for Booker T. Washington and his Tuskegee Institute. Would Carnegie's actions have put him in the vanguard of the Civil Rights Movement? I don't know, but it is crystal clear that Carnegie, too, saw the common humanity that bound us.

TEN THOUSAND RECIPIENTS

Consider **Vickie Tillman**. Ms. Tillman was driving to church one Sunday morning when she saw two men struggling on the side of the road. A police officer was struggling with a suspect who was on the officer's back, trying to get his gun out of the holster. Both men were white. It would have been easy for Ms. Tillman, a five-foot, two-inch, 56-year-old Black woman, to keep on driving down that road to her church. No one would have known, and even if someone did, who would have criticized her? But Vickie Tillman decided something was wrong, and she pulled over. The officer, Deputy Sheriff Billy Aime, asked her to call 911, which she did. Most of us would agree that at that point, she had done her civic duty and then some. This was not enough for Vickie Tillman. She jumped on the attacker, got her hand on the attacker's hand and the gun, and held on until help arrived. To give you an idea what Tillman and Aime were up against, the arriving officers stunned the attacker several times "without effect." For Deputy Billy Aime, Vickie Tillman's heroism meant he survived to be the one who presented her with the 10,000th Carnegie Hero Medal.

Now, are our heroes "outliers"? Was Vickie Tillman an "outlier"? Of course, that's why we give them the Carnegie Medal! But these "outliers" and their extraordinary actions are a challenge to all of us to conduct our everyday dealings with our fellow citizens on the same moral basis. The values of heroism and altruism that shine through their heroic acts are important threads in the fabric of our culture. The Hero Fund is determined to add the stories of these heroes to our national discussion about who we really are. That is why you hold this book in your hands.

Mark Laskow
Chair Emeritus
Pittsburgh, Pennsylvania
2023

These words were written by Andrew Carnegie in 1886 in honor of a young Scottish lad, William Hunter, who lost his life attempting to save a young boy from drowning in the town loch. These words gave life to a movement, in support of an idea that one individual, acting selflessly in behalf of another, can in itself not only save a life, but give life to hope for our future and the world.

Eighteen years after these words found their place on a memorial stone in Dunfermline, Scotland, they leapt again from Carnegie's consciousness to light a flame that still burns brightly in the work of the Carnegie Hero Fund—the body he created to ensure that those who risk, or lose, their lives through selfless action in behalf of others should be recognized, honored, and kept from further harm.

There is much evidence that the Hero Fund that Carnegie created, and those that would follow in distant lands, was especially dear to Carnegie's heart. More than that, it's strongly suggested that none of Carnegie's other creations so intimately express his private, inner self. The hero funds were expressions of the deep empathy and respect Carnegie felt for our society's heroes—those who would choose to put another's life before their own welfare. There was no profit to be gained from it (unlike the business world that occupied Carnegie earlier in life), no logic to drive it, and scant witnesses to applaud it. And yet, to Carnegie, it was the selfless actions of one individual in one moment in time that surpassed in purity and value all of the world's wealth, with which he was more intimately familiar than most.

Carnegie called the Hero Fund his "pet child." He alone conceived of it; his only collaborators were the muses of respect and compassion. Calling the Hero Fund, "the noblest fund in the world," he closely followed, and on occasion interjected into, its work throughout the rest of his life, to ensure that the capable men to whom he personally entrusted his pet child continued to recognize and support the hero, and widow, and orphan . . . so that they not suffer.

But it is important to remember that which gives the work of honoring heroes wings to fly: hope. Hope pushes this work beyond the here and now, beyond the scene of life-threatening chaos, across continents and even time itself. In spite of the realities of the challenges of both Carnegie's and our own world, hope is born through the glorious meeting of courage and the ultimate respect for another human being, regardless of cost. If applied over and over again, by countless individuals . . . by communities, by nations, by civilizations . . . it can only create peace among us. Hate, violence, intolerance—even war itself—cannot, by definition, exist in such an environment of universal individual selflessness. If we were to apply extreme individual altruism to the exercise of Immanuel Kant's Categorical Imperative, specifically, "acting according to maxims that we would will to be universal law," what a world it would be!

The Hero Fund has presented more than 10,000 Carnegie Medals for heroism. This number, while significant enough in its own right, is but a fraction of the nominated cases, roughly 100,000, in the Commission's 119-year history. Now I ask you to consider that large number not as a whole or from the perspective of hindsight or from a distance, but rather as 100,000 points of peril, fear, pain, loss; the undetermined outcomes of 100,000 horrific scenes, where life and death hung in the balance. And consider those who stood their ground or rushed in, because they refused to walk away, because they refused to leave a victim without hope. And never forget those among them who never returned to the arms of those who loved them. And consider those who were able to get home but bore scars both seen and unseen.

Now, as heavy as that leaves our hearts, remember that they did it. Despite the obstacles, the danger, the fear, the self-doubt, the confusion, and the peril, they did it, very often for complete strangers. They cared enough to risk all. We are told, and further profess in the awarding of each Carnegie Medal, that "no greater love hath man than this." Do any of us doubt it? Can that realization do anything other than give rise to hope? Hope for us, for our world, and for our future.

The fact that each hero, and each heroic act, changes not only those involved but all who share their experience through the honor is the true impact, and promise, of the Hero Fund. And I, for one, believe that no one knew this better than Andrew Carnegie.

Through all the years, we have found that the hero—and their mind and heart—is truly timeless. And though the cases considered by the Fund have evolved from rescues involving horse and buggies to jet planes, from steamers to powerboats, the heroic spirit endures—unaltered. Even now, in our disconnected, technology-driven world reportedly void of human compassion, heroes abound. And we need them more than ever. The Hero Fund Commission remains committed to recognizing and supporting them and, just as importantly, telling their stories.

When I think of these heroes, I am humbled. We ask ourselves if we could, or would, have done it. Their courage and sacrifice act like a mirror into which we cannot help but peer. What do we see in it, our fears, our insecurities, our limitations, and self-doubt? Or do we see our capabilities and the possibility of embodying hope for others, as they have done, not only for another in peril, but for all of us by their actions? If we are honest, most of us see all this and more.

I believe Carnegie wanted us to look into the mirror and note what we see—good and bad, ugly and beautiful, tragic and inspiring; to look closely—for the sake of the world, of ourselves, and of hope eternal. Perhaps, above all, he hoped we would see the power of each one of us, imperfect as we are, to make a difference, to change the world—for one moment and for all time.

Eric Zahren
President and Chair
Pittsburgh, Pennsylvania

Harwick Mine D

P.B.&L.E.R.R.

THE DAY
THE VALLEY WEPT

BY CAROL BLEIER

A TRAGEDY DEEP BELOW GROUND
INSPIRED ANDREW CARNEGIE TO ESTABLISH A FUND
TO HONOR THE "HEROES OF CIVILIZATION."

Shortly after eight o'clock on the morning of January 25, 1904, a day that dawned bitterly cold in southwestern Pennsylvania and in the hamlet of Harwick, a mining town 15 miles northeast of Pittsburgh and home to the Allegheny Coal Company's Harwick Mine, a massive explosion tore through the 200-foot-deep mine, claiming the lives of 179 miners, many of them teen-age boys. The accident—"as if the earth had suddenly parted and had broken in two"[1]—still ranks as one of the worst in U.S. coal-mining history. In the following days, the disaster laid claim to two more lives, men who had entered the mine in rescue attempts.

Andrew Carnegie, then retired and living in New York, was soon made aware of the disaster. It touched him deeply. By March 12, only six weeks after the explosion, he had penned a document—a "deed of trust"—that would serve as the philosophical basis for the establishment of his newest philanthropy, the Carnegie Hero Fund Commission. "Gentlemen," it began, "we live in a heroic age."

Southwestern Pennsylvania at the turn of the 19th century was rich in bituminous coal deposits. Numerous mines and company-owned towns to house the miners were developed to feed the great demand for coal by the iron and steel manufacturers of Pittsburgh. Selwyn M. Taylor, member of a prominent city family, was a well-known mining engineer and consultant to coal companies, including the Allegheny Coal Company, and it was he who had drawn the plans for the Harwick Mine. He had equipped it with powerful ventilation, and, by commencement of operations in the latter part of 1902, the mine was reputedly one of the safer ones. Nevertheless, the industry was especially dangerous. A lack of regulation, limited equipment, and inexperienced miners—often immigrants of differing tongues—led to mistake and accident. The workforce at Harwick was mainly Hungarian, but Italian, Polish, and German miners also labored alongside English and American ones. Contemporary reports also noted that the mine at Harwick was gas-filled and dusty.

AN EXPLOSION THAT SHOOK THE EARTH

On the morning of the disaster, the circulation of fresh air in the mine had been cut off by the formation of ice at the bottom of the airshaft, allowing the accumulation of methane, a highly volatile gas. Coal dust, which is extremely flammable, was also present. A dynamite charge used to break up the coal ignited the deadly combination. In the words of a report by the Department of Mines of Pennsylvania:

> The shot … lighted the gas, which, by the fine particles of coal dust suspended in the air, traveled into every place in the mine like a streak of lightening [*sic*], carrying destruction in its path, until it finally expended its force up the air and hoisting shafts … The entire population of the village was in an uproar, and the utmost excitement prevailed. The explosion had been one of terrific force. The tipple, which was built of iron, was wrecked, the cages were blown out of the shaft, and a mule that had been at the bottom of the shaft was caught by the force of the explosion and blown out and over the tipple, a distance of about 300 feet. The accident had destroyed the organization that existed among the officials, as the mine foreman and the fire boss as well as almost all the employees had been killed. The officials who were present and had escaped the disaster seemed to be dazed and without confidence in themselves.[2]

The village suddenly came to know horror, confusion, panic, fear, and dread. Weeping, grieving women and children milled about the mine complex. Scores of caskets filled with bodies burned beyond recognition were soon being taken on sleds to the town's frame schoolhouse, turned morgue. The entire local mine workers organization had been wiped out, and with the mine foreman and fire boss killed by the explosion, there could only be speculation as to what had happened. An investigation into the cause of the explosion quickly got under way.

Many of the killed miners, several of whose families could not afford a traditional burial, were buried in a mass grave on land donated by the Allegheny Coal Company.

ADOLPH GUNIA

Immediate calls went out for volunteers and aid. When Taylor, 42, learned of the disaster, he hurried from his Pittsburgh office to the site and offered his services. There are conflicting reports on when the first rescue attempt was made. One said it was at 4 p.m., but the two men involved were driven back by the foul air. Taylor and his assistant, James McCann, and another man were lowered into the mine an hour later. Some 40 minutes later, McCann was hoisted in the cage. With him was the explosion's sole survivor, 16-year-old Adolph Gunia. McCann reported that Taylor had collapsed from afterdamp, an asphyxiating mixture of residual gases after an explosion, and that he had attempted to bring him to the bottom of the shaft but had been driven back by the gas. Taylor was soon found and brought to the surface, but he died early the next day. The community was so taken by his sacrifice that many accompanied his sled-drawn casket from the mine to the Cheswick railroad station. A newspaper article said of Taylor: "Himself, he had not a single thought of. His way was to save or die. He died."[3] Taylor left a wife and stepson.

Gunia, a German immigrant, lost both his father and brother in the accident. Brought out severely burned—described as more dead than alive—he was semiconscious and at first thought to have been blinded by the explosion. He spent four months in the hospital and bore the resulting deep scars from head to toe throughout his life. Interviewed shortly after he was rescued, Gunia said, "I saw a sheet of flame coming from back in the mine. I ran. Something seemed to hit me in the middle of my back. I fell unconscious and cannot remember anything until McCann picked me up."[4] Eventually he returned to coal mining, but, according to his grandson Bruce Gunia, he never worked underground again, and he discouraged his three sons from becoming coal miners. Adolph Gunia died of cancer in 1935 at the age of 49.

The day following the explosion, coal miner Daniel A. Lyle, 43, answered an appeal for volunteers and rushed to the scene from Leechburg, a small town 15 miles away. Although he suffered asthma and was aware of the dangerous conditions in the mine, Lyle and two other men worked from late afternoon well into the night, going deeper into the mine than other volunteers to look for survivors. The other two men surfaced the next morning and reported that Lyle, like Taylor, had been fatally overcome by afterdamp.

DANIEL A. LYLE

SELWYN M. TAYLOR

The calamity was sensational news, and vivid photos and bold front-page headlines underscored its scope. Charges of negligence and inefficiency arose and were bitterly contested by the government and the coal company. There was controversy over the loss of the fire boss's inspection report and debate about whether the dynamite was misplaced, misfired, or incorrectly tamped. State mine inspector Frederick W. Cunningham and mine superintendent Wilfred Snowden were later arrested on charges of murder and held for a grand jury. Both men were eventually released.

Benevolence developed, as well. The Cheswick Relief Committee was organized and more than $40,000 was soon collected from the general public for the bereaved families. Carnegie responded with matching funds. But it was the rescue efforts of Taylor and Lyle that compelled him to put form to his idea of many years, that of recognizing acts of selfless heroism. A report Carnegie received on Lyle's death noted: "Lyle made a valiant effort to rescue entombed men. He left a widow and five children. What a tragedy that his life had to go with his deed! He was a hero."[5] Carnegie directed that gold medals be struck and presented to the families of the two fallen rescuers "in commemoration of the acts of heroism … wherein they sacrificed their lives in an endeavor to save their fellowman [*sic*]."[6]

HARWICK'S MINERS WILL ALWAYS BE REMEMBERED

One hundred years after the disaster, the Harwick Mine and miners are far from forgotten, kept in memory by poem and news feature. The *New Kensington Daily Dispatch* in the winter of 1958 ran a series on the explosion entitled, "This Was The Day The Valley Wept." The articles were reprints from a pamphlet written shortly after the disaster to raise funds for the families of the deceased miners. The son of a man who helped bury the dead in 1904 provided the pamphlet to the paper.

Monuments to the miners have also been erected over the years. A stone memorial was placed by the United Mine Workers of America in front of a plot donated by the Allegheny Coal Company for the bodies of many of the miners. It is adjacent to a power plant on the Allegheny River just a few miles from the mine and near where its coal was once burned. In 1996, the Pennsylvania Historical and Museum Commission placed a roadside marker just north of the small road leading to the mass grave. It commemorates the establishment of the Carnegie Hero Fund Commission and the heroic acts following the explosion that led to the Commission's founding. In 1999, the Harwick community dedicated a memorial to all of its miners. It is a large, handsome block of black granite, etched with a rendering of the mine's tipple and shaft buildings, and is situated in the center of a small parklet. Carved into the bricks surrounding the memorial are the names of individual miners.

Crumbling stone walls, a few rails, and some concrete pads—perhaps the floor of the iron tipple—are the only remains of the once busy mine. The entry shaft is covered with a concrete slab and enclosed with a chain-link fence. A cable cordons off a grassy, grown-over roadway leading through a few sparse trees and underbrush to the site. The mine was closed in 1970.

"…I intend some day
to do something for
such heroes as we have
been reading about.
Heroes in civic life
should be recognized,
as well as those whom
governments call he-
roes because they have
distinguished them-
selves in battle."
Andrew Carnegie

II

It crawled up my ain back,"[1] Andrew Carnegie said of the Carnegie Hero Fund Commission, his unique philanthropic endeavor to honor acts of heroism. "I cherish a fatherly regard for it since no one suggested it to me, and as far as I know, it never has been thought of."[2] He remained interested in the Commission's work for the rest of his life and took a special pride in its accomplishments. When he received letters from Carnegie Medal awardees or their families, he acknowledged, "These are the precious jewels of my life. I love the Hero Fund because it is my ain bairn [child]."[3]

Carnegie's meteoric rise in iron and steel manufacturing to become one of the richest men in the world at the turn of the 20th century is well known. Not as familiar is the far-reaching distribution of his wealth, and lesser still the establishment of the Carnegie Hero Fund Commission and his ideas behind it. One of his favorite quotations was an old proverb, "The gods send thread for a web begun."[4] Carnegie's web of honoring "heroes of peace" started gathering threads in childhood.

He was born on November 25, 1835, in the attic of a small stone cottage in the ancient town of Dunfermline, once the capital of Scotland. Carnegie cherished his humble birthplace, as he did his country's ballads, poetry, and the legendary courageous tales of Scotland's independence. In his autobiography, Carnegie said of his origins: "Even then, and till [one's] last day, the early impressions remain … They are always rising and coming again to the front to exert their influence to elevate his thought and color his mind."[5] He found literary heroes such as Robert Burns and heroes among the daring Scottish patriots, particularly William Wallace, and noted: "It is a tower of strength for a boy to have a hero."[6]

More personally, he thought of his mother, Margaret, as heroic. While his father, William, a handloom weaver, toiled in a declining occupation, his thrifty and practical mother took care of the family. She tended a small grocery shop in their home during the day and stitched shoes in the evening. She went on to play a dominant role in Carnegie's business and personal life, precluding his marrying until age 51, after she died. He dedicated his first book: "To my favorite Heroine My Mother."[7]

Carnegie revealed an instinct for his future business ventures while still a young boy in Scotland by organizing his friends to work for him. He kept pigeons and rabbits and wanted his companions to help with their care. Their compensation, since Carnegie had no money, was to bestow their names upon any new rabbits if they would feed them. His plan worked. "Precious knowledge this is for man to possess," he later wrote. "I did not understand steam machinery, but I tried to understand that much more complicated piece of mechanism—man."[8]

When Carnegie was 12, his family decided to follow relatives who had emigrated to America. With borrowed funds, the family, which included Carnegie's four-year-old brother, Tom, found its way in 1848 to Allegheny, a city just across the river from Pittsburgh and now its North Side neighborhood. The area the Carnegies now called home was dismally dirty, overcrowded, and disease-infested. Pittsburgh, without an adequate water system, had been devastated just three years earlier by a major fire. Yet new immigrants, especially Irish, Scotch, and German youths escaping from poverty in their homelands, were willing to take risks and work hard in their new land, where, despite the challenging conditions, they saw unlimited opportunities.

Enthusiastic, self-confident, and likable, Carnegie advanced rapidly from his first job, as a bobbin boy in a smelly, dank cotton mill, making $1.20 a week, to work as a messenger for a Pittsburgh telegraph office. Exhibiting his foresight and a willingness to try new things, he learned Morse code and became a telegraph operator. The job brought him at the age of 17 to the attention of Thomas A. Scott, superintendent of the Western

Division of the Pennsylvania Railroad, who hired him as his clerk and operator. Only six years later, in 1859, Carnegie took over Scott's position. He resigned that job in 1865 at the age of 29 to go into business for himself. "I was determined to make a fortune," Carnegie declared.[9] He chose an auspicious time to build his empire.

Pittsburgh after the Civil War was a busy, prosperous, and growing city. With railroads expanding westward and few or ineffectual government restraints, Carnegie was free to marshal his abundant talents. He accumulated wealth quickly, focusing initially on investing in companies that manufactured sleeping cars, built bridges, and expanded telegraphy. In 1867, a couple of years after he organized the first of his many companies, he left Pittsburgh and moved to New York. There, in a startling show of self-analysis in the midst of his business success, Carnegie sat down at a desk in his room at the St. Nicholas Hotel and reflected on the value of making more money. He wrote a note to himself: "Thirty-three and an income of 50,000$ per annum ... Beyond this never earn—make no effort to increase fortune, but spend the surplus each year for benovelent [sic] purposes ... Man must have an idol—The amassing of wealth is one of the worst species of idolitary [sic]... I will resign business at thirty-five."[10] The note, which surfaced after Carnegie's death, had remained in the desk forgotten. Instead of ending his career at the age of 35, he was about to move into the steel business, which would add exponentially to his wealth.

Though not physically imposing, at five feet three with sparkling pale eyes and a ruddy complexion, Carnegie was a fierce competitor. With innovative thinking and keen insight into human nature, he initiated a vertical business structure headed by family members, friends, and ambitious young men among whom he inspired loyalty. He frequently trusted them to manage his business affairs while he traveled abroad, often for months at a time.

Carnegie focused on new trends in manufacturing processes and techniques. He brought the Bessemer steel process from England to America, lowered the price of steel by keeping production costs down, and reinvested profits back into his businesses for improvements and expansion. He sought to produce the best products at the lowest costs. Carnegie pushed his workers hard; few workers survived in his plants past the age of 40. While he was starting to grow his fortune, he was not thinking of charity. "I was in business to make money. I was not a philanthropist at all. When rails were high we got the highest prices we could get. When they were low we met the lowest price we had to meet."[11]

His business acumen, however, was only part of a multi-faceted persona. Growing up among a lively family of readers and political activists concerned with theology and workers' rights, he became a self-taught Renaissance man who retained lifelong interests in literature, philosophy, and world politics. A voracious reader and a raconteur with a quick wit, Carnegie often expressed strong opinions on numerous subjects beyond his business expertise, writing and cajoling kings and presidents, and vigorously promoting ideas that ranged from the simplified spelling of the English language to pacifism. He was, however, pragmatic and adaptable. When Congress declared war on Germany on April 6, 1917, Carnegie wrote to President Woodrow Wilson, "You have triumphed at last. God bless you. You will give the world peace and rank the greatest hero of all."[12]

Although he seldom had doubts in making business decisions, Carnegie was periodically conflicted over his prosperity and how he was achieving it. Though not religious, he worried about his soul and self-respect. Another of his favorite quotations came from Robert Burns: "Thine own reproach alone do fear."[13] He was greatly anguished over the Homestead strike and was haunted by it until the day he died. The July 6, 1892, confrontation between workers of the Homestead mill and the Pinkerton National Detective Agency would later cause Carnegie to write: "Nothing I have had to meet in all my life, before or since, wounded me so deeply."[14] He had, paradoxically, great admiration for the common man, choosing his heroes and businesses' presidents from among them. Carnegie also admired those who treated others well. During the Civil War, he met and lauded Abraham Lincoln: "I never met a great man who thoroughly made himself one with all men as Mr. Lincoln. He was the most perfect Democrat, revealing in every work and act the equality of men."[15]

In 1886, Carnegie made his first overture toward rewarding heroic action. He contributed to the cost of a monument erected in a cemetery in Dunfermline in memory of a young man, William Hunter, who died while attempting to save a boy from drowning. In words very similar to those he used when founding the Hero Fund years later, he wrote, "The false heroes of barbarous man are those who can only boast of the destruction of their fellows. The true heroes of civilization are those alone who save or greatly serve them."[16]

At the age of 65 in 1901, Carnegie sold the Carnegie Company to investment banker J. Pierpont Morgan, who merged it into his recently formed United States Steel Corporation. "An opportunity to retire came to me unsought, which I considered my duty to accept," he wrote to the people of Pittsburgh in a letter published in the newspapers. "I have always thought that old age should be spent, not as the Scotch say 'in making mickle mair' but in making good use of what has been acquired …"[17] The plan to give away most of his fortune had taken root in 1889 when he wrote "The Gospel of Wealth," an essay in which he stated his belief that, beyond providing for a family's needs, excess wealth should be regarded as a trust fund to be used for the benefit of the community.

With this original concept that the rich have a responsibility for the improvement of society, Carnegie encouraged other millionaires to dispense of their wealth. "The man who dies thus rich, dies disgraced."[18] He frowned on indiscriminate handouts, or "soup kitchens," but believed instead that philanthropy should be for those who would help themselves or mankind, and should be organized as rationally and systematically as business. For the last 19 years of his life, he distributed most of his wealth with the same determination and organization that he used to acquire it, hoping it would benefit others and soften the criticism that had pursued him during his business career.

Carnegie's early thinking on heroism remained. A few years after retiring, he was having lunch with his friend, educator Dr. William J. Holland, on a day when news accounts were detailing a dramatic rescue from a burning building. "I intend some day to do something for such heroes as we have been reading about," Carnegie told him. "Heroes in civic life should be recognized, as well as those whom governments call heroes because they have distinguished themselves in battle."[19]

Thus, when Carnegie heard about the tragic coal mine accident in Harwick, he sent some of his former business associates to investigate. He could not get the disaster at the Harwick

Mine out of his mind, especially of the two men who had gone into the mine in separate rescue attempts and also lost their lives. Finally, after years of lamenting how little the world regarded heroic deeds by those in peaceful vocations, the tragedy in Harwick galvanized Carnegie to act.

It was fitting that Pittsburgh should be the headquarters for his new idea. There he could put in place a board composed of men he knew well and trusted completely to run the new institution, such as his second cousin Thomas Morrison and close friends and business associates Robert Pitcairn, Thomas N. Miller, and William L. Abbott.

Although he had left Pittsburgh for New York City 37 years earlier, Carnegie remained deeply involved and interested in the city's well-being: "Pittsburgh entered the core of my heart when I was a boy and cannot be torn out … how best to serve Pittsburgh is the question which recurs to me almost every day of my life."[20] He gave numerous gifts to the city, including Carnegie Institute, which comprises a museum, library, art gallery, and music hall, and a technical school, now Carnegie Mellon University. In a letter to a friend in 1897, Carnegie wrote, "Mrs. Carnegie and I derive the sweetest of all our satisfactions from our Pittsburgh benefactions."[21]

Since Carnegie envisioned the Hero Fund to include pensions for widows and children of deceased heroes, he turned to close friend and former business associate Charles L. Taylor, who then headed two pension funds established by Carnegie. In a letter to Taylor dated March 12, 1904, in which Carnegie touched on several issues concerning the soon-to-be-formed Hero Fund, he concluded, "I have thought over the idea for years, and the Harwick mine disaster brought it to a head, because in the interval I had found you, as the right man wanted, to put the idea into successful operation, another proof that 'The gods send thread for a web begun.'"[22]

Carnegie wanted to do something for those who with little thought risked their lives to save others, sometimes dying and thereby bringing financial hardship on their families. In correspondence, he made it clear that the purpose of the Hero Fund was "for watching, applauding, and *supporting*," emphasis his. The reward, he said, should be for "heroic action wherever displayed and [by] whomever displayed, white or black, male or female—at least this is my hope."[23]

Just as he had kept close watch on his business affairs, Carnegie scrutinized Hero Fund board minutes and maintained constant communications with the Commission. Through telegrams, transatlantic cables, and typewritten correspondence, often with added comments in a blunt lead pencil or black ink in the margins of the letters, he congratulated the board on its work, and urged its members to publicize their efforts and investigate cases quickly. Displaying his sense of humor, after dispensing some advice to the Commission's manager Frank M. Wilmot on how to handle newspaper reporters, he impishly added in the letter to the left of his signature: "No charge."[24]

He gave opinions on who should receive awards, made clear his intention was for "well-proved cases" and not "self-dubbed heroes,"[25] and urged that the Commission should not interpret his instructions too narrowly. In spite of his interference and prodding, he prophetically expected this board of trustees, like all his other boards, to conduct affairs as they saw fit. "Conditions upon the erth [sic] inevitably change; hence, no wise man will bind Trustees forever to certain paths, causes, or institutions. I disclaim any intention of doing so. On the contrary, I giv [sic] my Trustees full authority to change policy or causes hitherto aided, from time to time, when this, in their opinion has become necessary or desirable. They shall best conform to my wishes by using their own judgment."[26]

Carnegie was very fond of the Hero Fund. "It is the fund that may be considered my pet. I used to hate that word, because the children at school cald [sic] me Martin's [his teacher] pet, but now I like it."[27] At another time he wrote, "I don't believe there's a nobler fund in the world."[28] With the success of the Hero Fund, he created similar organizations in the United Kingdom, France, Germany, Belgium, the Netherlands, Sweden, Switzerland, Italy, Norway, and Denmark. All but the German fund remain in operation.

Carnegie died on August 11, 1919, from pneumonia at his summer home, Shadowbrook, in Lenox, Massachusetts. His wife, Louise, lived until 1946, turning over at her death their New York mansion at 2 East 91st to the Carnegie Corporation of New York. It is presently the Cooper-Hewitt, National Design Museum. On the walls of Carnegie's former library, now the museum shop, are some of his favorite quotations, including "The gods send thread for a web begun."

On the last day of the 19th century, Carnegie, still hoping for the existence of only heroes of peace and not of war, wrote: "All goes well, upward and onward. I believe that as the twentieth century closes, the earth will be purged of its foulest stain, the killing of men by men in battle under the name of war and that the profession of arms, hitherto the most and until recently the only profession thought worthy of a gentleman, will be held the most dishonorable of all and unworthy of any being in human form. To kill a man in that day will be considered as disgusting as we in this day consider it disgusting to eat one."[29]

While that belief has not been realized, Carnegie's vision for a better world is being kept alive through the trusts and institutions he endowed. Numbering 22, they were funded with $350 million—most of his wealth—to advance human endeavors in education, science, the arts, and world peace. The largest is the Carnegie Corporation of New York. Among the smallest is the Carnegie Hero Fund Commission, which is still following the Deed of Trust penned by Carnegie in 1904. "My chief happiness … lies in the thot [sic] that even after I pass away the welth [sic] that came to me to administer as a sacred trust for the good of my fellow men is to continue to benefit humanity for generations untold."[30]

31 May 1905
AN EXCERPT FROM A LETTER
TO CHARLES L. TAYLOR

Your cable made me very happy. You have made a start, and there is to be no finish—it goes on forever. There is not much good to be done in the world without publicity. You must attract the attention of the people. This leads them to think and to appreciate the work that you are doing, and finally to stir within themselves the desire to go and do likewise. In all cases where heroism is displayed, the action should be prompt so far as injury is concerned. Your agent should be on the ground by the first train, looking into matters.

Andrew Carnegie

12 March 1904
NEW YORK CITY, NEW YORK
TO THE HERO FUND COMMISSION

Gentlemen: We live in a heroic age. Not seldom are we thrilled by deeds of heroism where men or women are injured or lose their lives in attempting to preserve or rescue their fellows; such the heroes of civilization. The heroes of barbarism maimed or killed theirs.

I have long felt that the heroes and those dependent upon them should be freed from pecuniary cares resulting from their heroism, and, as a fund for this purpose, I have transferred to the Commission five million dollars of First Collateral Five Per Cent. Bonds of the United States Steel Corporation, the proceeds to be used as follows:

First. To place those following peaceful vocations, who have been injured in heroic effort to save human life, in somewhat better positions pecuniarily than before, until again able to work. In the case of death, the widow and children, or other dependents, to be provided for until she remarries, and the children until they reach a self-supporting age. For exceptional children exceptional grants may be made for exceptional education. Grants of sums of money may also be made to heroes or heroines as the Commission thinks advisable—each case to be judged on its merits.

Second. No grant is to be continued unless it be soberly and properly used, and the recipients remain respectable, well-behaved members of the community, but the heroes and heroines are to be given a fair trial, no matter what their antecedents. Heroes deserve pardon and a fresh start.

Third. A medal shall be given to the hero, or widow, or next of kin, which shall recite the heroic deed it commemorates, that descendants may know and be proud of their descent. The medal shall be given for the heroic act, even if the doer be uninjured, and also a sum of money, should the Commission deem such gift desirable.

Fourth. Many cities provide pensions for policemen, firemen, teachers, and others, and some may give rewards for acts of heroism. All these and other facts the Commission will take into account and act accordingly in making grants. Nothing could be further from my intention than to deaden or interfere with these most creditable provisions, doubly precious as showing public and municipal appreciation of faithful and heroic service. I ask from the Commission most careful guard against this danger. The medal can, of course, be offered in such cases. Whether something more can not judiciously be done, at the request of, or with the approval of, the city authorities, the Commission shall determine. I hope there can be.

Fifth. The claims upon the Fund for some years can not exhaust it. After years, however, pensioners will become numerous. Should the Commission find, after allowing liberally for this, that a surplus will remain, it has power to make grants in case of accidents (preferably where a hero has appeared) to those injured. The action taken in the recent Harwick Mine accident, where Heroes Taylor and Lyle lost their lives, is an illustration. The community first raised a fund of forty thousand dollars, which was duplicated by me after waiting until the generosity of the community had full scope. Here again the Commission should be exceedingly careful, as in this case, not to deaden, but to stimulate employers or communities to do their part, for such action benefits givers themselves as well as recipients.

Sixth. It seems probable that cities and employers on this continent will ultimately be placed under similar conditions to those of Britain, Germany, and other European States, and required to provide against accidents to employees. Therefore, the Commission, by a two-thirds vote, may devote any surplus that accrues beyond providing for heroes and their dependents (which provision must never be abandoned) to such other modes of benefiting those in want, chiefly caused through no fault of their own (such as drunkenness, laziness, crimes, etc.) but through exceptional circumstances, in such manner and to such extent as the Commission thinks advisable and likely to do more good than if such sums were given to those injured by accident, where the latter may be suitably provided for by law, or otherwise.

Seventh. The field embraced by the Fund is the United States of America, the Dominion of Canada, the Colony of Newfoundland, and the waters thereof. The sea is the scene of many heroic acts. No action more heroic than that of doctors and nurses volunteering their services in the case of epidemics. Railroad employees are remarkable for heroism. All these and similar cases are embraced. Whenever heroism is displayed by man or woman in saving human life, the Fund applies.

Eighth. No personal liability will attach to members for any act of the Commission. The Commission has power to fill vacancies.

Ninth. The Commission has full power to sell, invest, or reinvest all funds; to employ all officials, including Secretary, traveling agents to visit and oversee beneficiaries, etc. and to fix their compensation. Members of the Commission shall be reimbursed all expenses incurred, including traveling expenses attending meetings. The President shall be granted such honoraria as the Commission thinks proper and as he can be prevailed upon to accept.

Tenth. An annual report, including a detailed statement of sums and medals granted and the reasons therefor, shall be made each year and published in at least one newspaper in the principal cities of the countries embraced by the Fund. A finely executed roll of the heroes and heroines shall be kept displayed in the office at Pittsburgh.

Andrew Carnegie

Andrew Carnegie
Witness, Louise Whitfield Carnegie

THE FIRST HERO

17 July 1904
SULPHUR POND
WILKINSBURG, PENNSYLVANIA

C. H. 1

Sunday, July 17, 1904, was a warm, sunny day, and as was typical, boys from Wilkinsburg, a small community that borders Pittsburgh on its eastern side, decided to go swimming in nearby Sulphur Pond. The pond was in a deep ravine on a farm and had been created by the dumping of slack from a mine that had been abandoned 15 to 20 years earlier. When the mine was producing, the pond's water was used to operate some of its machinery.

Shortly after noon, brothers Charles and Harry Stevick came to the Baumann home and asked **LOUIS A. BAUMANN, JR.**, 17, and his brother Robert to go swimming with them. They agreed, and on the way to the pond they met up with six other boys, who joined them. Soon after reaching the pond, all of the boys except Charles took a quick dip. A short time later, when the boys were out of the water—Baumann and another boy on one side and the other boys on the opposite bank—Charles decided to dive into the pond. When he surfaced, he cried for help and then submerged.

Baumann immediately dived into the pond, but when he reached Charles, Charles grabbed his leg. Baumann broke free and returned to the bank to regain his breath. He swam back out and dived for Charles, then took him to the surface, but Charles again grabbed Baumann and both submerged. Again Baumann broke free and returned to the bank. A third time he swam out to Charles, that time managing to get Charles close enough to the bank for the other boys, who formed a chain, to drag both from the water.

Charles was unconscious, and thought dead by the other boys, but after several minutes he recovered. Baumann was winded and exhausted from his efforts. He was the first person to be awarded the Carnegie Medal *(see next page)*. FILE NO: 201

A 100-YEAR RELATIONSHIP

The case of Louis A. Baumann, Jr. first came to the attention of the Hero Fund in a letter written by his father on September 15, 1904, in which he briefly recounted his son's rescue act. Also signing the letter were six of the young Baumann's friends, who were at the scene and had witnessed the rescue.

Frank Wilmont, the Hero Fund's manager, responded by requesting additional information, and within two days the father wrote back providing a more detailed description of the rescue. The case was then investigated, and, at the May 15, 1905, meeting of the Commission's Executive Committee, the awarding of the bronze medal to Baumann was approved. Eight more medals were awarded that day, including one to Ernestine F. Atwood, 17, the first female awardee. Since the design of the medal and its manufacturer were issues still undecided, it was March of 1907 before Baumann received his medal.

The Commission and the Baumann family have been in contact with each other from time to time since the medal was presented. A long letter from Baumann's brother Robert arrived in 1911, explaining that Baumann was suffering from rheumatism and that his health was worsening. A doctor confirmed the illness in another letter at that time and further stated that Baumann was suffering from a chronic heart condition. Later that year, another doctor sent the Commission an invoice for $3 for a physical examination of Baumann, and the Commission assumed the cost.

It would be 47 years before the Commission again heard from the family. Baumann's sister, Anna, inquired in 1958 about her brother's heroic act, and the Commission confirmed that he was indeed the first recipient of the Carnegie Medal. Twenty years later, brother William wrote to inform that the medal had been stolen. Proof of the theft was provided, and the Commission had a duplicate medal struck.

In 1996, Baumann's nephew, Ronald Hitchon, made inquiry and was sent copies of documents from Baumann's file. In turn, Hitchon in 2003 provided the Commission with additional information on Baumann and his family. He also noted that Baumann died of heart disease at the age of 35 on March 14, 1925, and that his son, James, who was born the previous year, was living in the Arizona State Veterans Home in Phoenix.

Job Pa Sept 15
1904

To Whome it may concern

On the 17th of July 1904 While in swiming
With companions one Charls Stevick got
into the deep Watter and was drownding
Louis A Baumann jr of Penn township
rescud him after severe strugle. in the
First atempt was taken down with him but
succeded in getting away and made a
second atempt and got him out in time
to save his life. he was unconscious when
he got him out. the undersigned Were

Witness
Timothy Welsh.
Arthur Smeltz
Joe Welsh.
Harry Stevick
Robert Baumann.
Louis Möller -

Louis A Baumann

Job Pa

WILLIAM L.
ABBOTT

EDWIN H.
ANDERSON

EDWARD M.
BIGELOW

WILLIAM WALLACE
BLACKBURN

JOSEPH
BUFFINGTON

WILLIAM N. FREW

WILLIAM J.
HOLLAND

JOHN BEARD
JACKSON

THOMAS LYNCH

CHARLES C.
MELLOR

THOMAS N.
MILLER

THOMAS
MORRISON

FREDERICK C.
PERKINS

ROBERT PITCAIRN

HENRY KIRKE
PORTER

JAMES H. REED

WILLIAM LUCIEN
SCAIFE

WILLIAM SCOTT

WILLIAM H.
STEVENSON

CHARLES L.
TAYLOR

FRANK M.
WILMOT

Thread for a Web

by MARY BRIGNANO

III

CARNEGIE AND THE FIRST COMMISSIONERS
LAUNCH AN UNPRECEDENTED IDEA

When does an institution actually begin? While it is still an idea in the mind of its creator ... or when others bring that idea to life?

Perhaps the Carnegie Hero Fund Commission began in earnest on a winter day early in 1904 when Andrew Carnegie summoned two Pittsburghers, Charles L. Taylor and Frank M. Wilmot, to his New York mansion. Taylor (1857–1922), an innovative metallurgist, had been one of Carnegie's "young geniuses," his partners in building the largest steel operation in the world. Wilmot (1872–1930) was a gifted and dedicated administrator. The two were chairman and manager, respectively, of the Carnegie Relief Fund, and they had come prepared to discuss the terrible explosion that had occurred just days ago at Harwick, Pennsylvania. One hundred and seventy-nine coal miners had lost their lives, and two more men had died while heroically trying to rescue those underground.

Carnegie had created his $4 million Relief Fund in 1901, immediately after selling the Carnegie Company and receiving bonds worth $225,639,000 par value of the new United States Steel Corporation.[1] He intended the fund to aid workers injured in "his" mills and provide small pensions for needy, aged employees.[2] In his autobiography he would proudly describe "this first gift of surplus wealth, four millions in first mortgage 5% bonds, upon retiring from business, as an acknowledgment of the deep debt which I owe to the workmen who have contributed so greatly to my success."[3] To oversee the fund, he had appointed Taylor, one of his "original boys, a working, not merely a preaching apostle of the gospel of service to his fellow men."[4]

Now a special bank vault had been constructed to hold Carnegie's bonds, yielding five percent annually, and the "industrial Napoleon" had set off on an exhilarating new campaign: the distribution of a massive fortune "in the manner … best calculated to produce the most beneficial results for the community."[5] He was personally inventing philanthropy on a scale the world had never seen, and with a strategy dear to the heart of this complex, multifaceted man. He aimed to provide "ladders upon which the aspiring can rise."[6] Whether through research, public libraries, technical schools, or museums, Carnegie preached that philanthropy could promote ideas and alter (he would say improve) public attitudes. Only the millions accumulated by a few men like himself and John D. Rockefeller made possible such industrial strength, "scientific" giving.[7]

And he was launching this new philanthropy from a 64-room mansion as innovative as its owner, who was famous for seizing on any new technology that would push his mills to produce ever more steel at ever-lower cost. Built far from New York's then-fashionable neighborhoods, 2 East 91st Street was the first private residence in the United States with a structural steel frame and also one of the first in New York with its own push-button electric passenger elevator. In the sub-basement, a miniature coal car ran on its own railroad track carrying a quarter-ton of coal from the 200-ton bin to the furnace.

Slim and silver-haired, Taylor was still as fascinated by innovation as he had been back in 1880, when the 23-year-old graduate of Lehigh University first arrived in Pittsburgh to help transform the industrial world. A pioneer steel chemist, he went to work at the new, ultra-modern Pittsburgh Bessemer Steel Works at Homestead. Carnegie bought this plant in 1883—and set off yet another string of "firsts." Coupled with the Bessemer process, the nation's first basic open-hearth furnaces had enabled American steel production to outstrip any other country's by 1890, thanks largely to Carnegie's drive. Then Taylor and others had formulated lighter, stronger steels for new uses. The chemist had been among the first to develop steel for railroad-car construction, an advance that had made railroad transport safer and more profitable … and added millions to the Carnegie balance sheets.[8]

A secretary ushered Taylor and Wilmot into the great man's study, a personal room full of books, portraits, honors, awards, medals, and autographed photographs of kings, emperors, great writers, and statesmen. Beneath the coffered ceiling ran a panel painted with quotations that had inspired Carnegie over the years: "All is well since all grows better," "Thine own reproach alone do fear," "The highest form of worship is service to man," and another, particularly apt for this meeting, "The gods send thread for a web begun."[9] Carnegie was about to announce his plan for a wholly new benevolent purpose—a gift that would be "absolutely unique among the world's philanthropies of modern or ancient times."[10] He had decided to endow a fund of $5 million for heroes and their dependents, and he intended Taylor to supply the thread—the chemistry—that would put his idea into action.

"THE WHOLE IDEA OF MY HERO FUND IS IN THAT POEM"

The disaster at Harwick had struck him forcefully, Carnegie told his friends. He could not get the thought of the heroic would-be rescuers out of his mind, and he wanted to do something for the families they had left behind. These selfless men reminded him of a "true and beautiful poem" by "my dear, dear friend Richard Watson Gilder," the influential editor-in-chief of the *Century Monthly Magazine*. "I re-read it the morning after the accident, and resolved then to establish the Hero Fund," he would write in his autobiography.

Entitled "In the Time of Peace," the poem expressed Carnegie's conviction that just as much heroism was needed to save a life as to take one. The world was continually growing better, he believed, and in the progressive times to come, heroes would no longer be warriors. They would be women, children, scholars—"civic heroes" with "moral courage":

> 'Twas said: 'When roll of drum and battle's roar
> Shall cease upon the earth, O, then no more
>
> The deed—the race—of heroes in the land.'
> But scarce that word was breathed when one small hand
>
> Lifted victorious o'er a giant wrong
> That had its victims crushed through ages long;

Some woman set her pale and quivering face
Firm as a rock against a man's disgrace;

A little child suffered in silence lest
His savage pain should wound a mother's breast;

Some quiet scholar flung his gauntlet down
And risked, in Truth's great name, the synod's frown;

A civic hero, in the realm of laws,
Did that which suddenly drew a world's applause;

And one to the pest his lithe young body gave
That he a thousand thousand lives might save.

"We have got to show young men that there are just as great battles to be fought in peace-time as in war-time and just as much opportunity for the hero," Carnegie told another friend, Frederick Lynch.[11] "I thought by creating this fund it would be one way of setting the world to thinking upon the heroism of civilization, getting its mind off the association of valor and heroism with war only."[12]

This then was Carnegie's challenge to Taylor and Wilmot: around one unusual idea—a major philanthropic endowment that would promote a new view of heroism—they were to formulate an organization "without parallel in the history of human benevolence." From one inspiring concept they would have to forge a practical and enduring structure. At a time when no large foundations existed as we know them today, they had to organize and administer a new kind of philanthropy … based on a concept that few shared or understood. And they would have to do it in the glare of publicity that always surrounded any Carnegie action.

LENGTHENED SHADOWS

Fortunately, they did not have to accomplish all this alone. When Carnegie finished outlining his plan, he produced a list of 21 individuals he had chosen to serve as his Hero Fund's first commissioners. Within weeks, on April 15, 1904, nearly all would meet for the first time in the Carnegie Building in Downtown Pittsburgh—and few men on earth were better prepared to give flesh to Carnegie's altruistic idea. It seems fitting that they gathered in one of Pittsburgh's first steel-framed skyscrapers, for the structure they forged has endured solidly for a century.

"An institution is the lengthened shadow of one man," Emerson wrote. The Carnegie Hero Fund Commission is in large part the lengthened shadow not only of Carnegie but also those of the founding commissioners. They laid the foundations on which the Commission has carried out its work, and they are a key to understanding why it has endured with little change for 100 years. They created models of organization and set standards of operating procedure. Their achievements changed philanthropy in America.

Although each of these first commissioners stands out, all shared similar traits. Each in his way was an innovator who by 1904 had helped make Pittsburgh the most advanced industrial center in the world at that time—the Silicon Valley of its era. Each had demonstrated unusual ability in managing a business or advancing the newest endeavors of their time—steel, railroads, electricity, and such civic improvements as universities, museums, urban parks, a symphony orchestra, and scientific societies. They were hardheaded, practical men of wide-ranging interests. They welcomed new ideas.

Men who dealt in facts and numbers, the first commissioners were nonetheless captivated by Carnegie's vision of the heroic potential in every human being. Developing a new, large-scale organization to promote a very personal ideal, they became innovators in advancing the systematic analysis, administration, and distribution of great wealth in America.

Handpicked by Carnegie, the first 21 commissioners were socially prominent men who were personally and in many cases intimately known to him. He could trust them to manage his idea and his capital—just as he had counted on his employees to advance his business. Three had risen with him from impoverished boyhoods in Allegheny, today Pittsburgh's North Side. Six had been his partners. Two were related to him through blood or marriage.

Ten—almost half—of them served as trustees of Carnegie Institute, his first major philanthropic enterprise. Established in 1895, this "radically new and different approach to cultural philanthropy" by 1904 comprised the Carnegie Library of Pittsburgh, the Carnegie Museums, and the Carnegie Institute of Technology, today's Carnegie Mellon University.[13]

If the commissioners all knew how to work with Carnegie by executing his ideas with immediacy, they were also comfortable with one another. Many served on boards together, saw each other daily at the Duquesne Club, lived in the same East End neighborhoods, or attended the same churches. Some were related: Taylor, for instance, was married to the daughter of Commissioner Robert Pitcairn, a close boyhood friend of Carnegie.

Most important, the original commissioners were forward-looking men who set great store by science and new technology. They believed in the rational, detailed observation and analysis of information. Several were amateur scientists; one was a professional scientist. Nearly all had advanced or invested in new technologies. In their lifetimes they had seen railroads unite the country and open vast markets. They had watched the telegraph, telephone, and ocean cables shrink the world, and electricity light homes and streets and power great machines. They had witnessed the improvements in health care that followed groundbreaking research into germ theory. Many had helped make steel "the structural metal of modern civilization."[14] They had contributed to civic advances that enhanced their city's image and quality of life—culture and education, safe drinking water, and the amazing display of dinosaur skeletons. They were confident that science was carrying civilization to new heights.

Perhaps what the first commissioners shared most profoundly was their pride in knowing that Carnegie had personally chosen each of them to serve. This fact is crucial to understanding the Hero Fund and how it has evolved. The Commission was and is a uniquely personal organization. Only serving commissioners select new commissioners—and thus there is an unbroken link to Carnegie and his inspiring idea. Commissioners feel and have felt honored to be asked to serve. "There is satisfaction that the work has followed the wishes of the founder, and that it has prospered," a commissioner wrote in 1935. "There is pride that the Fund, in exalting the fine qualities of heroism, has given inspiration and nobility to daily life."[15] "It is a privilege and an honor to serve on this board," agrees Commissioner Ann M. McGuinn today.

Who then were these founding commissioners, who built so lasting and important a structure? On March 12, 1904, Carnegie sent Taylor "a list of suitable persons for the Commission, being

chiefly those whom we talked over." The first name was that of
Taylor himself, whom Carnegie described as "one of the best men
that ever lived."[16] Taylor also became the Commission's first president and served until his death in 1922. Next was Wilmot, who
had come to Pittsburgh from New Jersey in 1888 as a clerk for the
Pennsylvania Railroad Relief Fund. He was one of only two men
with access to safe-deposit box 675 of the Hudson Trust Company
in Hoboken, New Jersey, where the Hero Fund's $5 million in
bonds were stored (the other was Carnegie's longtime secretary,
Robert A. Franks, who later became a commissioner). Wilmot
would serve as the Hero Fund's manager for 26 years, until his
sudden death from a heart attack.

Carnegie's list continued with William Nimick Frew
(1854–1915), lawyer, banker, and first chairman of the board of
trustees of Carnegie Institute. The only son of a pioneer western
Pennsylvania oil refiner who had sold his interests to Rockefeller's
Standard Oil Company, the wealthy Frew was a cultural visionary.
He played a guiding role in launching the *Carnegie International*,
in 1896 the first annual art exhibition in the United States to be
multinational in scope. The fact that Pittsburgh, this "center of
materialism," could produce such an innovative event surprised
the world—and created a new image for the city "at a time when
many considered the encouragement of living artists as essential
to the nation's progress."[17] A catalyst in founding the Pittsburgh
Symphony, Frew also served as a member of the original board of
trustees of the Carnegie Institution of Washington, D.C., and the
Carnegie Corporation of New York.

Judge James H. Reed (1853–1927), a founder of the international law firm Reed Smith, figured as prominently on Carnegie's
list as he did in the industrialist's life. Reed had acted as Carnegie's
lawyer in the sale of the Carnegie Company's facilities to U. S. Steel
in 1901, and Carnegie had named him one of the original direc-
tors of the world's first billion-dollar corporation. An outstanding
business counselor, organizer, and manager, he also consolidated
Pittsburgh's new natural gas, electricity, and urban transportation
companies into one of the first energy giants. Judge Reed (he
had served briefly as a judge of the United States District Court
for the Western District of Pennsylvania) was "liked by everyone
because of his wonderful personality and fairness in all things he
did," according to banker Richard B. Mellon. This lean, dry-witted

lawyer also served as treasurer of Carnegie Institute, Carnegie Library of Pittsburgh, and Carnegie Institute of Technology.[18]

A pioneer manufacturer of light locomotives, the Hon. Henry Kirke Porter (1840–1921) was serving one term as a member of Congress when Carnegie named him to the Hero Fund Commission. Porter's hardworking machines, said to have been the only locomotives built solely for industrial purposes, helped "win the West" at quarries, logging operations, explosives works, grain processing plants, factories, and mines. Porter and his artist wife, Annie Decamp, owned a significant art collection and had built one of the few private galleries in Pittsburgh to display it.[19]

Carnegie's longtime friend Robert Pitcairn (1836–1909) was of course on the list. The two young Scottish immigrants had worked side by side as telegraph messenger boys, Carnegie liked to remember, "for the then magnificent salary of two and a half dollars per week." Like his friend, Pitcairn had learned how to operate the new technology of telegraphy, and he had succeeded Carnegie as a superintendent and general agent of the powerful Pennsylvania Railroad. Always seeking safer, systematic railroad operation, Pitcairn introduced a number of innovations and "gave to America the basic rules for train running"[20] in "the first modern rule book"[21] of 1874. According to one florid historian, "When Robert Pitcairn began his career, the science and art of railroad work were in their infancy. He was one of the … pioneers who blazed a pathway through the untracked wilderness, ceaselessly marching toward the goal of perfect systematized knowledge."[22] A broad-faced, disciplined man with an enormous mustache, Pitcairn is also credited with introducing a pension for retired Pennsylvania Railroad employees, one of the first pension funds anywhere.

Carnegie's next choice was William J. Holland, DD (1848–1932), who introduced the world's first "celebrity dinosaur."[23] Throughout his life this internationally known "churchman, educator, artist, traveler, scholar, scientist, and public-spirited citizen"[24] managed to find himself at the right place and among the right people. He had come to Pittsburgh as pastor of the fashionable Bellefield Presbyterian Church and soon officiated at the marriage of Henry C. Frick and Adelaide Childs. Once he met Carnegie, the two remained, in his words, friends for life. "We were like two brothers," Holland would tell a reporter in 1931. "No man living knew him like myself."[25]

In 1891, he became chancellor of the Western University of Pennsylvania (University of Pittsburgh) and increased the enrollment eightfold by starting the schools of law, medicine, and dental surgery, and the departments of electrical and mining engineering. Admitting women for the first time,[26] the university consolidated its campus in Oakland, near Carnegie Institute—of which Holland also became director in 1898.

In 1899, Holland oversaw the Carnegie Institute expedition to Wyoming to excavate a dinosaur skeleton that would be known worldwide as *Diplodocus carnegii*—the first dinosaur to be seen by millions of people. Carnegie and his museum would present casts of this 85-foot fossil to national museums in England, Germany, France, Austria, Italy, Russia, Spain, Argentina, and Mexico, and William Holland personally installed each one. The original went on display in Pittsburgh when Carnegie Institute expanded in 1907. Holland would later serve as the Commission's second president, from 1923 to 1932.

Charles C. Mellor (1836–1909) "was not an ordinary man," claimed Holland of his fellow commissioner and Carnegie Institute trustee. "He was an artist, but he possessed also the instincts and capacity of the man of affairs. He had scientific tastes, and by reading and observation had acquired a large fund of exact scientific knowledge; but he also possessed a poetic imagination, which scientific study did not deaden." An organist and amateur botanist, Mellor ran the music business started in 1831 by his father, a friend of Stephen Foster. The store was the first to sell a piano in Pittsburgh and, in 1877, one of the first to install a telephone.

By no means a steel millionaire, Commissioner Edwin H. Anderson (1861–1947) was the librarian who organized the Carnegie Library of Pittsburgh—and thus accelerated the trend toward an enormous expansion of library services in urban centers throughout the United States. Directing the library from 1895 until 1904, he shaped it into a multifaceted resource to serve the community—a new ideal for libraries at the time. Anderson created the first Department of Technology in any public library in the country, as well as the first Children's Department. He would serve as director of the New York Public Library from 1914 to 1934.[27]

A real-life Horatio Alger, William Wallace Blackburn (1859–1931) began working for Carnegie companies as a bookkeeper in

1880, became a partner, and rose to become vice president and secretary of Carnegie Steel Company, at that time the largest entity in the United States Steel Corporation. He was a graduate of Duff's Business College in Pittsburgh, the first such business accounting school in the United States.[28]

Thomas Lynch (1854–1914) had worked his way from a clerkship in a company store in Broad Ford, Pennsylvania, to the presidency of the H. C. Frick Coke Company by the age of just 42. He thus shared in the spoils after the notorious Frick–Carnegie lawsuit in 1899, coming away with $640,000 in Carnegie Company stock and bonds. Although Frick remained bitterly antagonistic to Carnegie, and Lynch was a friend of Frick, Carnegie wanted him on the Commission, perhaps because of his experience with coal mine safety. He is credited with being "the father of the 'safety first' movement in the coal industry" and with having drafted the first set of rules for minimizing the dangers of mining.

Carnegie considered the next two commissioners, Thomas Morrison and Frederick C. Perkins, "excellent men of our family, and as such I should like to have them on the Commission."[29] Born in Dunfermline and Carnegie's second cousin, Morrison (1861–1946) became general manager and superintendent of Carnegie Steel's Duquesne and Edgar Thomson Works. He and another machinist patented a successful new cooling process for rails, and he was responsible for several other steelmaking inventions.[30]

Perkins (1870–1935), a graduate of Yale University and Harvard Law School, was a lawyer, a banker, and an early investor in automobile sales. He married Florence N. Carnegie, a daughter of Carnegie's brother Thomas and Lucy Coleman Carnegie.

William Lucien Scaife (1853–1924), a mining engineer who had studied at Yale, in Germany, and in Paris, had also worked in a Belgian coal mine to gain practical mining experience. In Pittsburgh, he established the Scaife Foundry & Machine Company, Ltd. A trustee of the Western University of Pennsylvania, Scaife headed the committee that renamed it the University of Pittsburgh. He also edited *John A. Brashear: The Autobiography of a Man Who Loved the Stars* and served as a trustee of Carnegie Institute.[31]

Another commissioner who devoted time to public service was William H. Stevenson (1857–1930), president of George K. Stevenson Company, an importing grocery business, and a close friend of Carnegie. As a reform member of City Council, he brought about the selection and purchase of the site for Carnegie Institute of Technology, and he served on the "Tech" board from 1902 to 1909. He ran for mayor in 1909. An original board member of the Chamber of Commerce of the United States, he served as president (1912–1914) of the Pittsburgh Chamber of Commerce and as a director for 27 years.

"The father of Pittsburgh's parks," Edward M. Bigelow (1850–1916) was a visionary who, far ahead of his times, stemmed the tide of urban sprawl in the 1880s. The development of Highland and Schenley Parks, Bigelow Boulevard and the Boulevard of the Allies, miles of streets and sewers, the improvement of the water system, and plans for Phipps Conservatory and for the Liberty Tunnels all sprang from his vision for a greener, more livable Pittsburgh. In 1889, he helped persuade Mary Schenley to sell 300 acres of land to Pittsburgh for a public park at a discount price of $75,000, considerably below its $200,000 valuation. "It used to be said that Mr. Bigelow made the taxpayers spend money," stated his obituary. "He admitted the charge laughingly, often, but called attention to the fact that he was constantly urging rich men to spend their money for the benefit of the people."[32]

To Thomas N. Miller, a boyhood companion in the neighborhood they called "Barefoot Square," Carnegie owed his start in the iron business. As purchasing agent of the Ohio and Pennsylvania Railroad, Miller (1835–1911) became a partner in the Iron City Forge Company. In 1864, Carnegie purchased a one-sixth interest in this company, and it became the parent of his first iron and steel interests. Miller sold his own shares to Carnegie in 1867. Although some claimed Miller had been forced out, the two remained friends for life.

Carnegie's original list included four more names: Samuel H. Church, a Pennsylvania Railroad vice president who would succeed Frew as chairman of Carnegie Institute; John Caldwell, an officer in Westinghouse companies and a noted art collector; William McConway, president of McConway & Torley Company and a Carnegie Institute trustee; and John W. Beatty, whom Carnegie had personally appointed as Carnegie Institute's first director of Fine Arts.

Unable to serve, they were replaced on the Commission first by William L. Abbott (1852–1930). Starting as a clerk at age 19, he had risen to become chairman of Carnegie, Phipps & Co. by 37. "Abbott's chief contribution to the success of the Carnegie company was the organization of its unequalled system of sales agencies," according to *The Romance of Steel*. Before 1884, the company had relied exclusively on commissioned sales agents. "This was not satisfactory," Abbott would recall, "for the reason that a commission man makes deals with both sides. We decided that it would pay to send out salaried men who would work first and last for the Carnegie company." He had retired in 1892, "before the melon was cut," he joked.

The Hon. Joseph Buffington (1855–1947) had followed James H. Reed as judge of the United States District Court for the Western District of Pennsylvania when he became an original Hero Fund Commissioner. In 1906, President Theodore Roosevelt would name Judge Buffington to the Third Circuit Court of Appeals, and he would retire in 1938 with the distinction of having served longer, at that time, than any other judge in the history of the federal courts. A trustee of Carnegie Institute, he made important rulings in interstate commerce law, and in 1915 he would write the legal opinion denying the government's claim that U. S. Steel was a monopoly within the meaning of the Sherman Antitrust Act.[33] Additionally, he became known for his work in helping aliens to become citizens of the United States.

Ironically, another of the first commissioners was the son of an owner of a cotton mill—ironic in that Carnegie's first job at the age of 13 was as a bobbin boy in such a mill, at a salary of $1.20 a week. John Beard Jackson (1845–1908) was the cultured president of the Fidelity Title and Trust Company and also a stockholder in the Carnegie Company. A philanthropist and original trustee of Carnegie Institute, Jackson became the first Pittsburgher to donate a painting to the permanent collection of the Carnegie Museum of Art and was an original guarantor of the Pittsburgh Symphony. Also intrigued by natural science, he served as president of the Archaeological Institute of America, Pittsburgh Society.[34]

Last was William Scott (1850–1906), a Princeton graduate who had worked as a civil engineer out west before studying law in the firm of Knox & Reed, forerunner of Reed Smith. Serving as president of both the Allegheny County and the Pennsylvania Bar Associations, he joined an elite group of lawyers who represented Carnegie in the "Iron Clad Agreement" suit brought by Frick. Known as "one of the most gentlemanly lawyers at the Bar and of the Bar," Scott also served as general counsel of Fidelity Title and Trust Company.[35]

ACTUARIES, POETS, AND THE METHODS OF DOING GOOD

Thus the first Hero Fund Commission consisted of just the sort of people Carnegie most admired and could trust to make decisions about his philanthropy—hardworking, principled, active, multidimensional individuals with wide-ranging interests and experiences. *American Illustrated Magazine* would describe the commissioners in September 1905 as "shrewd" men "in whom [Carnegie] had very complete confidence, successful men of very large affairs and reasonably entitled to a very fair degree of confidence in themselves."[36] In part, this confidence rose from their commitment to the problem-solving scientific pursuits of their times. Thomas S. Arbuthnot, MD, president of the Hero Fund from 1932 to 1956, once described Carnegie's giving as "seasoned with the genius that marks the great scientist; that is, a meticulous zeal for pertinent organization, detail, and the ability to suspend judgment and abide by the slow accumulations of tedious, undramatic facts." This "scientific method" also marks the Hero Fund, which from the first has had to develop systematic, organized approaches for judging some of the most dramatic, uplifting, and selfless acts of which human beings are capable.

When Taylor called the first meeting to order on April 15, 1904, the commissioners' first task was the formal acceptance of Carnegie's Deed of Trust. Next they adopted a resolution prepared by Holland, expressing "to Mr. Carnegie our appreciation of the high honor which he has conferred upon us in inviting us to administer the affairs of the trust which he has created, and thus in some measure to share with him in the pleasure of doing good." Holland knew the value of praise where this patron was concerned.

Then came the serious business of formal organizing. How in fact should this unprecedented entity operate? Carnegie had given the high-minded idea and $5 million of his money in bonds paying $250,000 a year. Now his "employees" had to make the concept work—with few guidelines and no previous models to follow. "One great difficulty in carrying out Mr. Carnegie's wishes lies in the fact that the enterprise is so new, so lacking in the parentage of precedent," claimed *American Illustrated*. "And when it comes to deciding whether an act is really heroic or not, one is a little in doubt as to whether a poet or an actuary should be called upon to determine it."[37] Thanks to Carnegie's and Taylor's sagacity, the Commission seemed well endowed with both types.

Five commissioners were promptly named to a committee on permanent organization: Judges Buffington and Reed, Messrs. Taylor, Wilmot, and, as chair, Lynch. Within five days, this committee had recommended the name, submitted by-laws, and suggested monthly meetings of an Executive Committee to "consider cases and make its recommendations in respect to all benefits and medals. It shall cause to be made a résumé of each case and present same to the Commission for final action." Taylor appointed the Executive Committee: Holland as chairman, Anderson, Blackburn, Morrison, Wilmot, and himself.

Meanwhile Carnegie was pushing for publicity, firing off hastily handwritten, penciled notes from his castle in Scotland. "It does not do to have such new ideas fall still-born—I regret the delay," he chided Wilmot in April 1904. "The idea being new, to create an interest in it and let all men feel the Heroes are to be taken care of must be widely known."[38] Carnegie had a very modern understanding of the media's power to shape public opinion, and he knew that the daily papers' appetite for news could quickly date a fresh idea.

The Hero Fund did indeed attract widespread attention in the United States and abroad, and most journals praised the new concept. But Carnegie's "robber baronetcy" and memories of the violent labor confrontation at Homestead in 1892 had made him a divisive figure. A number of voices ridiculed his new philanthropy and questioned "the possibility of administering such a trust in a way to benefit mankind," as Holland later put it. Quite a few criticized what they misinterpreted as the "commercialization" of heroism. Another later dismissed it as a branch of Carnegie's "peace propaganda."[39]

The publicity gave the commissioners even more incentive to move with care, intending to prove the skeptics wrong.

It also made their job harder, because few outsiders grasped the purpose of the Hero Fund. Within weeks, 244 letters would arrive at the Commission's offices, asking for jobs and soliciting investments (some people thought the Fund supplied venture capital). Many also reported alleged acts of heroism, mostly undertaken by the writers themselves.

The Executive Committee quickly realized that the Commission's toughest job would be defining, evaluating, and codifying the nature of a heroic act, in line with Carnegie's Deed of Trust and their own experience. "Whether or not Mr. Carnegie had any idea that he was giving his Commission a rather large order is a matter of surmise purely, as also whether the Commission undertook its task in fear and trembling," claimed *American Illustrated Magazine* in 1905. "However they regarded it at the beginning of their labors, it is safe to say that by now they have discovered how difficult a task is cut out for them."[40]

Even Carnegie had to do some rethinking. When Taylor sent letters from self-acknowledged heroes, Carnegie replied, "I think the claims of unknown heroes will have to be thoroughly investigated, if considered at all. Men who write urging their claims appear in court under a cloud. I had in view well-proved cases—known to the public—seen and admired by their fellows—heroes who had attracted public attention,—not such as have only admired themselves. As you say much study and thought will be required to arrive at a working basis."[41]

Not until October 19, 1904, did the full Commission define and approve the Hero Fund's limitations and scope. The commissioners had discussed, debated, and resolved the following:

- The Fund was to be limited to "acts, in which conclusive evidence may be obtained showing that the person performing the act, voluntarily risked his own life in saving, or attempting to save, the life of a fellow being." As Holland would write in 1929, "it will be observed that this regulation, while not removing heroic acts from the field of impulsive effort, nevertheless provides that the performer of the deed must at the time have been conscious of the fact that its performance involved peril to himself."

- Such acts must be performed by persons the nature of whose duties in following their regular vocations, does not require them to perform such an act, i.e., the person must go beyond his duty.

- The heroic acts must be performed in the USA, the Dominion of Canada, the Colony of Newfoundland, and the waters thereof.

- Such acts must be performed on or after April 15th, 1904.

- Mr. Carnegie having directed that, in case of death, the widow and children, or other dependents, are to be provided for until the widow remarries and until the children reach a self-supporting age, and, in the event of disability, the disabled to be provided for until again able to work; the maximum death or disablement benefit to be paid in any one year to any one family or dependent, shall not exceed $1,000, the amount and manner of payment in each case to be fixed by the Commission, upon the recommendation of the Executive Committee, provided in no case, however, shall death or disablement benefits be paid unless it shall clearly be shown that the dependents or disabled need such assistance.

- Medals when awarded shall be presented, in death cases, to the widow or next of kin, and in disability and non-disability cases, to the person performing the act.

- Heroic acts may be brought to the attention of the Commission by applications by the friends of the persons performing them, and through the public press. Death and disablement cases shall be certified to by the attending physicians, and the Executive Committee shall have power to employ a traveling investigator to ascertain the facts in any given case.

By now the Carnegie Hero Fund Commission had in place its first official employees: Sara E. Weir, assistant treasurer, at a salary of $20 per month, and Wilmot, secretary, who earned $2,000 per year.

"THE MEDAL QUESTION"

Next the Executive Committee took up "the medal question"— and it seemed to perplex these capable men more than any other. Carnegie had made it clear that he intended a medal to be the hero's reward. He enjoyed presenting and receiving medals. But— what sort of medal should the Commission award? What would be its design? Should there be categories of medals? The commissioners first discussed soliciting the services of leading American sculptors for an appropriate design. Among those suggested were Augustus Saint-Gaudens and Daniel Chester French.

Talks went on. The January 1905 minutes reported that the Executive Committee was working on the design for a medal "illustrative of Mr. Carnegie's idea of a hero, as defined in his deed of trust, and as a motto the scriptural text, 'Greater love hath no man than this, that a man lay down his life for his friends'" (John 15:13). The committee had now visited leading jewelry firms. And in quite a modern way they recognized that the medal should "tell its own story, without explanation, to persons in all walks of life." They wanted the wording to appear in English rather than in Latin, a "dead language."

Even by May, however, the commissioners found the designs for the medal still not satisfactory in portraying Carnegie's idea of a hero. They took it upon themselves to change the design: the obverse side of the medal would contain only a bust of Carnegie encircled by the words, "Carnegie Hero Fund Commission, established April 15th, 1904." The reverse side would contain the coats of arms of the United States, Canada, and Newfoundland, suitably enwreathed, and the tablet for the inscription, with the motto. They awarded the commission to the fashionable J. E. Caldwell & Company of Philadelphia. This firm had shown "the greatest effort and ability of any of the competitors toward the desired object." And they decided to create three categories of medals: gold, silver, and bronze. All would be three inches in diameter, and three-sixteenths of an inch in thickness.

A HUNGER FOR HEROES

In the meantime, the able Wilmot had devised a system for tabulating and organizing the cases to be presented to the Commission. By May 1905, he had reclassified all cases received since the establishment of the Fund. More than 230 cases had been refused, and 174 were pending.

On May 24, 1905, the Carnegie Hero Fund Commission approved and granted its first 12 awards. The awards included death benefits, disablement benefits, and "betterment benefits," bestowed upon the recipients of medals whom the Executive Committee had deemed worthy of financial help. Three widows of heroes received annual awards, and the sole woman hero received scholarship help so she could continue her studies.

Announcement of these first awards silenced the doubters. The public and the media responded enthusiastically to the Hero Fund. All the awards are for "acts of a fine, fearless sort, worthy of thought and memory," wrote H. K. Webster. "Every time that Mr. Carnegie's Commission can hold up before us, in a way that commands our attention, a man of our own day and our own or a humbler walk of life, who in some great moment has squarely turned his back upon the Main Chance, they have done us a service. The sight may not make heroes of us, but at least it will melt off something of the crust of cynicism and selfishness which has been blinding our eyes."[42]

"In a time when every possible crime, every form of meanness and selfishness, is exploited at great length by the newspapers, it is well that the story of good deeds should be told as often and as completely as possible," wrote *The Outlook* in 1913.[43]

And in 1996: "Local heroes may never have been as important as they are today, an era when there are so few national heroes. Today the national hunger for heroes may be best satisfied on a small scale, where a single man, woman, or child may exemplify the selfless bravery America has long honored."[44]

And so it was that the Carnegie Hero Fund passed "from the experimental stage to the permanent," in Taylor's words, "where the Hero Commission takes its stand firmly among the great benevolences of the age."

Over a century of amazing change, the Carnegie Hero Fund Commission has naturally met and dealt with extraordinary challenges. The commissioners have also wisely managed Carnegie's "princely" gift of $5 million so that at the end of 2021 the Fund totaled $66 million. And they have carried out these responsibilities with respect for the original, founding commissioners who wrote the first "road map" for modern philanthropy.

A hundred years ago, Carnegie hoped to change the world with large-scale, systematically distributed philanthropy. The Hero Fund Commission was one of his very first attempts to do so. And although his later gifts eclipsed it in size, he always cherished the Hero Fund—perhaps because he recognized the unchanging nature of humanity's hunger for heroes. As Carnegie himself wrote with typical optimism to Taylor in 1905, "You have made a start, and there is to be no finish. It goes on forever."

Excerpts from Hero Fund booklet by Mary Brignano

Andrew Carnegie sent a clear signal in 1904 when he appointed Charles L. Taylor to be the first president of the Carnegie Hero Fund Commission. He wanted his unique philanthropic venture to be administered as efficiently, systematically, and scientifically as his steel plants had been. A metallurgical chemist, Taylor had helped turn steelmaking into a science rather than a craft.

CHARLES LEWIS TAYLOR

Charles Lewis Taylor (1857–1922) was born in Philadelphia and educated at the new Lehigh University, where he studied mining engineering and graduated first in his class in 1876. He went to work as assistant chemist in the first chemical laboratory associated with an iron and steel firm in America—the Cambria Iron Works of Johnstown, Pennsylvania. In 1880 he moved to Pittsburgh to be chemist, then superintendent, of the state-of-the-art Bessemer Steel Company at Homestead. When Carnegie Steel took over this huge plant in 1883, Taylor stayed as superintendent and helped make the world-famous Homestead Steel Works one of the most technologically advanced and efficient in the world. The rest of his career would be spent with Carnegie.

Upon retiring from the steel business, Taylor, at Carnegie's request, took on the oversight of the $4 million Carnegie Relief Fund, Carnegie's "first use of surplus wealth." Taylor in 1911 became a founding board member of the $125 million Carnegie Corporation of New York, the largest single philanthropic trust established up to that time. What Taylor most contributed in his work with the Carnegie Hero Fund was the objective, scientific approach that had characterized his work with steel. He and his fellow commissioners had been handed the difficult, complex job of defining, evaluating, and codifying the nature of a heroic act. Taylor took it upon himself "to so plan the work that in future years the far-seeing wisdom and the genuine beneficence of the Founder should be vindicated." Within a few months his "administrative sagacity" had helped build a methodology around an ideal—and had created the first road map for modern philanthropy.

In addition to his work with the Hero Fund, Taylor served as a trustee of the Western Pennsylvania Institute for the

Blind, the Carnegie Library of Pittsburgh, Carnegie Institute of Pittsburgh, Carnegie Institute of Technology, and the Carnegie Endowment for International Peace. "One of the best men that ever lived" is how Carnegie described his silver-haired friend— despite the fact that Taylor was not afraid to stand up to his former employer. In 1906, when the two men had a friendly difference of opinion about whether or not to send money to victims of the San Francisco earthquake, Taylor announced to Carnegie, "You are not a member of the Commission. You have parted with your money and left it in the care of your friends, and the decision in this case will have to rest with them." Just as Charles L. Taylor, the first president of the Hero Fund advanced Pittsburgh as a great industrial center, its second president, the amazingly multifaceted William J. Holland, who became president of the Hero Fund in 1923, worked incessantly to translate the philanthropic vision of his friend Carnegie into action.

A Renaissance man who studied natural science, languages, art history, literature, theology, architecture, law, economics, and education, Holland wrote three books and more than 130 articles about butterflies and moths; read Greek, Latin, Hebrew, Arabic, Japanese, and all the romance languages (many of which he also spoke); and was at various times during his long life (1848–1932) a teacher, high school principal, medical student, Presbyterian minister, chancellor of the University of Pittsburgh, and first director of the Carnegie Museum of Natural History. He was "there at the creation" of the Carnegie Hero Fund and, with Taylor, understood better than anyone how best to bring it to life.

William Jacob Holland was born in Jamaica, where his parents were missionaries and naturalists. Before the age of 18, he completed studies at Moravian College at Bethlehem, Pennsylvania, and in 1869 he graduated from Amherst College. After earning a degree at Princeton Theological Seminary in 1874, he was assigned to Pittsburgh's new Bellefield Presbyterian Church. In 1879 Holland married Carrie Moorhead, youngest daughter of wealthy iron manufacturer John Moorhead. Through this union and the prominent members of his church, he moved in Pittsburgh's leading social circles. Summering with the Moorheads in Cresson, Pennsylvania, for example, he got to know Andrew Carnegie, who liked the ambitious young minister's

WILLIAM J. HOLLAND

zeal for learning. On walks through the woods around Cresson, Holland taught the industrialist the names of plants and birds. Their friendship would continue for the rest of Carnegie's life.

By 1891 Holland became chancellor of the Western University of Pennsylvania (today the University of Pittsburgh), where he helped transform this undergraduate men's college into a coed university and laid the groundwork for its move to Oakland. Added during his tenure were schools of medicine, law, mines and mining engineering; colleges of pharmacy and dentistry; and a department of electrical engineering.

Then, while he was still chancellor, Carnegie appointed him as the first director of the new Carnegie Museum of Natural History. Serving as director until 1922 and director emeritus until his death, Holland more than fulfilled Carnegie's desire that his museum be a dynamic cultural force that would reach out, educate, and take its place among the great museums of the world. He turned a raw, virtually empty building into a world-class institution and launched one of the four or five most important dinosaur collections in the United States.

A founding trustee of Carnegie Institute and an internationally known entomologist, Holland also started the scientific publishing program of the Carnegie Museum of Natural History. He served as trustee of a number of colleges and universities, was a member of numerous national and international scientific societies, and took the initiative in founding the American Association of Museums.

A leader as well in public health, he headed the initiative to build a water purification system for Pittsburgh that lowered the city's typhoid fever death rate from 65 per 100,000 in 1908 to 2.7 by 1920.

Holland was among the first people to whom Carnegie revealed his ideas for the Hero Fund. He was the Commission's first vice president, and he was perhaps the foremost torchbearer for Carnegie's unprecedented, wide-ranging philanthropic vision.

The Carnegie Hero Fund Commission elevated Pittsburgh's civic image as the 20th century unfolded, revealing the altruistic side of the city of metal, money, and smoke. The Commission's presidents, in their various professions, did the same. In his effective, good-humored, and likeable way, Dr. Thomas Shaw

Arbuthnot was a generous and public-spirited leader for the Hero Fund and the many other organizations he served. Its longest-serving president (1932–1956), he guided the Commission through the momentous years of the Great Depression, World War II, and the birth of modern America in the 1950s. Arbuthnot (1871–1956) had an infectious gusto for life. A prominent physician, he enjoyed classical music, sports (especially golf), art, adventurous travel, and his many friends. A man of ideas and action whose zest for big game hunting invited comparison with Theodore Roosevelt, he was equally at home on safari or in the operating room. He was a member of the medical staffs of four hospitals, served as president of the Pittsburgh Art Society, wrote books and articles, starred in a film, and in 1936 helped to incorporate the University Hospital Board to represent the interests of the hospitals associated with the Medical Center in Oakland.

Arbuthnot was born into a comfortable family in Allegheny City, today Pittsburgh's North Side, and grew up in the family home in Pittsburgh, where he would live the rest of his life. He graduated in 1894 from Yale University, where he played third base on the University Nine, performed with the Glee Club, and was president of the Banjo Club. He earned his medical degree in 1898 from Columbia University College of Physicians and Surgeons. Because no U.S. physician could at that time be considered properly educated until he had studied in Europe, Dr. Arbuthnot went abroad for two years of post-graduate work in Edinburgh, Dublin, and London. Returning to Pittsburgh in 1900, the good-looking, socially prominent young surgeon found his services much in demand. He was invited to join the medical staffs of West Penn, Mercy, Tuberculosis, and Children's Hospitals. In 1909, at the age of 38, he was appointed dean of the underperforming University of Pittsburgh School of Medicine and charged with converting it into one of the most prestigious medical schools in the nation. In 1913 the School of Medicine received an A+ rating from the American Medical Association's Council of Medical Education, putting it in a league with medical colleges at Johns Hopkins, Harvard, and Yale.

The good doctor would be equally hardworking and unselfish in his work for the Hero Fund, which he joined in 1912.

To commemorate the 100th anniversary of Andrew Carnegie's birth, in 1935, Arbuthnot produced the elegantly written *Heroes of Peace*, a history of the Carnegie Hero Fund Commission he served with such generous spirit for 44 years. He praised Carnegie's giving, and the Commission's work, as "seasoned with the genius that marks the great scientist; that is, a meticulous zeal for pertinent organization, detail, and the ability to suspend judgment and abide by the slow accumulations of tedious, undramatic facts." If the first three presidents of the Carnegie Hero Fund Commission gave form to an unprecedented philanthropic vision, its fourth arrived at the right moment to establish a gratifying sense of tradition. The cordial and gracious Charles Arbuthnot McClintock (1883–1968), the nephew of the Commission's third president, Thomas S. Arbuthnot, was a leading banker and a generous citizen whose interests centered on history—especially western Pennsylvania history. He became president as Pittsburgh celebrated its bicentennial and the Hero Fund had passed its half-century mark. His wide-ranging knowledge of and his family's historic contributions to the Pittsburgh region gave him an uncommon understanding of the importance of the people and institutions that made the city unique.

Prominent among these, certainly, was the Hero Fund, and, as its leader, McClintock imparted not only his financial counsel but also his appreciation of its enduring value. Known to many friends as "Spook," McClintock was born in Pittsburgh to Jonas Roup McClintock, Jr., and Elizabeth Arbuthnot McClintock, the sister of Thomas Arbuthnot. His grandfather McClintock was Pittsburgh's first elected (not council-appointed) mayor. McClintock entered Princeton in 1903 and played football; although an injury forced him to the sidelines, he remained a loyal booster. At important games he often was called from the stands to lead the singing and cheers, and he also lent his rich bass voice to the Glee and Triangle Clubs. He loved Princeton, and Princeton loved him: He served as vice president of his class and, as president of the Princeton Alumni Association of Western Pennsylvania, became one of the association's best known and most enthusiastic members for more than 60 years.

McClintock started his career in the insurance business and then became associated with the Commonwealth Trust

Company. During and after World War I, he served briefly with combat troops as a captain in the 1st Infantry Division and as a major in the 1st Battalion of the 7th Infantry, 3rd Division, American Army of Occupation. In his banking career he rose to the presidency of Colonial Trust Company, one of the largest trust companies in Pittsburgh. In that role he took part in creating what has become one of the largest banks in the United States. Colonial Trust merged in 1954 with Fidelity Trust Company to create Fidelity Trust, and McClintock served as chairman of the board of the bank formed by the union. When Fidelity Trust merged with Peoples First National Bank & Trust Company in 1959 to create Pittsburgh National Bank, he became a director of the institution that has grown to become PNC, one of the leading financial services organizations in the country today.

McClintock became a member of the Carnegie Hero Fund Commission in 1938, four years after joining the Historical Society of Western Pennsylvania. These two organizations would occupy much of his time in coming years.

Spook McClintock died unexpectedly in 1968 while reading an issue of the historical society's magazine. In a resolution marking his death, the Hero Fund recorded, "His greeting had the warmth of the morning sun. To the work of the Commission he brought integrity, perception, and a generous measure of practical value. His judgment was keen and his decision firm. He was, perhaps above all, a loyal friend who will long be remembered with the greatest respect and deepest affection."

Presidents of the Carnegie Hero Fund Commission have brought many talents and proficiencies to their position, but perhaps none was better trained to analyze facts and technicalities to arrive at the essence of heroism than the self-effacing Stewart McClintic, who played a secret role in what one historian called "the most significant intelligence enterprise in the history of warfare."

During World War II, he served in London as a lieutenant colonel in the U.S. Strategic and Tactical Air Forces, working with the British Air Ministry to analyze intelligence reports to support strategic bombing campaigns over Nazi-occupied Europe. Thousands of lives depended on his ability to evaluate an array of information—an experience that fortified this courtly civil engineer's renowned respect for structure and precision. Stewart McClintic (1904–1982) was born in Pittsburgh to Howard Hale McClintic and Margaret McCulloch McClintic. His father co-founded the McClintic-Marshall Construction Company with fellow Lehigh University engineering classmate Charles D. Marshall in 1900; it would develop into the largest independent steel-fabricating firm in the country, producing structural steel for the Panama Canal locks, the Empire State Building, and the Golden Gate Bridge.

In his intelligence work, McClintic had to be not only smart and reliable but also diplomatic and social. In London he had his uniforms made on Savile Row, lived in the glamorous Claridge's hotel, and shared a flat in Belgravia with two colleagues. It was in London that McClintic met his future wife, Pamela Gresson, an elegant British war widow who drove an ambulance for the Red Cross. They were married in 1946 and had two children, Miranda and Howard—who both remember how seriously their father took his responsibilities at the Hero Fund.

STEWART McCLINTIC

"He would read the case reports out loud to us," recalls Miranda. "He cared very much about each one. That was part of his philosophy of life: recognition for every individual. He treated everyone the same."

McClintic served for a number of years as president of the board of the Eye and Ear Hospital in Pittsburgh. He became a member of the Commission in 1947, succeeding his father, a member from 1912 until his death in 1938. As treasurer, he oversaw its finances for almost 30 years.

"His frequent memoranda are classics in revealing the dedication of this man to the efficient operation of the Fund," read the Commission minutes.

He believed in the Carnegie Medal as the highest symbol of civilian heroism, and he refused to award it lightly or without a thorough examination of the facts.

"We must pursue the truth," he insisted over and over. "Perhaps we will never have an opportunity to be dramatically heroic," this dignified, thoughtful, courteous man once wrote. "Yet, every day we can be responding to the needs of others; in specific ways we can be mentally preparing ourselves to be truly useful in case of the chance emergency. This predisposition of the mind and nerve to help others will speed the reactions necessary when the crisis happens. We may be a hero, in the eyes of some. But for those who know, it will be the natural, spontaneous act of one who has prepared himself to love his fellow men wherever the need."

The Commission's fourth president, Robert W. Off (1919–2010), was a quiet banker who led the Carnegie Hero Fund Commission for longer than anyone since Thomas Arbuthnot, the Commission's third president, who served from 1932 to 1956. Born two months after the life of Andrew Carnegie ended, Off led the Fund into the 21st century in ways Carnegie would heartily have approved. He oversaw a 237 percent increase in the Commission's portfolio and the institution of asset allocation and spending limitation policies. He upgraded staff salaries and benefits and modernized operations, computerizing office procedures and records and reducing operating costs by streamlining case investigation procedures. He broadened public relations. Moreover, during Off's tenure the board gained 11 new members of decided expertise, enthusiasm, and commitment, including its first women. His daughter Augusta Moravec described Off as "a peach of a guy."

He was born in Winnetka, Illinois, to businessman and investor Clifford Off and Helen Willock Off. His mother was a Pittsburgher, the daughter of Samuel M. Willock, founder of the Waverly Oil Works Company. Off graduated from The Hun School of Princeton in 1938 and the University of Virginia in 1942, with a degree in geology. Immediately after the attack on Pearl Harbor in 1941, he enlisted in the U.S. Army Air Force and served first as a flight instructor. He then reported to southern Italy to join the new 15th Air Force, created in 1943 to carry out strategic daytime bombing of precise targets in Germany and occupied Europe— exactly the kind of precision bombing that Stewart McClintic's intelligence work in London was helping to plan and assign. Off completed 29 combat missions in the European Theater and 23 missions as a group or squadron leader. His airtime totaled over 2,100 hours. He received the Distinguished Flying Cross—the third highest award for valor in aerial combat—for the destruction of the Köln Oil Refinery, a mission in which he returned home on one engine, three having been lost to ground fire. And then the fighting was over, and Captain Off, along with 12 million of his

ROBERT W. OFF

fellow Americans, took off his uniform and "became once again ordinary people."

In 1946 he went to work at Mellon Bank as a loan officer and remained at Mellon for 33 years, retiring as a senior vice president in charge of commercial lending. In 1946 he also married Mary Augusta "Polly" Bickel. The Offs lived in Pittsburgh and had three children, Robert, Augusta, and Helen. A modest and private person, he became even more devoted to his family when Polly contracted polio in the early 1950s and was in a wheelchair for the rest of her life. He cared for her until her death in 1990.

Off joined the Hero Fund Commission in 1973 and served first as treasurer. With his retirement from the bank, he became Commission president in 1979 and began the work of bringing the Hero Fund up to date. He worked on the staff payroll until 1990 (forgoing benefits) but continued without salary as president until the age of 82. At Off's memorial service, the rector said, "There is a time to receive medals and a time to give medals." He was alluding not only to the familiar passage from Ecclesiastes 3 but also to two widely differing elements of Off 's life: his heroic military service during World War II and his long oversight of a foundation that recognizes civilian heroism. Although he had demonstrated heroic courage in war, he loved the Hero Fund because it honored the heroes of peace.

"As well-suited as Bob was for the various disciplines of management," observed Mark Laskow, Off's successor, in 2001, "his greatest asset was his devotion to the ideals of the mission of the Hero Fund. His hallmarks were integrity, loyalty, and affability—certainly worthy to the task of honoring those who selflessly serve others." Shortly after he was elected Commission president in 2001, Mark Laskow was interviewed by a young reporter who asked, "What changes do you expect to be making at the Carnegie Hero Fund?"

Surprising his questioner, Mark answered, "None." He went on to explain that, in 1904, Carnegie made a clear statement of what he considered to be of enduring value in human character and that no alterations were necessary to the Hero Fund's mission. "Modern society still needs heroes, and the Hero Fund still finds them and still honors their acts and spirit."

Laskow, whose title changed to Board Chair in 2013, is the most recent former leader in a line of extraordinary leaders of the Carnegie Hero Fund. His inauguration as president was baptized by fire, coming three months after 9/11 as the Commission formulated its response to the unprecedented degree of selfless heroism exhibited at the terror sites in Manhattan, Shanksville, and Washington, D.C. Additional circumstances that demanded Laskow's attention in his early years as president included preparation for the Commission's centennial, the instituting of the Carnegie Medal of Philanthropy with its call for involvement by all of Carnegie's benefactions, and the widespread use of the Internet with its seemingly limitless opportunities for communication.

Laskow took advantage of all these developments to raise the profile of the Hero Fund and its work while at the same time honoring and acting on its cherished principles. A native of Philadelphia, Laskow graduated from the University of Pennsylvania and the University of Pittsburgh School of Law. Formerly an associate at Reed Smith, he was vice president and director of The Hillman Company and the chief executive officer of Greycourt & Co., an independent investment advisor. He and his wife, Lisa, are the parents of two sons, Paul and Thomas. In addition to his work with the Hero Fund, Mark is active in health care. As a board member, director, chairman, and trustee of hospitals and health care foundations, he has made the case for elimination of hospital-borne infections and medication errors, and improved efficiency, safety, and retention by challenging the status quo and building consensus among hospitals and health plan administrators, physicians, business leaders, and health care advocates.

A trustee of UPMC Shadyside (formerly Shadyside Hospital) since 1983, Laskow was vice chair of the University of Pittsburgh Medical Center. He chaired the Shadyside Hospital Foundation and also the UPMC Health Plan. In 2011, the Allegheny County, Pennsylvania, Medical Society presented him with the Benjamin Rush Individual Public Health Award, which honors a lay individual who has made an outstanding contribution to the betterment, health, and welfare of citizens in the county.

Laskow's civic engagement extends to The Dietrich Foundation, a Pittsburgh-based, $550 million fund that supports higher education and charitable organizations primarily in Western Pennsylvania. He was named board chair in 2012.

Laskow became a member of the Hero Fund Commission in 1993, serving on the finance and executive committees and chairing the latter. The commemoration of the Hero Fund's centennial in 2004 provided an opportunity for its new administration to recognize the value of history both as a course-steadier and a map for the future. Laskow was convinced that the occasion merited memorable events of lasting value: a speech by David McCullough in the Carnegie Music Hall, a dinner, a book and video, and the presentation of a commemorative medal, all centered on the heroes. The 250 people who attended the elegant dinner in the grand Hall of Architecture of the Carnegie Museum of Art brought together Commission members, community leaders, and a number of medal awardees, some of them traveling from the west coasts of both the United States and Canada.

For Laskow, the Carnegie evening also spawned ideas on how the Hero Fund could be more effective, more inclusive, and more open. These ideas revolved around greater outreach, both to integrate the awardees into a cohesive unit—a "family"— and to elevate their status as merited by their selflessness. The Commission began to publish a quarterly newsletter. Presentations of the medal by Commission members, staff, and local awardees became regular events. The Hero Fund enhanced its website and introduced a bronze grave marker to be provided to the families of deceased awardees. The Commission then broadened this outreach by revitalizing the Hero Fund's relationships with the more than 20 other Carnegie institutions, including the European hero funds.

The Hero Fund was strengthened through measures Laskow oversaw to guard its financial security.

"We combine flexibility with a frugality that would make our founder proud," he wrote in the midst of the economic downturn of 2008–2009. Quick to commend the leadership of the Hero Fund's finance committee, Mark concluded that investment management changes made early in the decade resulted not only in record-high portfolio levels but in major defenses against the collapse of equities and against inflation while retaining the opportunity to participate in recovery. But for all his big ideas and broadening of the Hero Fund's interactions with the world, Laskow always nodded back to the unchanging nature of humanity's hunger for heroes. As he wrote, "The Carnegie Medal represents a considered judgment in which the heroic act was weighed against an exacting standard and found worthy. History steadies our course. When Commission members deliberate, they are well aware of the Hero Fund's history and of their own responsibility in adding to that history. Year by year we are building our next great century, confident that there will be no shortage of heroes, no shortage of those willing to act in the face of danger to aid others."

At its annual meeting in June of 2022, newly elected Chair Eric Zahren nominated, and the Commission elected, Laskow the first-ever Chair Emeritus of the Commission.

In Andrew Carnegie's Deed of Trust he specified, "A medal shall be given to the hero, or widow, or next of kin, which shall recite the heroic deed it commemorates, that descendants may know and be proud of their descent."

Numerous documents in the Commission's files tracing the history of the development of the medal from this directive to the first one struck, more than two years later, attest that the process was painstakingly thorough. A reference to this process can be found on pages 40–41, as can other details about the medal's early history, including that they were to be struck in gold, silver, and bronze.

Without any evidence of a formal policy, and without a precedent to follow, it is unclear how in its formative years the Commission decided to award the three medals. Beginning in the early 1920s, however, a policy was adopted that stated that the gold medal would be awarded for heroic acts involving several rescuers, the silver for rescuers who repeatedly risked their lives in the persistent performance of their acts, and the bronze for all other rescues. In early 1981, the Commission decided that the bronze medal would be the only one awarded. The last gold medal to an individual was awarded to **Charles L. Coe** (⸸ *C. H. 1865*), posthumously, who died in a fire rescue act on February 6, 1923. An account of Coe's rescue is on page 132. The last silver medals were awarded to **Brian Mervyn Clegg** (*C. H. 6476*) and **Robert Stephen Grant** (*C. H. 6475*) for their rescue of three individuals from exposure in a downed airplane in Lake of the Woods, Kenora, Ontario, in March of 1979.

In all, 19 gold, 617 silver, and 8,128 bronze medals were awarded in the Hero Fund's first 100 years.

Carnegie Medals awarded in 2004 include a banner to mark the Commission's centennial year, which replaces "Established April 15, 1904." The word Commission has been added. On the reverse, the biblical verse has been attributed to John 15:13. The seal of Newfoundland has been removed, and the flora detail has been simplified.

Medals struck in 2005 and beyond will revert to the "Established April 15, 1904" embossing.

(ABOVE) Luigi Badia, an artist from Somers, New York, works on the sculpture of the 2004 Carnegie Medal.

(FACING PAGE) Carnegie Medal Obverse: Several strikes of a bronze blank are necessary to gain the final relief. Reverse: In low relief is the geographical outline of the United States and Canada. In higher relief are the seals of the United States on the bottom, Canada on the top left, and Newfoundland on the top right. When the medal was designed, Newfoundland was a separate colony. The passage encircling the margin, "Greater love hath no man than this, that a man lay down his life for his friends," is from the New Testament, John 15:13. On the inscription plate, or cartouche, a brief description of the rescue is embossed, along with the name of the rescuer, the rescued, and where and when the act occurred. Relief work under the plate contains sprigs of laurel, typifying glory, and above are sprigs of ivy, oak, and thistle, for friendship, strength, and persistence.

Frank M. Wilmot,
Commission manager,
seated, center,
with special agents.
Photograph is undated,
but is thought to have
been taken in the early
1910s.

BY MARY BRIGNANO

IV

There is no branch of detective science which is so important and so much neglected as the act of tracing footsteps," announced Sherlock Holmes in 1887. In that year, just 17 years before the creation of the Carnegie Hero Fund, Holmes made his first appearance in detective fiction, and the reading public took to him immediately. Here was a "scientific" detective whose exacting, uncanny observation and deductive reasoning made him a force for justice—a hero who could snare a murderer and right society's wrongs by studying facts and evidence. "There is," Sherlock Holmes says time and again, "nothing like first-hand evidence."

In his insistence on the facts and facts alone, this hero of detective science could be a model for the Carnegie Hero Fund's special agents, later known as field representatives and now case investigators. These men and women have studied and authenticated nearly 9,000 heroic acts since January 1905, and have investigated countless more. For a century, they have worked to fulfill Andrew Carnegie's charge to celebrate the noblest, most unselfish behavior of which human beings may be capable. And the best way they and the Hero Fund's commissioners have found to honor such heroism is through the unwavering, objective search for facts. Rigorously documenting each extraordinary act, case investigators and their dedicated scrutiny give heroism its rightful recognition.

In the words of Herbert W. Eyman, who spent 25 years as an investigator with the Hero Fund, "Essentially field work is a quest for truth. Within the framework of our organization a man … is a hero only if, in our opinion, he risked his life and that fact can be conclusively established." Heroism cannot be proved "through an accumulation of assumptions," Eyman added. "It can only be achieved through thoroughness in the investigation to the point that all doors to speculation are closed." Or, as Holmes put it, "It is a capital mistake to theorize before you have all the evidence. It biases the judgment."

EXTRAORDINARY INVESTIGATORS

Struggling to wrestle Carnegie's philanthropic ideals into a functional, enduring organization, the first commissioners quickly realized that they could not by themselves verify reported acts of heroism taking place over the 7.4 million square miles of the continental United States, Canada, and the then-British colony of Newfoundland. Frank Wilmot, the Fund's manager, announced in October 1904 that, although seven cases had been investigated, 52 more were still pending. How could the commissioners properly judge these cases without trustworthy evidence to guide them? "In all of these cases it is the feeling of the Executive Committee that before reaching a final decision it is desirable that the localities where the alleged acts of heroism were performed should be visited by a representative of the Commission, who may ascertain the facts more clearly," state the minutes for October 1904.

William L. Abbott, who had so successfully launched the Carnegie Company's force of salaried sales agents, moved that the Executive Committee be "empowered to engage the services of such persons as might be necessary to investigate cases for the Commission." Thus in January 1905 the Commission hired its first traveling special agent, George A. Campsey, formerly a reporter for the *Pittsburg Times* newspaper. His salary was $100 a month plus expenses, to be raised to $125 at six months if his services proved satisfactory. His living expenses on the road were not to exceed a thrifty $3.50 per day. A year later, with 195 cases in line for investigation, the commissioners hired a second special agent. He was John P. Cowan, a reporter for the *Pittsburg Gazette*. By 1912, there would be 10 agents, all former journalists.

Why reporters? "Newspaper reporters with college training seemed to be the combination best suited to the work," wrote Commission President Thomas S. Arbuthnot in 1935. Quoting a 1909 magazine article, he claimed that the commissioners found their training and previous experience "conducive to thoroughness of investigation and lucidity of statement."[1] Another writer singled out the educated reporter's ability "to detect fraud and exaggeration."[2]

Again the Carnegie Hero Fund commissioners had demonstrated their innovative approach to problem solving as well as their desire to please their "boss." Carnegie had shown quite a modern ability to shape popular opinion through mass media. He treated reporters well, putting up New York journalists at Pittsburgh's elite Duquesne Club, for instance, when they covered the opening of Carnegie Institute in 1895. He wrote essays for popular magazines. He had shrewdly insisted on publicizing the Hero Fund in order to promote its reach and effectiveness—unlike his rival John D. Rockefeller, who preferred to keep his giving more private.

The commissioners also seemed to understand the trends that had so changed journalism in the late 19th century, when mass communications began to shape popular culture. Technology had dramatically lowered the cost of newspaper publishing, and publishing rivals like Joseph Pulitzer and William Randolph Hearst drove up sales with sensational stories. They also launched journalistic crusades against social injustice and ran exposés of political and economic corruption. Although the targets of these investigations called them "yellow journalism" and "muckraking," reporters like Pittsburgh's Nellie Bly (the pen name of Elizabeth Cochrane) courageously opened readers' eyes to cruelty in mental institutions, sweatshops, and jails, and to bribery in the legislature. The "new" reporters made journalism a profession that appealed to adventurous, idealistic men and women—just the sort of eyes and ears the Carnegie Hero Fund Commission needed.

"The hero hunter must be a good interviewer," stated a *Harper's Weekly* article in 1912. "He must be a keen judge of people. … He must know how to get evidence and how to sift it. Above all, he must have good judgment. He must be young and energetic. And since the job entails months of travel yearly, unmarried men are preferred."[3]

And, by recommending a thorough investigation of each case of reported heroism, the commissioners revealed their own bias for the scientific method. Only by strict documentation of the facts could the elusive nature of heroism be *proved* to a skeptical public. These special investigators also opened yet another new field in American philanthropy. They were in some ways the first scientific program officers. Advocating the case study method to determine a hero's eligibility, they became the experts on whom the commissioners relied to guide their policy.

TO KINGDOM COME WITHOUT A MURMUR

"Facts, and facts only" became the special agent's Holmesian mantra. The Commission outfitted each with the latest equipment: a pocket Kodak camera, instruments for measuring distances, and a typewriter—the camera and the typewriter being fairly new technologies. "With these accoutrements he was ready for the road, wherever it might lead—to the banks of Newfoundland or to the swamps of Georgia," enthused Commissioner Arbuthnot.

The first special agents spent as many as 11 months on the road each year, a routine that changed only in the 1950s. *Harper's Weekly* described a typical travel schedule in 1912:

> The investigator starts from the office in Pittsburgh on a regular itinerary. Perhaps his itinerary will read something like this: Pittsburgh to Steubenville, to Youngstown, to Warren, to Cambridge Springs, to Erie, to Ashtabula, to Cleveland, to Toledo, to Detroit, to Benton Harbor, and thence to Chicago. When the investigator reaches Cleveland, perhaps he finds instructions to go to Louisville, thence to Mansfield, to Indianapolis, and so to Benton Harbor. Arriving at Chicago, he finds orders to go to Milwaukee, then to points in Wisconsin, Minnesota, and North Dakota, and so back to Chicago. From here he is sent through Illinois, down into Missouri and Tennessee, and thence back to Pittsburgh. Thus a trip that was intended to extend from April to June lasts until the end of December. The best hero hunter … will go to kingdom come without a murmur.[4]

Until the 1950s, the investigators traveled just about every mile by rail—and Carnegie steel plants had produced many of these rails. In each town or city, they followed the same routine, registering at a hotel (never revealing the purpose of their visit and always requesting a room at or near the minimum rate), studying the documents relating to the case, interviewing those who had reported the case, interviewing eyewitnesses, studying, measuring, and photographing the site of the act, and finally interviewing the "hero," if he or she had survived. "An experienced investigator quickly scents a case that amounts to nothing, and he as quickly gets to the bottom of it and drops it," *Harper's Weekly* informed its readers. "But on a genuine case he spends anywhere from two to three days to as many months."

"Although the job required you to talk to everybody from millionaires to people who lived in chicken coops, it could get kind of lonely out there," admits retired investigator William A. Dillon. After spending all day in the field and eating a solitary dinner, the investigator used the evening hours to write and type his daily log and detailed report. The report included (and still includes) the time, place, and circumstances of the rescue, along with pertinent facts such as weather conditions or tidal stages. If, for example, the special investigator discovered that the tide had been out at the time of a reported near drowning, he might become suspicious that the "rescue" took place in six feet of water. Each report had to include statements from all those interviewed and information about the witnesses' reputations. Were they honest, reliable people? How old was the rescuer (always listed as RR)? How much did the RR weigh? How much did the rescued (QD) weigh? Exactly how many feet from the approaching train did the QD fall? Exactly how fast was the train traveling? How many seconds did the RR have to save the QD? How far from the riverbank was the QD? How many miles per hour was the current flowing? "When possible," stated an early investigator's manual, "current speeds should be measured by timing a floating object over a measured distance." And, "in runaway cases carefully develop and state clearly *how* the horse was going, i.e., whether running wildly, on a gallop, rearing and plunging, panic-stricken, etc." And, "to determine width of river, etc., from Point A sight object C on a line forming a 60-degree angle (ten minutes on your watch) with the bank. Pace off distance AB, B being opposite C. Distance BC equals AB x 1.7321."

Every question, every measurement, and every judgment led toward one goal: to answer the question, Can it be *conclusively established* that the RR *knowingly risked his or her life* in the attempt to save another human being?

The investigators' single-spaced reports, often accompanied by photos and drawings, are as remarkable today as they were a century ago. In factual, uninflected, even dry language, they recount extraordinary acts of ordinary people. Composed by solitary men in the banal rooms of hotels throughout North America, these disciplined descriptions can bring a reader to tears, and to a new reverence for human nobility.

COLORED TACKS AND CARGO PLANES

Meanwhile, back in the Hero Fund's Pittsburgh office, by 1911 H. A. Pickering had been brought in from the field to "criticize and condense" the special investigators' reports, while a home office manager deployed the travelers from alligator-infested bayous of Louisiana to remote encampments in Alaska. To plot an economical itinerary for each investigation, the manager relied on sectional maps of the United States, Canada, and Newfoundland, each stored in a single shallow drawer of a specially built cabinet. Colored tacks studded each map, blue for the site of the act to be investigated, red and black for the residence of persons who had witnessed the act, green for the residence of persons to be interviewed in regard to acts in another state, and pink for the residence of an original reporter of an act, not living near the scene.

What colored tacks could not reveal were the adventures of the wandering life, a job that would eventually carry investigators by hay wagon, motorcycle, jet plane, "from a roomette in a luxury night train to a dusty seat in a Star Mail Route station wagon, from a deck chair aboard a glittering lake steamer to the bow seat of a small outboard motorboat, from the generally ubiquitous taxicab to self-propelled shoe leather."[5]

Suburban growth, highway construction, and the decline of public transportation led to the use of rental cars in the 1970s. But by the mid-1980s the investigators came in from the field. The Commission's three case investigators now work almost entirely from the Pittsburgh office, relying on telephones and computers and fax machines and the mail to conduct their research and correspondence.

But whether on the road or at a desk, as the *Wall Street Journal* wrote in 1966, "The occupational hazard of working in the field of heroism is an unblinking awareness of the fragility of life and the dangers underlying even mundane activities." Investigators have at times risked their own lives to uncover acts of heroism, and in the Commission office the memories live on. There was the day Eyman had to take a 17-foot mail boat from Rockland, Maine, across a stormy open sea to Vinal Haven Island—and he made the four-hour trip lashed to the mast. Once he flew on a tiny cargo plane from an island off the Alaska coast to Juneau, lying on crates loaded with fresh salmon. One day he walked a mile-long Florida lane to the home of a reputed moonshiner; wide enough for one car, the road was flanked by deep, water-filled ditches— home, he surmised, to poisonous snakes and alligators. A pack of hounds threatened to tear him apart when he reached the house. But Eyman got his interview—as did Walter Rutkowski when he investigated a "bear case" in the Yukon, traveling on puddle jumper planes from one Inuit town to the next, then chartering a pickup truck and driving into the tundra to track down the peripatetic gold miner who had saved a young woman by taking his ax to the bear that attacked her. The miner received a bronze medal and $2,000 for his valor. Rutkowski received his regular paycheck. But had he not persisted, this heroic act would have gone unrecognized.

RESPECTING THE MISSION

Case investigators are not charged to speculate about or judge *why* some people risk their lives for others. For 100 years, their loyalty has focused on the discovery and distillation of the facts, and they maintain a deep-seated respect for their mission—a respect, even reverence, often missing in today's ironic mood. Agent Eyman believed that a "sacred trust" existed among the Carnegie Hero Fund heroes, the commissioners, and the investigators. As he would write eloquently:

> The establishment of the case, including the environmental features that relate to the risks to which the rescuer exposed himself, must be pursued to the conclusive level. This can be achieved only if the field representative holds conviction that anything less is a betrayal of his responsibilities to the Commission, the individuals recommended for rewards, and just as importantly, himself.
>
> The partly investigated case, like a little knowledge, is a very dangerous thing. It can lead the Commission astray in its evaluation, it can result in unworthy cases receiving awards and worthy acts being rejected.

Attainment of the ideal, which should motivate the field representative in his approach to each case assigned to him, is not easy. Nothing worth doing ever is.

It involves an investigative zeal embracing willingness to go the extra mile to establish the conclusiveness of an important point. It involves unflinching confrontations with all obstacles and barriers to investigative progress. It involves a determination on the part of the field representative to make the case which he currently has under study better covered in all areas than any other he has ever done.

Heroic in its own way, this quest for the truth of each act continues to define the Carnegie Hero Fund Commission's investigators as they begin a new century of "scientific detection." Like Sherlock Holmes's, their work is rooted in justice—the opportunity to reveal and celebrate the greatest altruism a man or woman may achieve. The "hero hunters" offer us hope about our fellow humans and the world we live in—just as Carnegie knew they would.

Hero hunter rescues youth

By GEORGE S. STUTEVILLE

James L. Rethi hunts heroes for a [liv]ing. After rescuing a drowning 13-[ye]ar-old boy Monday night he has to [loo]k no farther than his mirror.

Rethi, 28, is an investigator for the [Ca]rnegie Hero Fund Commission of [Pi]ttsburgh. He searches the nation for [m]en and women who have proved [th]eir valor by jeopardizing their lives [to] save another.

The foundation, created by the late [in]dustrialist Andrew Carnegie, bestows [aw]ards upon worthy heroes. It may [ha]ve to strike a medallion for Rethi.

THE PITTSBURGH resident had [be]en in Indianapolis three days re[se]arching the events around a near-[dr]owning at an apartment complex in [19]30.

Rethi left his room at the Sheraton-[Me]ridian to go to the hotel pool for a [rou]tine half-mile swim. He sat at the [poo]lside watching two boys play in the [wa]ter about 9 p.m.

R[o]y L. Halsell, 13, 653 West 30th Street, pulled himself out and dived back in.

"I ALWAYS notice children, I guess I'm that way," Rethi commented. "After a short amount of time I didn't see the boy surface." Halsell had been underwater about three minutes.

"I looked over the edge and he was laying on his stomach on the bottom."

Rethi, who has a slight paunch pushing at his trunks, plunged to the bottom. He scooped Halsell into his arms.

He lifted the youth to the surface with the aid of Jerry E. Kleber, 28, Pheonix, Ariz., who was attending a conference at the hotel.

RETHI PERFORMED mouth-to-mouth recusitation. The fourth time he blew into the boy's lungs Halsell began breathing, Rethi said.

Halsell was in serious condition in Methodist Hospital.

The boy sneaked into the pool, his mother, Linda O. Halsell, 31, said. "He was somewhere he was not supposed to be."

Doctors said her son was having respiratory problems, but should recover, she said. Mrs. Halsell also became a hero hunter, saying she wanted to meet Rethi and thank him.

"ME AND Roy's father are so thankful," Mrs. Halsell said at Methodist. "God put him (Rethi) there at that particular time."

During his three months as an investigator, the former newspaper reporter learned timing is a crucial ingredient to heroism.

"It amounts to being in the right place at the right time and doing the right thing."

Rethi said he doubts his life-saving effort would meet the Carnegie foundation's standard of heroism — risk.

"I DON'T feel that I actually risked

So read the headline on the front page of the Indianapolis Star *on June 15, 1982. The rescuer was James L. Rethi, an investigator for the Hero Fund. Rethi had been in Indianapolis for three days investigating the case of a near drowning. He was staying at a hotel, and at 9 p.m. on June 14 was sitting at the hotel's pool watching two young boys play in the water. One of the boys got out of the water and dived back in, and when Rethi noticed that the youngster did not surface, he went to investigate. The boy was face down on the pool's bottom. Rethi plunged in, scooped the boy in his arms, and with the aid of another man brought him to the surface. Rethi performed mouth-to-mouth resuscitation and the boy soon started breathing, but was then taken to the hospital where his condition was listed as serious. Doctors said at the time that he should recover.*

Rethi told the reporter for the Star *that he doubted his actions would earn him a Carnegie Medal since he didn't think he risked his life. He was right. After giving him a hero's welcome and free lunch back in Pittsburgh, the staff promptly assigned the case a file number—58473— then TD'd it (Turned Down, in Hero Fund parlance).*

James L. Rethi

my life. I just lifted the boy out of the water."

Rethi had dried off, but could not shake off the excitement from the danger.

"My nerves are still on edge, but I'm all so thankful. Here is a young life that will continue on."

For better or worse, the Hero Fund is inextricably linked to disasters. After all, the impetus that spurred Andrew Carnegie's desire to honor civilian heroes from an idea into action lay in the settled dust and debris of the Harwick Mine Disaster of 1904. The mine disaster left a lasting impression on Andrew Carnegie. In particular, the potential for reverberating damage to the families of those lost in the accident weighed heavily on his heart. In a letter to his close friend and future first president of the Carnegie Hero Fund, Charles L. Taylor, Carnegie said, "I cannot get those widows and children of the mine out of my head." Carnegie had long contemplated forming an organization dedicated to recognizing those "heroes of civilization" who risk their lives to save others. In a letter to a close business partner, Carnegie wrote, "I have thought over the idea (of a Hero Fund) for years, and the Harwick Mine

disaster brought it to a head." Thus, wheels were set in motion that would culminate in the creation of the Carnegie Hero Fund Commission as we know it today.

As the Hero Fund grew, so too did its philanthropic reach. Initially, the Commission focused on individuals who risked death or serious injury to save another, but, quickly, the Fund's scope expanded. It soon began responding to disasters, as allowed for by Carnegie in the Deed of Trust (*"in case of accidents (preferably where a hero has appeared) to those injured. The action taken in the recent Harwick Mine accident, where Heroes Taylor and Lyle lost their lives, is an illustration"*), by donating money toward relief efforts and charitable organizations and providing direct monetary compensation to victims and dependents affected by disasters.

The first of such contributions was made after the Grover Shoe Factory disaster in Brockton, Massachusetts, in 1905. On a chilly afternoon in March, an old boiler used to heat the Grover

Shoe Factory exploded, sending massive pieces of metal shrapnel straight up through all four floors of the factory and starting fires throughout the building. Broken gas lines exacerbated the situation, while flames, aided by hundreds of open windows, funneled upward, creating a chimney effect that resulted in the highest temperatures recorded inside a burning building in Brockton.

In recognition of the brave individuals who risked their lives attempting to save others, the Commission donated $10,000 to support a community marred by devastation and loss. Through the years, the Commission continued to support widows, children, and those disabled by the accident with annual payments to help ease their suffering. All in all, the Commission allotted $104,187.87 (about $3.5 million in today's dollars) in relief funds after that fateful day in 1905.

The Fund continued to provide disaster relief in the years to come, including one-time payments made in response to the California earthquakes of 1906 ($29,462) and 1989 ($25,000); hurricanes Hugo and Andrew ($25,000 each); and the Monongah ($154,350), Darr ($97,062), Lick Branch ($26,708), Jed Coal & Coke Co. ($10,000), and McCurtain ($53,115) mine disasters among others.

Up until 1912, disaster relief and commemoration of heroics on a widespread scale had been contained to the geographic parameters set out in the Deed of Trust, namely, "the United States of America, the Dominion of Canada, the Colony of Newfoundland, and the waters thereof." A disaster of epic proportions would expand the Commission's field of operation for the first time in its short history.

On April 15, 1912, the luxury steamship *Titanic* tragically sank in the waters of the North Atlantic Ocean; the Carnegie Hero Fund Commission convened a meeting of the Board of Trustees to debate the Fund's role in recognizing and mitigating the effects of tragedies outside the geographic scope of the organization's sphere of influence. After deliberation, it decided that, in rare circumstances, the Carnegie Hero Fund Commission would publicly recognize and commemorate the actions of heroes and heroines who acted selflessly to save another, regardless of whether it fell into the boundaries set out in the Deed of Trust. In recognition of those brave individuals who risked their own lives to save sur-

The New York Times.

VOL. LXI...NO. 19,806.   NEW YORK, TUESDAY, APRIL 16, 1912.—TWENTY-FOUR PAGES.   ONE CENT In Greater New York, Jersey City and Newark.   Elsewhere TWO CENTS

TITANIC SINKS FOUR HOURS AFTER HITTING ICEBERG; 866 RESCUED BY CARPATHIA, PROBABLY 1250 PERISH; ISMAY SAFE, MRS. ASTOR MAYBE, NOTED NAMES MISSING

Col. Astor and Bride, Isidor Straus and Wife, and Maj. Butt Aboard.

"RULE OF SEA" FOLLOWED

Women and Children Put Over in Lifeboats and Are Supposed to be Safe on Carpathia.

PICKED UP AFTER 8 HOURS

Vincent Astor Calls at White Star Office for News of His Father and Leaves Weeping.

FRANKLIN HOPEFUL ALL DAY

Manager of the Line Insisted Titanic Was Unsinkable Even After She Had Gone Down.

HEAD OF THE LINE ABOARD

J. Bruce Ismay Making First Trip on Gigantic Ship That Was to Surpass All Others.

The admission that the Titanic, the biggest steamship in the world, had been sunk by an iceberg and had gone to the bottom of the Atlantic, probably carrying more than 1,400 of her passengers and crew with her, was made at the White Star offices, 9 Broadway, at 8:20 o'clock last night. Then P. A. S. Franklin, Vice President and General Manager of the International Mercantile Marine, conceded that probably only those passengers who were picked up by the Cunarder Carpathia had been saved. Advices received early this morning tended to increase the number of survivors by 200.

The admission followed a day in which the White Star officials had been optimistic in the extreme. At no time was the admission made that every one aboard the huge steamer was not safe. The ship itself, it was confidently asserted, was unsinkable, and inquirers were informed that she would reach port, under her own steam probably, but surely with the help of the Allan liner Virginian, which was reported to be towing her.

As the day passed, however, with no new authentic reports from the Titanic or any of the ships which were known to have responded to her wireless call for help, it became apparent that authentic news of the disaster probably could come only from the Titanic's sister ship, the Olympic. The wireless range of the Olympic is 500 miles. That of the Carpathia, the Parisian, and the Virginian is much less, and as they neared the position of the Titanic they drew further and further out of short range. From the Titanic's position at the time of the disaster it is doubtful if any of the ships except the Olympic could establish communication with shore.

Titanic Sunk at 2:20 A. M. Monday.

In the White Star offices the hope was held out all day that the Parisian and the Virginian had taken off some of the Titanic's passengers, and efforts were made to get into communication with these liners. The White Star officials refused to recognize the possibility that there were more of the Titanic's passengers aboard them.

But by nightfall came the message from Capt. Haddock of the Olympic to Cape Race, Newfoundland, telling of the foundering of the Titanic and of the rescue of 655 of her passengers by the Cunarder Carpathia, which, the wireless message said, reached the position of the Titanic at daybreak. All they found there, however, was lifeboats and wreckage. The biggest ship in the world had sunk at 2:20 A. M. yesterday morning.

Mr. Franklin admitted late last night that the Parisian and the Virginian, though they were among the first to answer the Titanic's calls for help, could not have reached the scene before 10 o'clock yesterday morning, seven and a half hours after the big Titanic buried her nose beneath the waves and pitched downward out of sight. The Carpathia, so the wireless dispatch from Capt. Haddock to Cape Race announced, reached the scene of the Titanic's foundering at daybreak, several hours before the expected arrival of the Virginian and the Parisian.

First Reported Titanic in Tow.

It is unbelievable, said White Star Line officials were compelled to concede finally, that the Carpathia should have failed to pick up every lifeboat which still floated on the waves. If they failed to pick up more than 655 passengers, it was because the crew of the ship's complement had gone with her to the bottom.

But it was not until nearly nightfall that the extent of the disaster was realized. Before that the reassuring nature of the bulletins issued by the White Star line was sufficient to quiet the fears of those who had relatives or friends aboard the unfortunate ship and to prevent widespread belief in a serious disaster.

Capt. Haddock's message from the Olympic, which is printed in another column of The Times, strongly indicated that none but the 655 taken from life boats by the Carpathia had been saved. This message was relayed immediately to the White Star offices, but Mr. Franklin positively declined to make the text of the message public. He offered still the hope that passengers were aboard the Parisian and the Virginian, and even when the admission was wrung from him that there seemed little hope of the saving of any other than the 655 aboard the Carpathia, he clung to the hope that in some unexplained way there were other passengers aboard the two Allan liners.

Throughout the day there had been reassurances that the Titanic was being towed to port by the Virginian.

The Lost Titanic Being Towed Out of Belfast Harbor.

CAPT. E. J. SMITH,
Commander of the Titanic.

Biggest Liner Plunges to the Bottom at 2:20 A. M.

RESCUERS THERE TOO LATE

Except to Pick Up the Few Hundreds Who Took to the Lifeboats.

WOMEN AND CHILDREN FIRST

Cunarder Carpathia Rushing to New York with the Survivors.

SEA SEARCH FOR OTHERS

The Californie Stands By on Chance of Picking Up Other Boats or Rafts.

OLYMPIC SENDS THE NEWS

Only Ship to Flash Wireless Messages to Shore After the Disaster.

LATER REPORT SAVES 866.

BOSTON, April 15.—A wireless message picked up late to-night, relayed from the Olympic, says that the Carpathia is on her way to New York with 866 passengers from the steamer Titanic aboard. They are mostly women and children, the message said, and it concluded: "Grave fears are felt for the safety of the balance of the passengers and crew."

Continued on Page 2.

PARTIAL LIST OF THE SAVED.

Includes Bruce Ismay, Mrs. Widener, Mrs. H. B. Harris, and an Incomplete name, suggesting Mrs. Astor's.

Special to The New York Times.

CAPE RACE, N. F., Tuesday, April 16.—Following is a partial list of survivors among the first-class passengers of the Titanic, received by the Marconi wireless station this morning from the Carpathia, via the steamship Olympic:

Mr. JACOB P. — and maid.
Mr. HARRY ANDERSON.
Mr. ED. W. APPLETON.
Mrs. ROSE ABBOTT.
Miss G. M. BURNS.
Miss D. D. CASSEBERE.
Mrs. WM. M. CLARKE.
Mrs. B. CHIBNACE.
Mr. R. G. CROSBIE.
Miss H. ROSEBIE.
Miss JEAN HIFACK.
Mr. HY. B. HARRIS.
Mr. ALEX. HALVERSON.
Miss MARGARET BAYS.
Mr. BRUCE ISMAY.
Mr. and Mrs. ED. KIMBERLET.
Mr. F. A. KENNYMAN.
Miss EMILE KENCHEN.
Mr. A. F. LEADER.
Miss BERTHA LAVORY.
Mr. ERNEST LIVES.
Miss MARY CLINES.
Miss SINGRID LINDSTROM.
Mr. GUSTAVE J. LESNEUR.
Miss GIORGETTA A. MADILL.
Miss. MELICARD.
Mrs. TUCKER and maid.
Mr. J. B. THAYER, Jr.
Mr. HENRY WOOLMER.
Miss ANNA WARD.
Mr. RICHARD M. WILLIAMS.
Mrs. F. M. WAHNER.
Miss HELEN A. WILSON.
Mrs. MARY WICKR.
Mrs. GEO. D. WIDENER and maid.
Mr. J. STEWART WHITE.
Miss MARIE YOUNG.
Mr. THOMAS POTTER, Jr.
Miss EDNA S. ROBERTS.
Countess of ROTHES.

Mr. C. ROLMANE.
Mrs. SUSAN P. ROGERSON. (Probably liverpool.)
Miss EMILY B. ROGERSON.
Mrs. ARTHUR ROGERSON.
Master ALLISON and nurse.
Miss M. T. ANDREWS.
Miss NINETTE PANHART.
Miss E. W. ALLEN.
Mr. and Mrs. D. BISHOP.
Mr. H. BLANK.
Miss A. BASSINA.
Mrs. JAMES BAXTER.
Mr. GEORGE A. BAYTO——
Miss C. BONNELL.
Miss RUTH TAUSSIG.
Miss ELLA. THOR.
Mr. and Mrs. E. Z. TAYLOR.
GILBERT M. TUCKER.
Mr. J. B. THAYER.
Mr. JOHN B. ROGERSON.
Mrs. M. ROTHSCHILD.
Mrs. MADELEINE NEWELL.
Mrs. MARJORIE NEWELL.
HELEN W. NEWSOM.
Mr. FIENNAD OMOND.
Mlle. OLIVIA.
Mr. D. W. MERVIN.
Mr. PHILIP EMOCK.
Mr. JAMES GOOGHT.
Miss RUBERTA MAIMY.
Mr. PIERRE MARECHAL.
Mr. W. E. MINHAN.
Miss APPIE RANELT.
Major ARTUR PEUCHEN.
Mrs. KARL H. BEHR.
Miss DESSETTE.

Mrs. WILLIAM BUCKNELL.
Mrs. O. H. BARKWORTH.
Mrs. IO B. STEFFASON.
Miss ELSIE BOWERMAN.

The Marconi station reports that it missed the word after "Mrs. Jacob P." In a list received by the Associated Press this morning this name appeared well down, but in The Times list it is first, suggesting that the name of Mrs. John Jacob Astor is intended. This supposition is strengthened by the fact that, except for Mrs. H. J. Allison, Mrs. Astor is the only lady in the "A" column of the ship's passenger list attended by a maid.

NAMES PICKED UP AT BOSTON.

BOSTON, April 15.—Among the names of survivors of the Titanic picked up by wireless from the steamer Carpathia here to-night were the following:

Mr. and Mrs. L. HENRY.
Mrs. W. A. HOOPER.
Mr. MILE.
Mr. J. FLYNN.
Miss ALICE FORTUNE.
Mrs. ROBERT DOUGLAS.
Miss HILDA SLAYTE!!
Mr. F. SMITH.
Mrs. BRAHAM.
Miss LUCILLE CARTER.
Mr. WILLIAM CARTER.
Miss CUMMINGS.
Mrs. FLORENCE MARE.
Miss ALICE PHILLIPS.
Mrs. PAULA MUNGE.
Mrs. JANE ——
Miss PHYLLIS O——
HOWARD B. CASE.
Miss MINEHAN.
Miss BERTHA.

Special to The New York Times.

CAPE RACE, N. F., April 15.—The White Star liner Olympic reports by wireless this evening that the Cunarder Carpathia reached, at daybreak this morning, the position from which wireless calls for help were sent out last night by the Titanic after her collision with an iceberg. The Carpathia found only the lifeboats and the wreckage of what had been the biggest steamship afloat.

The Titanic had foundered at about 2:20 A. M., in latitude 41:16 north and longitude 50:14 west. This is about 30 minutes of latitude, or about 34 miles, due south of the position at which she struck the iceberg. All her boats are accounted for and about 655 souls have been saved of the crew and passengers, most of the latter presumably women and children. There were about 2,100 persons aboard the Titanic.

The Leyland liner California is remaining and searching the position of the disaster, while the Carpathia is returning to New York with the survivors.

It can be positively stated that up to 11 o'clock to-night nothing whatever had been received at or heard by the Marconi station here to the effect that the Parisian, Virginian or any other ships had picked up any survivors, other than those picked up by the Carpathia.

First News of the Disaster.

The first news of the disaster to the Titanic was received by the Marconi wireless station here at 10:25 o'clock last night [as told in yesterday's New York Times.] The Titanic was first heard giving the distress signal "C. Q. D.," which was answered by a number of ships, including the Carpathia,

vivors of the shipwreck, the Hero Fund commissioned a 22-karat gold medal to be mounted on a bronze base to commemorate the stories of heroism that came out of the failed voyage.

In response to the September 11, 2001, terrorist attacks, the Commission donated a total of $100,000, split between the Todd M. Beamer Memorial Foundation, which sought to provide counseling to traumatized children of 9/11 victims and survivors, and the September 11, 2001, Children's Fund Inc., which provided educational opportunities to children affected by the terror strikes. September 11, 2001, marked another tragic moment in the nation's history, prompting the Commission to publicly acknowledge and commemorate the tremendous courage shown by many first responders and everyday citizens.

Most recently, in response to the Covid-19 pandemic, the Commission recognized the efforts of first responders and medical personnel to mitigate and manage the coronavirus's deadly toll. The Carnegie Hero Fund Commission donated $100,000 to the Brave of Heart Fund, established to provide financial and emotional support to the surviving family members of frontline healthcare workers and volunteers who lost their lives as a result of treating Covid-19 patients.

"No action (is) more heroic than that of doctors and nurses volunteering their services in the case of epidemics," wrote Carnegie in the Hero Fund's Deed of Trust.

"Andrew Carnegie clearly and specifically applauded such heroic action in establishing the Hero Fund over 100 years ago," then-chair Mark Laskow said. "Through the Hero Fund, Carnegie wished to ensure that neither those who sacrifice for others through heroic action, nor their dependents suffer as a result."

Although the Carnegie Hero Fund Commission is dedicated to recognizing and supporting those civilians who risk their lives or severe injury saving or attempting to save the lives of others, it has also grown into a steadying force willing to help, when disaster provides heroes an opportunity for selfless action. Often taking a flexible, pragmatic approach to disaster relief, the Carnegie Hero Fund Commission continues to recognize heroism individually and collectively whenever the opportunity presents itself.

On the evening of June 12, 2018, more than a decade after the centennial celebration of the founding of the Carnegie Hero Fund Commission by Andrew Carnegie, 275 invited guests returned to Carnegie Music Hall to honor his philanthropic legacy and 10,000 Carnegie heroes.

The event, themed as "The Power of One—A Tribute to the Power of the Individual," marked the second in a year-long series of events around the world to commemorate the 100th anniversary of Carnegie's death in 1919. The evening's program celebrated Carnegie's enduring impact in Pittsburgh, and included Pittsburgh's four Carnegie institutions—the Carnegie Hero Fund Commission, Carnegie Library of Pittsburgh, Carnegie Museums of Pittsburgh, and Carnegie Mellon University.

Master of Ceremonies Scott Simon, a decorated journalist, author, and host of *Weekend Edition Saturday* on NPR, welcomed guests to the festivities. The Chicago native proved he had indeed done his homework with his expert pronunciation of the Carnegie name. Following Simon's introduction, William E. Hunt, then-chair of the museums' Board of Trustees, and Mark Laskow,

THE CARNEGIE MUSIC HALL FOYER IN PITTSBURGH IS SET FOR THE CARNEGIE HERO FUND'S POWER OF ONE EVENT HELD JUNE 12, 2018. THE EVENT—ATTENDED BY ABOUT 275 GUESTS—CELEBRATED ANDREW CARNEGIE'S LEGACY IN PITTSBURGH AND THE HERO FUND'S 10,000 CARNEGIE HEROES.

then-chair of the Carnegie Hero Fund Commission, provided additional introductions.

Laskow noted Carnegie's legacy of benevolence. "More than a century ago, Andrew Carnegie built a series of organizations in North America and Europe through which he intended to do nothing less than make the world a better place. That's an ambitious goal, but he was an ambitious man. His building materials were money and ideas, and he built well," he said.

After dinner, guests moved into the intimate auditorium of Carnegie Music Hall to hear words on the educational impact and legacy of Andrew Carnegie from Farnam Jahanian, president and Henry L. Hillman President's Chair of Carnegie Mellon University, and Mary Frances Cooper, then-president and director of Carnegie Library of Pittsburgh.

Carnegie Hero Fund President Eric P. Zahren spoke of the strength of character and altruistic bravery ingrained in Carnegie's heroes. He referenced the selfless actions of William Hunter, a Scottish boy who lost his life attempting to save another child from drowning in a lake in 1886, believing it gave "life to a

movement—the very same we celebrate tonight—in support of an idea that one individual, acting selflessly in behalf of another, can in itself not only save a life, but give life to hope for our future and the world."

At the end of his address, Zahren revealed a Roll of Honor of Carnegie Medal–awarded heroes and heroines, completed with meticulous attention and in accordance with the Deed of Trust, which calls for a "finely executed roll." This timely tribute to the more than 10,000 past and present Carnegie Heroes not only indicated the unwavering sense of bravery and self-sacrifice found in humans, but also the Carnegie Hero Fund's commitment to sharing the stories of individuals such as VICKIE TILLMAN and JIMMY RHODES, who were the guests of honor at the gala as the commission's 10,000th and 10,001st Carnegie Medal awardees, respectively.

Following Zahren's words, keynote speaker and Pittsburgh native Michael Keaton returned home to recognize the 10,000th and 10,001st Carnegie Medal awardees. During his

C. H. 10000, 10001

long and impactful acting career, he has embodied heroes such as Batman, but spoke of the importance of the Fund's deferent treatment of the title "hero" and the recognition of true noble acts of valor, evident in Carnegie heroes.

He noted that the common denominator of heroism is courage. "Courage shows up all the time in this world and often without any fanfare," he said.

Before the presentation of medals, the audience viewed a short video about the commission's history, in addition to a moving reflection of the heroic actions of guests of honor, Tillman and Rhodes. As the videos played, the audience pensively looked on; the stories of Tillman and Rhodes taking hold.

In 2017, Tillman, a 56-year-old school cafeteria clerk, stopped her car after seeing a wounded police officer, Deputy Sherriff Billy Aime, struggling to take a man into custody. The five-foot, two-inch woman rushed to the men, removed the suspect's hand from the officer's holstered gun and held it behind his back. As the man continued to punch the officer, Tillman impeded his attack until other police officers arrived. It took two other police officers to subdue the assailant and take him into custody.

As Simon read the details of Tillman's acts aloud, Aime, who towered over Tillman, placed the Carnegie Medal over her head.

"Ms. Vickie saved my life. Anything for her, I'm willing to do," Aime said.

Carnegie Hero No. 10,001, Jimmy Rhodes, 38, rescued Patrick E. Mahany, Jr., 64, from a burning medical helicopter on July 3, 2015, in Frisco, Colorado. After hearing of the helicopter crash in the hospital's parking lot, Rhodes, a radiographic technologist employed by the hospital, ran to the helicopter's nose with a fire extinguisher, spraying Mahany and attempting to reach for his legs to free him from the burning wreckage. Two nurses aboard the helicopter escaped. Although Rhodes successfully pulled Mahany from the burning wreckage, Mahany did not survive the severe burns, blunt force, and internal thermal injuries he suffered. Rhodes received medical treatment for smoke inhalation and burns, and recovered.

At the event, Mahany's widow, Karen Mahany, in an emotional moment, presented the Carnegie Medal to Rhodes, both of their eyes wet with tears. The audience members, many of whom were also moved to tears, stood and applauded Tillman and Rhodes for several, heartfelt minutes.

Andrew Carnegie's dedication to honoring civilian heroes continues to be fulfilled by the Carnegie Hero Fund. More

than 114 years after the Hero Fund's founding, the presentation of the 10,000th and 10,001st Carnegie Medals are testament to the steadfast, inherent capability of humans to act selflessly and bravely at times when they are needed most.

TWICE A HERO

For nearly all Carnegie Medal awardees, risking their own lives to save another is a once-in-a-lifetime experience. But in the more than 100-year history of the Commission, there are six men who, remarkably, met the challenge again and became awardees of a second medal.

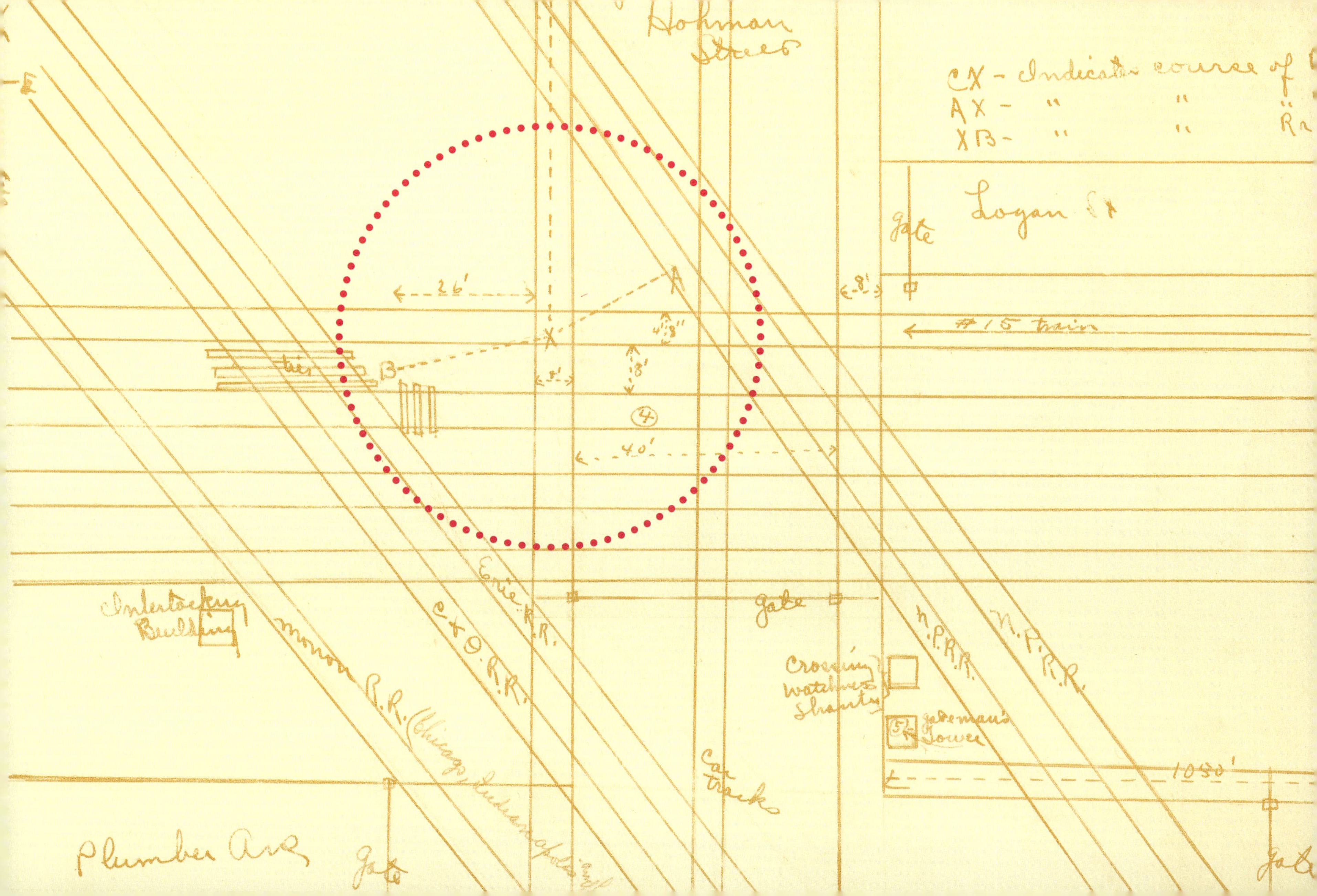

Hofman Street
CX - Indicates course of
AX - "   "
XB - "   "   R..
gate   Logan St
←8'→
← #15 train
26'
A
X
4'.8"
3'
B
ties
4
40'
Erie R.R.
gate
Interlocking Building
monon R.R. (Chicago, Indianapolis)
C&O.R.R.
Crossing watchmans Shanty
n.P.R.R.
N.P.R.R.
car track
gatemans Tower
5
1050'
Plumber Ave
gate
gate

HENRY NAUMANN, 46, was a watchman at the Hohman Street crossing of several railroad tracks in Hammond, Indiana, at midday on June 16, 1924. In addition to Naumann, 10 mechanical gates controlled pedestrian and automobile traffic as an average of 318 trains a day passed through the crossing that summer.

C. H. 1972, 2278

Naumann considered himself quite agile and boasted that he could outrun a man 10 years his junior. His fitness was more than a boast. It proved to be of life-saving quality when he dashed 25 feet in just a few seconds to push a woman, 56, from the track on which a train was quickly bearing down. Naumann's timing was nearly perfect. Only his foot was clipped by the train's engine as both he and the woman fell in a heap at the track's side, largely uninjured.

Just shy of three years later, in late March 1927, and within feet of the same spot, Naumann and another woman were not nearly as fortunate. This woman, 52, who had ducked under a crossing gate and was hurrying to beat an oncoming train, tripped on a rail and fell with her body across the track. When Naumann first saw her there, he was about the same distance away as when he started his first rescue, and the train was traveling at about the same speed as the first. This time, however, he reached the woman when the train was only 10 feet away. He grabbed at her clothing and pulled, but the train hit them both. They were hurled 30 feet. The woman was severely injured and died three hours later.

A fellow worker was the first to reach Naumann, who instructed him, "Look at my leg." His right leg was badly crushed. Naumann was taken to the hospital, where the leg was amputated during a stay that lasted more than two months. Naumann told the Hero Fund's investigator that he thought he and the woman had not much chance of getting out of the way of the train and that he was "all done." Ironically, Naumann, tired from the strain of his job, had recently tendered his resignation, and the day after the rescue attempt was to be his last at work. FILE NOS: 24477, 69361

(PREVIOUS SPREAD AND BELOW) PHOTOGRAPHS OF THE HOHMAN STREET CROSSING IN HAMMOND, INDIANA.

(FACING PAGE) COMMISSION INVESTIGATOR'S SKETCH SHOWING COURSE OF HENRY NAUMANN'S FIRST RESCUE.

SYDNEY
WORLD
ELIMINATION
RUDELL ST
WORLD'S
VE
RALPH DU
WORLD'S

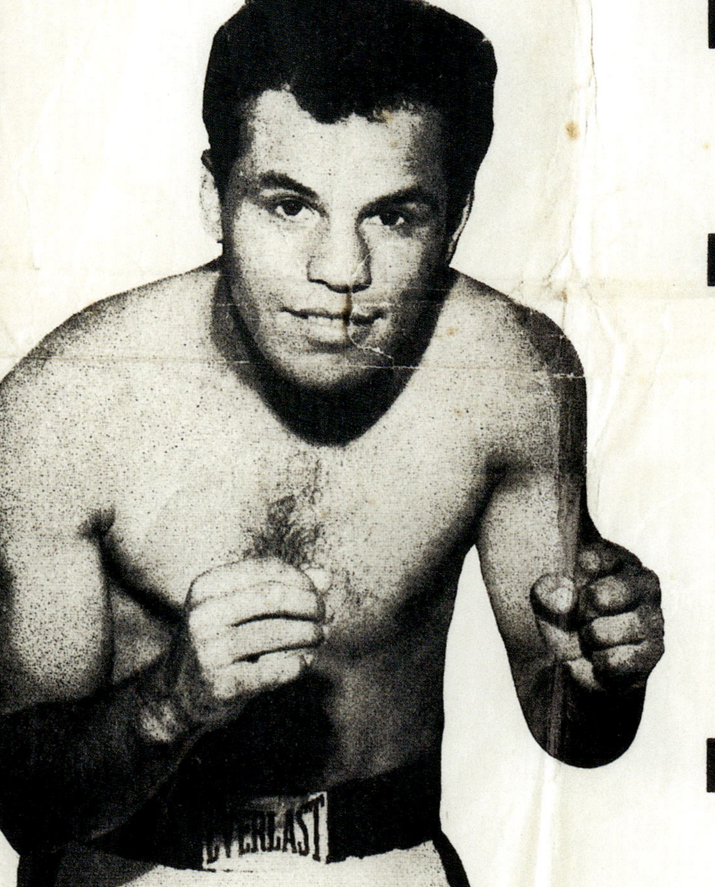

OVERLAST
RALPH DUPAS

RINGSIDE   TERRACES   BLEACHERS
dmission Prices: 70/- 30/- 15/- Reserves -
MONDAY - MAY

STADIUM

TITLE

OUT — 12 Rounds

ITCH

o. 2 WELTERWEIGHT

SUS

PAS

o. 3 WELTERWEIGHT

lan Kippax & Stadium

RUDELL STITCH

2 AT 8.00PM

16 September 1958 and 5 June 1960
DAM, OHIO RIVER
LOUISVILLE, KENTUCKY

C. H. 4230, 4350

RUDELL STITCH was a 26-year-old professional welterweight boxer ranked number three in the nation on September 16, 1958, when he became a hero by rescuing Joseph Schifcar, a workman at a dam on the Ohio River near Louisville, Kentucky.

Schifcar, 37, was standing on the dam's sill, plugging leaks, when he lost his footing and was swept over the eight-foot drop to the water below, where he broke his leg on a rock. He struggled to keep his head out of the swift current but was hampered by his injury and the weight of his boots and wet clothes.

Stitch, fishing on the rocks below the dam, quickly waded into the river to where he could grab Schifcar, who by then was nearly submerged. But Stitch also lost his footing, and both men were pulled into deeper water. Although a strong swimmer, Stitch could not overcome the fast-moving current. Instead, he supported Schifcar while they drifted 68 feet across submerged rocks into shallower water, where another fisherman was able to wade in and help Stitch tow Schifcar to safety.

Less than two years later, in early June of 1960, at the same dam, Stitch would attempt to save another man. Neither survived.

Stitch and Charles Oliver, 25, another boxer, were fishing at the dam. They were walking across the sill when Oliver, who couldn't swim, slipped and was washed into the river, pulling Stitch with him. The two became separated in the 10-foot-deep water, and the current quickly carried Oliver downstream toward a bridge. Stitch, who somehow had removed his boots, raincoat, and pants while submerged, surfaced just in time to see Oliver, now several yards farther downstream, get carried beneath the bridge and then sink near one of its piers. Swimming to where Oliver had disappeared, Stitch dived but came up empty-handed. He dived again, but this time did not surface. Several hours later, both bodies were recovered downstream. Stitch's second Carnegie Medal was awarded posthumously. Stitch's last bout was on May 24, 1960. At the time, he was ranked the number two welterweight in the world. FILE NOS: 44528, 70049

Stitch and wife, Rosa,
with sons
(l. to r.) Rudell III,
Rodney, and Donald
Charles.

C. H. 4038, 4127

JOHN JAMES O'NEILL, SR., 46, would easily have been excused from helping in the rescue of a woman who had jumped from the Yonkers City Pier into the Hudson River on May 5, 1954. In addition to several other men being present and witnessing the jump, O'Neill had a "long-established medical history of cardiac condition," which was known to the other men.

Not only did O'Neill jump from the pier, 14 feet above the river, he had just run about 500 feet after hearing the commotion over the woman's leap, which was described by police as a suicide attempt. He then swam several feet, submerged, grasped the woman around the waist, surfaced, and made his way to a ladder that was being suspended over the pier's side for him. Removed from the water, the 41-year-old woman was quickly revived. O'Neill was treated for shock and exposure and was hospitalized for a day.

Another woman, 62, reported to be despondent over the death of her husband, caused O'Neill to perform his second heroic act two and a half years later. Although the scene was the same, conditions this time were considerably different. It was late December, 1956, at 8:30 in the evening. The temperature was 27 degrees, ice was forming on the pier's walls, the wind was blowing at or above 40 mph, and waves in the river were striking the pier with "force and severity."

O'Neill, a municipal road worker, would normally not have been working at the time, but due to the foul weather he was asked to return for emergency duty. While waiting for a truck to be loaded with salt, O'Neill and a fellow worker noted the woman walking rapidly past them and out to the pier's edge. Concerned, both started after her, but before they reached her, she jumped into the darkness of the river. O'Neill's companion, a poor swimmer, ran to get a rope and ladder and to summon additional help. He was fearful O'Neill would attempt another rescue.

O'Neill this time did not jump from the pier but from a nearby structure he thought would take him closer to the woman. Swimming an irregular course and hampered by his wet, heavy clothing and the waves, he eventually spotted the woman's coat, which was floating above her head. Growing weary, he reached her with difficulty. Her weight, the heavy wind, a backwash from the pier's walls, and his waning strength all contributed to his taking five minutes to swim only 25 feet with her to a retaining wall. There, men with ropes pulled the woman from the river. O'Neill, ice forming on his face and clothing, was then helped from the water, 30 minutes after beginning the rescue. He was treated for shock and exposure, and a cardiogram revealed "severe effect" on his heart. He convalesced for two months at home before returning to work. FILE NOS: 43682, 69414

CASE OF JOHN J. O'NEILL, SR., FILE NO. 43682-A.

AB - Course of John J. O'Neill, Sr., as he hastened to
     stringpiece in rescue of ▋▋▋▋▋▋▋▋▋▋▋▋▋.

BC - Course as O'Neill jumped from stringpiece into water.

CX - Irregular course of O'Neill as he sought for, then
     reached ▋▋▋▋▋▋▋▋▋.

XY - Slightly irregular course of O'Neill as he towed
     ▋▋▋▋▋▋▋ to wall where man aided him until other
     help arrived.

YZ - Course of O'Neill to safety after ▋▋▋▋▋▋▋▋▋ later
     had been removed from water by men with rope.

H U D S O N   R I V E R

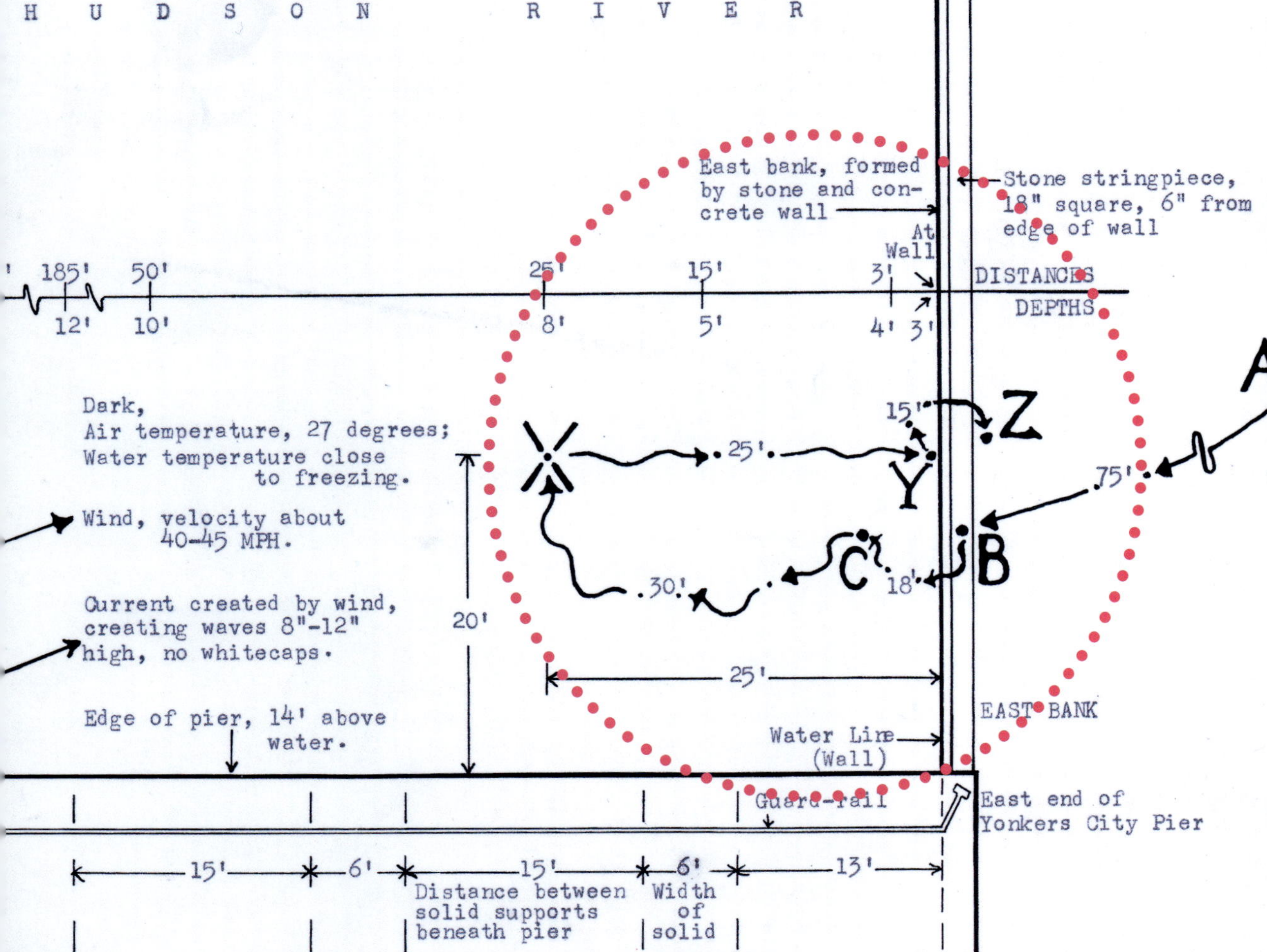

12 May 1963 and 15 October 1991
PHIPPSBURG, MAINE
EAST SWANZEY, NEW HAMPSHIRE

C. H. 4723, 7657

Unlike the rescues of the other twice-awarded heroes, **DANIEL STOCKWELL**'s were as different in type as they were far removed from each other in years and miles. The first, when Stockwell was a 20-year-old college student, took place off the rocky shore of the Atlantic Ocean in Phippsburg, Maine. Steven L. Quattropani, also 20 and a student, was swimming in the ocean in mid-May of 1963 when he was carried seaward by waves four- to six-feet high. From shore, **DALE ARNOLD HATCH**, 18, another student, attempted to toss Quattropani a lifeline made from articles of clothing, but Hatch was swept into the ocean by a large wave.

C. H. 4722

Stockwell then ran to a small beach almost directly opposite the two men in the water. He tied a rope around his waist, entered the surf, and swam to Quattropani, who was by then unconscious. With others pulling on the rope, both were towed to shore. The body of Hatch, who had submerged, was later washed ashore. Hatch and Stockwell were each awarded the Carnegie Medal, Hatch posthumously.

Twenty-eight years later, on October 15, 1991, Stockwell, now the principal of a high school in East Swanzey, New Hampshire, learned that a shooting had occurred in the school's cafeteria, which was crowded with 900 students. A 16-year-old boy armed with a .30-caliber rifle had shot and wounded two students there, then ordered 15 others into a classroom. When Stockwell reached the classroom door, he saw through the window that the armed student was reloading the rifle.

Stockwell knocked on the door and entered. The boy pointed the gun at him, but Stockwell calmly talked him into letting the other students leave the classroom in exchange for him becoming the boy's hostage. For nearly 40 minutes, all the time with the gun pointed at him, Stockwell discussed the boy's demands with him. Positioned outside the doorway, the chief of police then entered the classroom and ordered the student to put the rifle down. Stockwell left the room, another officer entering to subdue the student. FILE NOS: 46697, 46551, 66972

Daniel Stockwell

21 February 2007 and 14 November 2011
TAMPA, FLORIDA
LAKELAND, FLORIDA

C. H. 9151, 9691

CHARLES T. CARBONELL, SR., was awarded the Carnegie Medal twice four years apart: in 2007 after rescuing a police officer from assault, and in 2011 after partially entering an overturned and burning sport utility vehicle to remove its driver.

Carbonell, 50, was driving on February 12, 2007, in Tampa, Florida, when he saw a 57-year-old police officer fighting for control of his handgun with another man. He ran to the scene and peeled the assailant's fingers from the gun, enabling the officer to reholster it. The assailant continued to struggle violently as Carbonell and the officer attempted to subdue him. Taking him to the ground, they placed him in handcuffs before backup officers arrived.

On November 14, 2011, 41-year-old Denise Guzman was trapped in a sport utility vehicle after an accident in which the vehicle rolled off the highway and came to rest upside down in a stretch of wetland in Lakeland, Florida. Flames erupted in the engine compartment and spread to the car's exposed undercarriage. Carbonell ran to the burning vehicle and pulled on the driver's door, which was unlocked but blocked with mud. After some struggle, he succeeded in opening the door wide enough to lean in, headfirst, despite the growing and spreading flames outside and inside the car. Carbonell took hold of Guzman and pulled her out of the vehicle. He stood her on the ground, but as her feet sank partway into the mud, he picked her up and carried her back to the highway. FILE NOS: 80117, 84511

CHARLES T. CARBONELL

MICHAEL ROBERT KEYSER was the sixth person in Hero Fund history to receive a second Carnegie Medal. Keyser received the Carnegie Medal at the age of 19, when he risked electrocution to pull a 37-year-old driver from his vehicle that had struck a utility pole in Apple Valley, California. The pole broke off and hung from the lines. Flames erupted at the front end of the car. Although two other passersby had been shocked while in proximity to the car, Keyser reached through the open driver's door, pulled the 37-year-old driver from the vehicle, and took him to safety.

On January 19, 2020, also in Apple Valley, California, Keyser, now a 49-year-old mine worker, was driving at night when he saw an overturned semitruck, with its tractor extending about three feet into the roadway. Keyser stopped, and on foot, crossed the highway and approached the scene. At the truck, he pounded on the truck's windshield with a flashlight as the truck driver stood inside the cab, unable to lift himself out of the opened driver's window. Within seconds, another semitruck hauling two trailers containing hundreds of pounds of flammable lighter fluid struck the overturned semi, pushing it and Keyser off the highway into the desert. The trucks immediately erupted in flames. Keyser, and the man he was trying to rescue, died. FILE NOS: 65375, 90960

C. H. 7617, 10209

Posed as they are—four late-middle-aged men lined along a rusty railing on the north bank of the Potomac River, their gaze fixed by command to the far end of the Fourteenth Street Bridge—the moment transforms them into something of a monument, yet another one on these banks in Washington, D.C. They are common in appearance and no one recognizes them, this Mount Rushmore of American heroes, these men who defied a blizzard and its awful effects to save what would be the only survivors of a downed jetliner. Willing to pit human strengths against the raw forces of nature, the forces that determined that this plane should not clear that span, they listened to a primal stirring that dared them to think they might triumph.

They did. They gave hope, then life itself, back to three women and two men, who, clinging to sinking wreckage, survived the impact only to face sure death in the ice-clogged, fuel-poisoned waters of the Potomac on a winter afternoon in early 1982. Though to a man they shunned the notion, they were immediately and widely deemed heroes, and then they largely went their separate ways, seemingly linked by only 20 minutes and one overwhelming desire to achieve a common goal. A score and two years have passed, and they reunite for the first time. Like buddies from the trenches of a distant war, there is no space between them. They are familiar as they slap backs and give bear hugs, the sun kinder this day, the sky in full view.

It had snowed all morning and into the afternoon, and, in the 24-degree air, the accumulation was paralyzing Washington, D.C. By early afternoon, schools, offices, and businesses were closing, and the roadways became choked with the traffic of the storm's refugees.

ROGER OLIAN, 34, a sheet-metal worker, was among those attempting to evacuate the city. His usual route was across the Fourteenth Street Bridge, and on that day it took him two hours just to get there. Traffic was bumper-to-bumper, and Olian had the additional worries of running on a near-empty tank and a low battery. It was around 4 p.m. In another car on the span, **MARTIN L. ("LENNY") SKUTNIK III**, 28, was making the same trek. With him were his father and other carpool members. They too had been excused for the day from their jobs, Skutnik's as a government office services assistant. Skutnik recalled six to eight inches of snow on the bridge, and then people out of their cars looking over the railing.

A few miles to the east, at the headquarters of the Aviation Section of the U.S. Park Police, Chief Pilot **DONALD W. USHER**, 31, and Rescue Technician **MELVIN E. ("GENE") WINDSOR**, 31, were sitting out the storm, Usher having concluded it was "absolutely inconceivable that we would fly. Not in this stuff." Visibility was severely restricted and cloud cover was about 250 feet, conditions that required a craft certified in IFR—Instrument Flight Rules, or, in the vernacular, "I Follow Roads." Indeed, the unit's jet-powered Bell Ranger helicopter was snug and dry inside the hangar.

The storm had disrupted operations at Washington National Airport, hard by the Virginia bank of the Potomac, just south of the bridge. At about 1:40 p.m., the airport was shut down for snow removal, causing delays, including that of Air Florida's Flight 90, which was to depart for Fort Lauderdale at 2:15 p.m. Deicing of the plane was commenced, and by 4 p.m. it was cleared for takeoff. Aboard were 79 passengers and crewmembers, Kelly L. Duncan, Priscilla K. Tirado, Bert D. Hamilton, Joseph Stiley, and Patricia Felch among them.

Witnesses later reported an unusually heavy accumulation of snow or ice on the plane, and that its takeoff was labored and it lifted off too far down the runway. The plane lost altitude immediately and, less than a mile from the runway, it descended to the level of the northbound span of the bridge. It struck seven vehicles there, killing four people and injuring four others, then took out a length of bridge structure and crashed into the ice-covered Potomac and sank. Seventy-four persons aboard the jet died in the accident. Duncan, Tirado, Hamilton, Stiley, and Felch were not among them; miraculously, they and another male passenger surfaced amidst wreckage and ice floe at points about 120 feet from the Virginia bank.

Olian learned of the crash from another motorist and, abandoning his vehicle, ran to the riverbank, en route hearing the survivors' cries and seeing the plane's tail section above the water. *For a small plane, that's a large tail*, he concluded initially, and then a staggering realization: *If it's not a small plane, where is everyone?* Thinking as he ran, Olian knew he had a choice to make: "If I did nothing, I couldn't have lived with myself. But I knew I could live with myself if I tried and failed, even if I died. Figuratively speaking."

Other people had responded to the bank and were assembling a makeshift line from whatever was available—rope, belts, battery cables, even pantyhose. The situation to Olian was as desperate as it could be, but he thought a visible rescue attempt would buy the survivors time by giving them a measure of hope. He was right; Stiley later said that seeing Olian in action gave a "wonderful psychological feeling." Olian descended the steep bank, then entered the "electrifyingly cold" water. Handed one end of the line, he tied it to himself and continued out. He maneuvered between ice slabs and tried to crawl across the larger ones, often falling and submerging. He shouted encouragement to the victims but knew they were "miles and hours" away. Still, strength waning, he stayed focused. When he was halfway to his goal, the line became taut, and he tried to free himself of it. And then there came a welcome sound: a chopper was approaching.

Within minutes of the crash, Usher and Windsor took calls from the airport inquiring of their unit's availability to fly. There were reports of a missing aircraft, the men were told. Usher's no-fly edict rescinded, the men assembled lines and life jackets and had the ramp plowed. Near-whiteout conditions prevailed when they lifted off, Usher looking through the helicopter's floor windows—its "chin bubbles"—to follow highways to

(LEFT TO RIGHT) WINDSOR, SKUTNIK, AND USHER AND THE HELICOPTER USED IN THE RESCUE.

the scene. The trip took five minutes, a part of which was through freezing rain, which threatened the craft's rotor system and iced its windshield. As they approached the bridge, a letup in the snow enabled the men to view the carnage below, first the wrecked vehicles, then the broken ice of the river, then the debris in the water. There were people everywhere—*were they the passengers?*—but only a few in the water, including Olian, who was being reeled to the bank. At the jet's exposed tail section, they saw the six partially submerged victims.

Although Usher had extensive flying experience both with the Park Police and during four years in Vietnam, conditions this day provided new tests. In the water, the chopper's downdraft raised debris to threaten its rotor system, the river and immediate atmosphere were contaminated by the jetliner's fuel and its fumes, and ice floes clogging the surface could impinge on the skids should the craft be taken low. On land, the bank was choked with people and emergency vehicles, and small trees lining it had to be minded, even as firefighters pushed branches out of the way. In the air, Windsor would work unsecured through an open door. *If he falls out*, Usher thought, *we're really in trouble*. He knew that further help arriving in time was unlikely: *We were it*.

Windsor dropped the end of a line to the victims. Although suffering from a shattered right wrist and broken arm and ribs, Hamilton put the line around himself, and Usher flew him dangling to the bank. The effort was repeated for Duncan, who sustained leg and arm fractures. Windsor had dropped the line to an obviously injured man at the wreckage, but the man passed it to Duncan. Two lines were dropped on the third trip, and again, the injured man passed one of them off. Stiley secured a line to himself, then he grasped Tirado, who had sustained leg-fracture injury. Felch clinging to the second line, Usher started toward shore, dragging the victims through open water and floating ice. Halfway there, Felch lost her grip and settled back into the water, where she was kept afloat by a life vest. Suffering fractures to both legs, Stiley maintained his hold of Tirado until they became separated on the ice, Tirado left behind as Stiley was pulled to the bank. Weakened, dazed, and blinded by jet fuel, Tirado made futile attempts to swim as she mouthed, *Help!* Usher and Windsor returned and dropped the life ring to her, and with great difficulty she maintained the barest of holds as she was dragged ever closer to safety. Her hold gave out again.

Enter Skutnik, literally. Having watched the rescue from its start, he could bear no more—*I was going crazy*. Unlike his father, Skutnik was untrained in water rescue, but that mattered little. Shucking coat and boots, he plunged into the river and swam to Tirado. After working to secure a hold, Skutnik started to swim in with her. They were met by a firefighter, who took Tirado the rest of the way, Skutnik following. Less than two hours later he was world news, and by the end of the month he was at the State of the Union address, where President Ronald Reagan told the nation that he represented "American heroism at its finest."

With Tirado's safety assured, Usher and Windsor turned to Felch, who had sustained a broken leg, arm, and wrist. As Windsor, unsecured, stepped from the cabin to stand on a skid, Usher took the helicopter to the water, so low that both skids were at times submerged and at other times in contact with floating ice. Bracing himself against the craft, Windsor reached down and grasped Felch, using both hands to secure her while warding off the helicopter's flapping door with a shoulder. With both of them delicately perched on the skid, Usher returned to the bank. Felch was the last survivor out of the water, having endured 30 minutes of its numbing effects.

Their final trip to the wreckage, for the remaining passenger, was a heart-rending one for Usher and Windsor. The man had sunk by then, and their search for him was fruitless. Their successes, however, went on to be widely acknowledged. Along with Olian and Skutnik, they received numerous awards for their heroism, including the Carnegie Medal. Although in a profession "charged with the safety of the public," a Hero Fund regulation that might ordinarily have disqualified them, Usher and Windsor were thought by the Commission to have gone clearly above and beyond the line of duty—unfavorable conditions aside, they had acted outside their agency's jurisdiction.

But to ask *them* if they are heroes? Convinced that his was a human reaction, Skutnik shuns the term, believing that if he didn't act, someone else would have. Consequently, he remains puzzled, sometimes annoyed, by all the attention, the media viewing him as a "prop caught on video-tape." Olian too sees his reaction as the result of his humanity: *Heroes are no different—we all have the capability, and when people get to see that, that's good.* Still, he does not embrace the designation. "I've been called a hero," he said, "but I don't believe it about myself."

Usher and Windsor are likewise unimpressed by the title. Windsor maintains that training, experience, planning, teamwork, the skills of his pilot, and even participation by a "higher power" all played pivotal roles. "A hero is spontaneous," he says. "A hero is untrained." Similarly, Usher suspects heroes are "not paid, not expected" to act, and that "they are in hiding until they are actually needed. I don't think I fit into the definition." Having long ago concluded that modesty must be innate in the souls of the bravest, the Commission decided that Usher *did* fit in, as did his three corescuers. In the Hero Fund's thinking, the men assumed extraordinary risk while helping to save others when they had no obligation to do so, the Commission's traditional description of a hero.

"Whatever moved these men to challenge death on behalf of their fellows is not peculiar to them," wrote *Time Magazine* essayist Roger Rosenblatt. "Everyone feels the possibility in himself. That is the abiding wonder of the story. That is why we would not let go of it." FILE NOS: 58226, 58143, 58225, 58224

V

C. H. 3969

In a letter addressed to the Commission in 2011, the daughter of awardee and World War II veteran GEORGE D. HEMPHILL wrote, "George said, not long ago, one thing he was grateful for: We have been able to keep the family farm. You helped us do it." When he passed away in 2019, the 64-year relationship between the Hero Fund and his family came to an end. The many letters, holiday cards, and boxes of homemade cookies sent over that time reveal more than a professional correspondence; to the Hemphill family, the staff at the Commission had become family.

From his heroic act in 1954 in which he attempted to save the driver of a tanker truck that was struck by a train and burst into flames, Hemphill was severely burned, and even after medical treatment, struggled with everyday tasks such as eating and getting dressed. In his later years, he suffered from arthritis, Parkinson's disease, hearing loss, and frequent memory lapses. Despite these impairments, he continued his farm work—because maintaining the 367 acres of land was one of his greatest joys. His daughter Donna Hemphill Robbins wrote that even at the age of 95, "He remain[ed] ever the farmer, watching the weather, eager to talk to my son about the cows, hay, poultry, etc., happy to know the farm will carry on."

Hemphill demonstrated exceptional humility in his life. In a 2016 financial report, Robbins said he'd worried that the Commission's help over the years had taken away from other needy families and stated that George and his wife would still be grateful to the Commission regardless of whether the grant continued or not. Even beyond finances, Hemphill had never inquired into his missing World War II Purple Heart medal until it was returned to him by someone who purchased it at an antiques store.

Because of both George and his wife Athala's physical and mental decline, Donna was forced to retire from her teaching job in 2010 and then five years later quit a part-time job to devote all her time toward their general care and finances. Despite this tireless effort, her letters to the Hero Fund were always cheerful and optimistic toward the future, and she concluded all of them by thanking the Hero Fund for everything that had been done for them.

The Carnegie Hero Fund has distributed more than $44 million in grants, tuition, funeral expenses, and other support. Hero Fund founder Andrew Carnegie's original intent was to mitigate the negative financial harm resulting from an awardee's death or disability. At the time the Fund was established, work-men's compensation laws were not yet in existence to help the disabled or those killed or their dependents.

With the designation of the first heroes on May 24, 1905, the beneficiary story began to unfold. Pensions were granted to widows until they remarried and orphans until they reached the age of 16. That first year, three widows of heroes were voted to receive annual grants "to relieve them to some extent," and one hero was awarded money to continue her studies.

As it grew in experience during the first 10 years, the Commission crafted more specific guidelines, creating three cate-gories of pecuniary awards: death benefits, disablement benefits, and betterment benefits. Death benefits were designed to assist widows and other dependents of deceased heroes. Disablement benefits offered similar assistance to heroes injured in their acts. Betterment benefits included seven types of support: business establishment, educational expense, health restoration, home purchase, indebtedness liquidation, living expense, and miscella-neous aids. Offered in cases where no losses resulted from heroic acts, betterment benefits nonetheless sought to "improve the con-dition in the life of the beneficiaries in a permanent way."

Graduate John Thanos is a son of Mark John Thanos and grandson of John Mikel Thanos, both of whom were posthumously awarded the Carnegie Medal in 2009 in recognition of their attempts to save a boy from drowning in a flooded culvert in 2008 in Chesterton, Indiana.

Today, initial grants are given without stipulations. Additional benefits for medical expenses or ongoing stipends require a more stringent review of finances, including a series of forms seeking financial information such as real estate and personal property holdings, income from all sources, debts, and expenses. Renewals for ongoing benefits are typically made for three- to five-year periods, but beneficiaries are required to provide an annual financial report.

In the case of the family of **Mark John Thanos** and **John Mikel Thanos**, Mark's sons Michael and John both received more than \$100,000 in scholarship grants toward their college educations and John's daughter Alexis received a \$5,000 grant.

Mark and his father, John, both drowned in 2008 while attempting to save an 11-year-old boy who was caught in a swift current flooding a drainage ditch in his Chesterton, Indiana, neighborhood.

In 2009, Alexis wrote, "It has truly [been] the most difficult year of my life but because of you folks at the Carnegie

C. H. 9285, 9286

A350
2 LIFE VESTS

Commission, you have made it bearable. Why I am writing this letter is to truly thank you for your thoughtfulness on honoring my father and brother. You helped me by acknowledging just how great they both were and honored as such. They are missed horribly but you have helped me cope with their absence. Again, I Thank You.”

Rudell Stitch, one of six people to have been awarded the Carnegie Medal twice, died during his second act in 1960 and, four years later, his wife was murdered. This left Stitch's mother-in-law to take care of his six children. The family received a monthly stipend for 16 years and through the Hero Fund's scholarship assistance, Darryl L. Stitch and Janet L. Stitch were able to afford semesters at college.

To maintain the scholarship grants the Commission offers, beneficiaries send grades, progress reports, and plans for future education. The Thanos boys and Stitch children all kept up this correspondence so the Hero Fund could know how to best support their career goals.

“I truly believe that I would have not fulfilled my dream of becoming a pilot if your Fund was not a part of my life,” wrote Michael Thanos in one such report. “For this, I wanted to say how grateful I am for your help thus far in my career.”

Carnegie Hero **Francis C. Skinner**'s widow, Mary F. M. Skinner, received a monthly stipend from the Commission after her husband died attempting to rescue two men after an explosion in a Salineville, Ohio, mine caused it to cave in. His death left her to care for their six children, and in 1909, the Commission provided $40 per month, plus $5 per child. That amount steadily increased every few years until she was receiving $145 monthly at the time of her death in 1968. The stipend then continued with their daughter, Margaret. In her later years, Margaret's only source of income was the Carnegie pension. After her passing in 1981, Margaret's niece Betty wrote: “I want to thank you for all your kindness and the money she has received from you all these years.”

The Skinner family was on the Commission's beneficiary rolls for a total of 72 years.

Hero Fund Beneficiaries remain as such until their passing or when it's deemed that continued financial support is no

C. H. 4230, 4350

C. H. 234

June 2, 1967

Mrs. Mary F. M. Skinner
Washington Street
Salineville, Ohio 43945

Dear Mrs. Skinner:

Enclosed is our check for the month of
May and you will notice it is payable in
the amount of $145 rather than the $120
sum that has been coming to you since
early in 1963.

This further increase in your pension has
been made with the thought that it will
be of significant help in assisting you
to cover rising living expenses. We hope,
furthermore, that it will encourage you
to buy a television set. We feel that
many television programs would provide
pleasure and interest for you and your
daughter, and that you should be able to
enjoy them.

With appreciation for your kind words of
thanks to the Commission and for your warm
welcome to Mr. Swartzlander during his
recent visit with you, we are,

Sincerely,

David B. Oliver,

dbo c
enc.

January 11, 1969

Mr. David B. Oliver
Carnegie Hero Fund Commission
Pittsburgh, Penna.

CARNEGIE HERO FUND COMMISSION
OFFICE OF MANAGER
JAN 1969
OLIVER BUILDING, PITTSBURGH, PA.
FILE 2772

Dear Mr. Oliver,

This is in answer to your letter sent
to me by my sister, Margaret Skinner, of
Salineville, O.

It is with deep gratitude that I wish
to thank you for her and myself. The increased rate of her pension is most
generous and she is deeply grateful.

Margaret was very pleased to have your
representative call on her and he will be most
welcome at any time.

I feel this is a fine tribute to my mother
for the many years of her association with
you.

Sincerely,
Francis C. Skinner

(LEFT) MALCOLM R. ASPESLET WITH HIS WIFE, BARBARA ASPESLET. ASPESLET WAS MAULED BY A GRIZZLY BEAR WHILE SAVING CO-WORKER BARBARA (THEN BECK). THEY LATER MARRIED.

(BELOW) A NOTE FROM CARNEGIE HERO MALCOM R. ASPESLET, AFTER HE RECEIVED A MONTHLY PENSION FROM THE HERO FUND FOR MORE THAN TWO DECADES.

C. H. 5917

longer appropriate. In **MALCOLM R. ASPESLET**'s case, monthly grants were greatly appreciated when he sustained severe injuries while rescuing his then co-worker Barbara Beck from a grizzly bear in 1971. He and Barbara were unable to work for a period of time and struggled with medical bills, previous debts, and their wedding costs; in a 1973 letter, Malcolm wrote, "We find it hard to meet our obligations . . . We would appreciate any help you could give us in any way." The couple had declared personal bankruptcy in 1976 and were surprised to find that a prosthetic ear surgery was not covered by their Canadian health insurance. In assistance, the Commission gave several extensions to Malcolm's monthly grants over the years and paid for the surgery. This support ended in 2019 when, despite still being eligible for support, Malcom stated that he was "doing great" financially and wasn't in need of any further assistance, "Thank you for your assistance for all of these years. All is well with my life, family, and health. If possible, I still do enjoy your newsletters. Again, thank you very much."

CARNEGIE · HERO · FUND

· ESTABLISHED   APRIL 15TH 1904 ·

In the Hero Fund's history, Carnegie Medals have been awarded to more than 10,000 individuals. The heroes profiled on the following pages are representative of this group as to age, gender, geographical location, and date and type of act. The Fund's awardees all met the Commission's principal requirement for being awarded the medal: They voluntarily risked death or serious physical injury while saving or attempting to save the lives of others.

C. H. 4240

SHIRLEY F. O'NEILL, an 18-year-old-student, became a hero on May 7, 1959, when she risked her life to rescue the victim of a shark attack.

Albert Kogler, also 18, was swimming in San Francisco Bay near the Golden Gate Bridge about 150 feet from shore when a shark attacked him, tearing off parts of his arm, shoulder, and back, and causing severe bleeding.

O'Neill had gone to the beach with Kogler and, swimming nearby, was the only other person in the water. She heard Kogler's cries, then saw the water churning and reddening around him. O'Neill started to shore but then turned and swam back to Kogler. The attack having ceased, O'Neill put her arm around Kogler's chest and, aided by the current, began paddling them through two-foot swells back toward shore. When they were within 60 feet of the beach, a fisherman cast out a weighted line, which O'Neill wrapped around her wrist and Kogler's uninjured arm. They were then pulled in to where two other bystanders could wade out and get Kogler.

Kogler was rushed to the hospital, but died two hours later in spite of transfusions and emergency surgery. O'Neill was not injured.

News of the attack—termed unprecedented in San Francisco by marine experts—took up almost half of the front page of the following day's *San Francisco Examiner*, and it was reported in *Time* magazine and the *Congressional Record*. The case was called to the attention of the Hero Fund by, among others, the mayor of San Francisco, a former "special agent" of the Hero Fund, and Carnegie Medal awardee **MILEY B. WESSON, M.D.**, of San Francisco, whose own act of heroism 27 years earlier had its special measure of drama *(see below)*.

The Hero Fund's response to O'Neill's act may have been as unprecedented as the shark attack. Three weeks after the rescue, Special Agent Irwin M. Uhrling had a case report filed with the office and in mid-June the Hero Fund announced its award. Executive Committee members had been queried by mail, and the award was decided without the formality of the committee's meeting, its usual procedure. FILE NO: 44705

(FACING PAGE, TOP) SHIRLEY O'NEILL'S RESCUE WAS FRONT-PAGE NEWS THROUGHOUT THE UNITED STATES.

(BOTTOM) COMMISSION INVESTIGATOR'S SKETCH SHOWING COURSE OF O'NEILL'S RESCUE.

C. H. 2805

Wesson, too, knew to respond immediately in a life-threatening situation. While he was operating on a child, an x-ray technician in the room seized a bare wire charged with 30,000 volts and fell unconscious to the floor. Knowing the live line would kill the technician and probably the child if it came into contact with the metal operating table, Wesson, 50, grasped the line to pull it away. He lost consciousness briefly and fell to the floor, his weight pulling the wire free, breaking the circuit. Recovering, although having sustained fractures to vertebra and right clavicle, he regained his footing and completed the operation. FILE NO: 32051

Killed
e Shark
e Beach

d Braves Attack
ow Youth Ashore

ar old San Francisco State College fresh-
tally mangled and all but devoured, ap-
a great white shark, while swimming at
ch off the Presidio with a girl companion

perts said the
unprecedented
isco Bay or ad-
s, at least in
ory.
Albert Kogler
Ave., a former
otball and base-
Paradise, Butte
at Letterman
ral hours after
attack despite

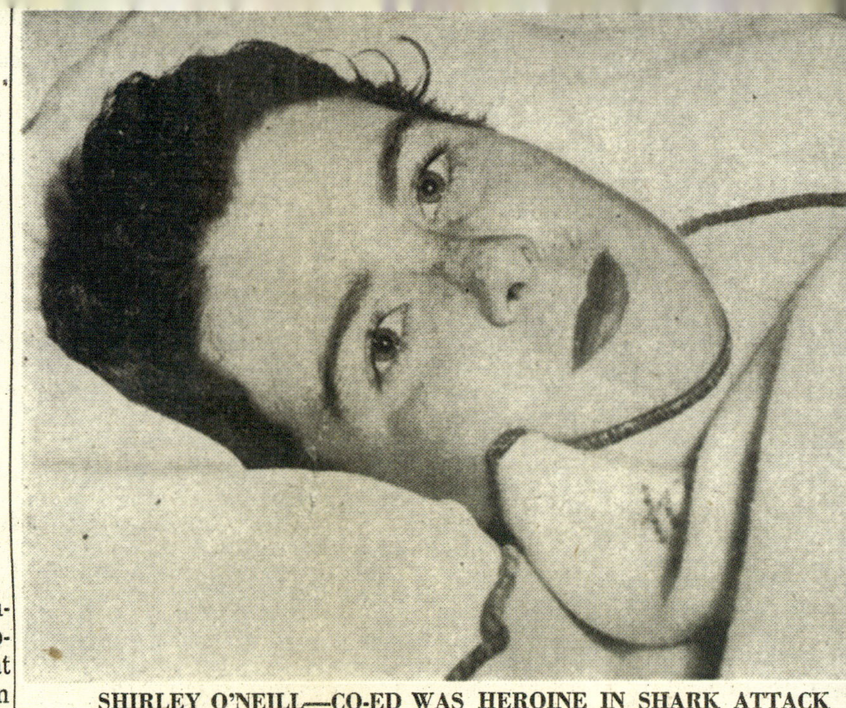

SHIRLEY O'NEILL—CO-ED WAS HEROINE IN SHARK ATTACK
... *resting in Letterman Hospital after nightmarish adventure*

'Couldn't Leave Him!'

Heroic Girl's Stark Tale Of Tragedy at Beach

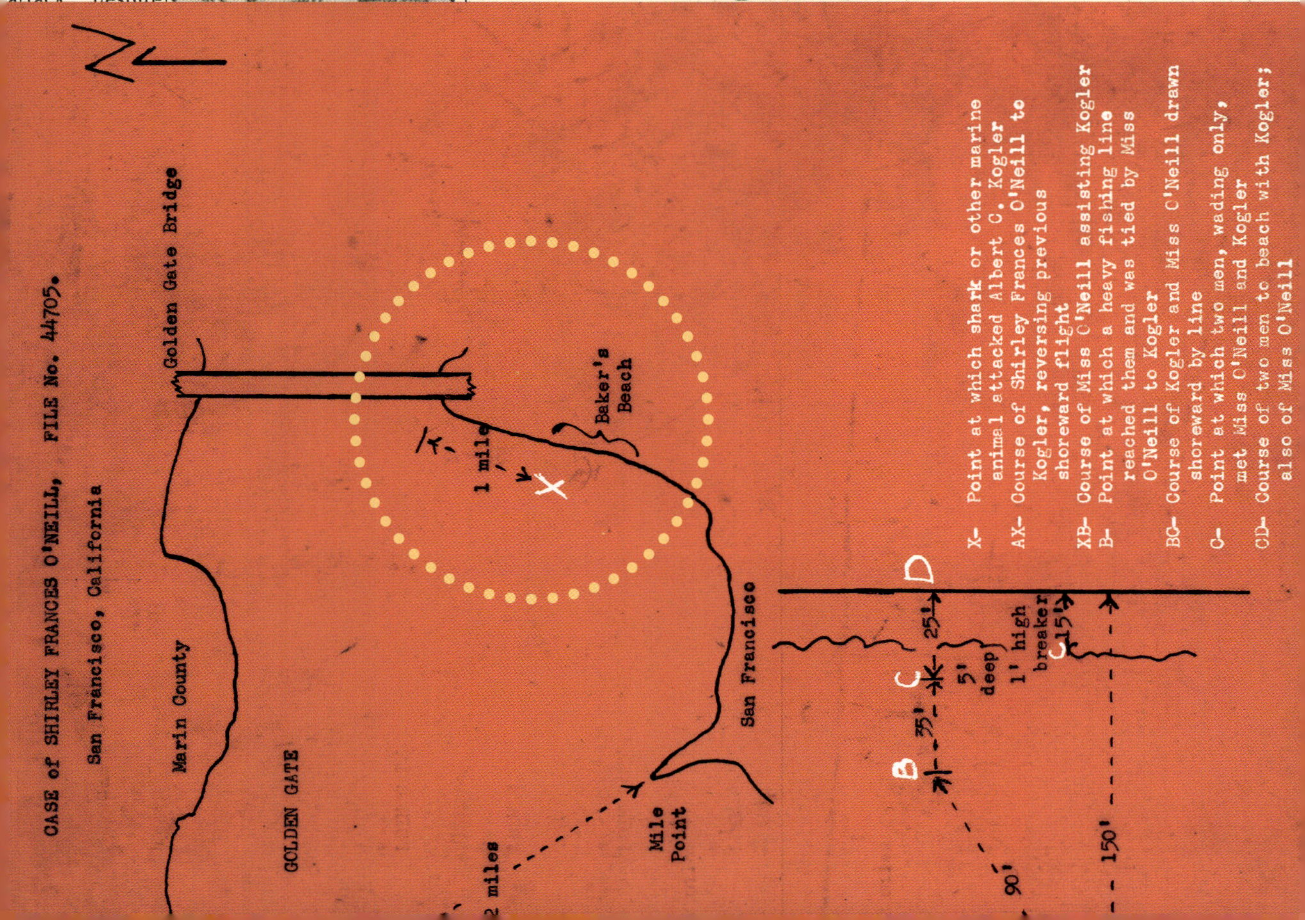

Charles Zolninger and
Julius B. Gordon, not
visible, were working
under the debris, while
William H. Reed, barely
visible under the shoring
planks, was providing
assistance.

On October 28, 1913, **Charles Zolninger**, **Julius B. Gordon**, **William H. Reed, Sr.**, and **John F. Steinbock** worked tirelessly in the 16-hour rescue of two men from the collapse of an industrial water well.

C. H. 1065, 1066, 1067, 1068

Seven men were working in the well, a hole that was 45 feet deep and 20 feet in diameter. The circumference of the well was lined with two walls of cemented brick, the inner wall rising just several feet from the well's bottom. Two platforms supporting pumping machinery weighing 4,500 pounds were imbedded in the outer wall 20 and 32 feet below the surface. At about 9 a.m. the outer wall began to collapse from the bottom up. Within seconds, a tangled mass of bricks, sand, timbers, and machinery fell in on the workers, killing four of them almost instantly. A fifth man died a few hours after the collapse, but two others survived and remained trapped under tons of unstable debris.

Zolninger, a 30-year-old plumbing contractor, Gordon, a 22-year-old laborer, and Reed, a 39-year-old laborer, arrived on the scene shortly after an alarm was sounded. A ladder was lowered to the top of the debris pile, and Zolninger and Gordon descended into the well, even though others warned them that portions of the wall were likely to collapse. Reed followed the two shortly thereafter. The men cut through the wooden debris to create an 18-inch hole, and then managed to reach one of the victims and help him out of the hole. It was now 10:30 a.m.

Zolninger and Gordon then entered the hole to look for the second victim, Reed taking a position at the mouth of the hole. They began cutting away more timbers to reach the other victim, who had been calling for help and telling the rescuers he was pinned under timbers and unable to move. Meanwhile, men at the top were shoring the well's wall. Zolninger and Gordon took turns working on cutting and removing timbers and debris in the cramped space, aided by Reed who provided tools and other assistance.

Around 2:30 in the afternoon, the men were able to free one of the victim's legs, but his other leg was pinned in the timbers. A doctor was persuaded to enter the hole to determine if amputation was possible, which after viewing the scene he said would mean death for the victim. So all climbed back out and, working with others, they removed sand and other debris from the top of the pile of rubble. After eight hours of work, however, a great quantity of sand caved in to the well. Discouraged, Zolninger said there was no chance now to rescue the victim, and said he was going home. Soon, though, he was encouraged to make another rescue attempt, and Gordon volunteered again to accompany him. Others were asked to assist, but only Steinbock, a 45-year-old farmer, agreed. After three more hours of dangerous work, and nearly 16 hours after the cave-in, the second victim was freed and transported out of the well.

FILE NOS: 11973, 13258, 13260, 13259

C. H. 3125

Thirteen-year-old **Norma Bedell** saved a baby from being killed by an enraged pig on June 12, 1941.

For three years, Bedell had been living on the farm of her foster parents, Mr. and Mrs. Ernest McKenzie, near Salineville in east central Ohio. In the late afternoon, the ninth-grade student was doing chores, tending cows in the barn. A toddler, 22-month-old James Ferguson, whose parents were visiting the McKenzies, had accompanied Bedell into the barn. A 450-pound sow, mother of 10 piglets, attacked young Ferguson, knocking him onto his back, and began biting him on the head.

Bedell immediately ran to the pig and pushed it away far enough to hoist the child onto the top of a box nailed to the wall. The sow charged Bedell, knocking her over and biting her on the side and stomach. The girl fought back, pushed the pig's head away, and struggled back to her feet. She took shelter in a nearby feed bin, but was unable to close the door, because the sow was in the way. Twice then it tried to get at the child, who was slipping off the box. Bedell grabbed a pitchfork and struck at the sow. The pig backed far enough away to allow Bedell to go to Ferguson and protect him until his mother arrived. Bedell fled the barn with them, the sow still menacing.

Though cut badly on his head, Ferguson healed with no ill effects. Bedell sustained four long gashes, but she recovered within a week.

FILE NO: 39131

C. H. 1826

On May 29, 1922, **Harley W. Pullen**, a 12-year-old schoolboy in Big Creek, Mississippi, rescued a young farmer who was being dragged by a runaway mule.

Pullen's neighbor and friend, Max Doolittle, 24, had been returning from the field riding sideways on a plow mule. When the 850-pound animal reared, Doolittle tumbled off its back. One of his feet got caught in a trace chain, and the frightened mule galloped off, dragging the boy 1,500 feet over a plowed field and a road.

When Pullen saw the mule dragging Doolittle, he immediately ran some 500 feet toward the approaching animal. When they met, Pullen tried to grab its bridle, but the mule struck him in the chest hard enough to knock him to the ground. The mule then took several steps past Pullen and stopped. Not injured by the blow, the young boy got up, stepped up to the mule, seized its bridle, and released Doolittle. Although Doolittle was disabled for five days from his injuries, he made a complete recovery.

FILE NO: 23002

At just past midnight on September 26, 1925, **TEODORO O. RIOS**, 30, and **MATILDE ROBLEDO**, 46, put their lives at risk to save a fellow worker from an explosion.

C. H. 2200, 2199

Rios and Robledo were part of a four-man powder gang setting a grid of dynamite charges on large rocks of ore at a copper mine near Santa Rita, New Mexico. Only the light from the men's lanterns illuminated the area. The fuses of 25 to 30 charges had been lit when the foot of a third powderman, 25-year-old Alfonso Sias, was caught under a rock measuring eight feet in diameter. Seeing that Sias was trapped, Rios, Robledo, and an older brother of Sias, who was the crew's foreman, ran to him. After trying unsuccessfully to free Sias, the three men began to throw away the lit charges near Sias. After they had each pitched four to five sticks as far as they could, one of the charges exploded. The last charge Rios threw exploded in the air.

The concussion flung the three men to the ground and extinguished their lanterns, but they were able to crawl 35 feet and take shelter under a steam shovel. Other explosions followed, and one, which Sias said seemed to be just 10 feet from him, shifted the rock holding him, allowing him to also crawl to the steam shovel and safety. None of the men was seriously injured.

FILE NOS: 25675, 25676

YOLANDA FABBRI displayed courage, strength, and determination, and refused to allow a deranged man to drown himself and his two children.

C. H. 3152

On July 2, 1939, the 24-year-old Chicago housewife was walking along the shore of Lake Michigan when she came upon a harrowing scene. A despondent 36-year-old laborer was trying to drown himself, along with his seven-year-old son and two-year-old daughter. He had already thrown the boy off the concrete wall into deep water and then jumped in with the baby in his arms.

A strong, trained swimmer, Fabbri reacted quickly and got the boy to safety. By then, the man was 20 feet from the wall, still holding his daughter. Fabbri swam out and got a grip on the baby. The man resisted and punched Fabbri in the jaw. When he went under the water, Fabbri wrestled the child away and swam back to the wall.

Then she swam back toward the man. The would-be suicide was now weakened, so Fabbri was able to get her arm around his chest and tow him to shore. Bystanders hauled the pair out, but the man leapt right back in. Fabbri leapt in the water and towed him to safety again. He went back in a third time, but a lifeguard who had arrived got him out and restrained him until police could take him away.

Fabbri risked her life to prevent a triple tragedy. FILE NO: 37845

(ABOVE) ON AUGUST 23, 2016, THEN HERO FUND EXECUTIVE DIRECTOR ERIC P. ZAHREN PRESENTS THE CARNEGIE MEDAL TO ASHLEY MARIE ALDRIDGE IN A CEREMONY IN THE PRESENCE OF FAMILY AND FRIENDS HELD AT AUBURN CITY HALL IN AUBURN, ILLINOIS.

15 September 2015
WASHINGTON STREET RAILROAD CROSSING
AUBURN, ILLINOIS

On an average day, as many as 30 trains can pass through the town of Auburn, Illinois. The residents there have always lived with trains speeding their way to Chicago, nearly 200 miles away, as well as to other parts of the United States.

Earl Moorman was one of those Auburn residents who was familiar with life near the railroad, and he routinely crossed the tracks to make his way around town. But Moorman had it tougher than most: At 75 years old, he did not have use of his legs and used a motorized wheelchair to get around.

One afternoon, on September 15, 2015, as Moorman was making his way over the tracks at the Washington Street crossing near his home, both rear wheels of his motorized chair got stuck on the rails. He struggled to free the jammed wheels to no avail. Despite being a big man and strong in his youth, Moorman could not muster the strength to get his wheelchair over the rails. He yelled for help. He knew the danger: a speeding train could come at any moment.

A short distance from the crossing was a collection of mobile homes. In one of the homes, 19-year-old **ASHLEY MARIE ALDRIDGE** was busy making lunch for her two young children, a one-year-old and a two-year-old. She happened to glance out of her kitchen window and saw Moorman in his wheelchair sitting on the tracks. She didn't know Moorman and wondered if the man had simply stopped to take a rest since it was a hot day. After she saw a motorcycle go around Moorman, she became curious and went outside to check on him. That's when she heard the man's desperate shouts. She quickly went over to the home next-door and asked her neighbor to watch her kids while she went to see if she could help a man caught on the tracks.

At that moment, the railroad crossing gates lowered, red warning lights were activated, and loud bells rang out, signaling that a train was fast approaching. The municipality in that part of Auburn permits trains to travel 80 miles an hour through the city, and trains are required to activate the crossing gates when they are 20 seconds from the crossing. So, by the time Aldridge heard the warning bells and saw the gates begin to close, Earl Moorman had mere seconds to live if he did not get freed from the rails.

Aldridge took off toward him in her bare feet. She lived more than 100 feet away from the crossing. The train, which consisted of one engine and five passenger cars, barreled closer and closer. Aldridge was not trained for this. The nearest police station was two blocks away. Before she knew it, Ashley Aldridge, stay-at-home mom of two, went from quietly making lunch for her two children to sprinting over hot asphalt, dirt, and rocks toward a speeding train.

Moorman's frantic attempts to free himself were futile, and he panicked as the train closed in on him, blaring its horn. That's when he saw Aldridge running toward the crossing. When she reached the lowered gates, Aldridge ducked underneath them and ran to Moorman. She told him everything was going to be okay as she crouched behind his wheelchair and tried unsuccessfully to lift it over the rails. She knew immediately she could not lift the heavy chair with Moorman in it. Her mind raced, then she thought of another option—she would try to lift Moorman out of the chair. With the train now bearing down on both of them, she grasped Moorman from behind, putting both of her arms under his, and pulled him up with all her might. Her first attempt did not work so she tried again. The train was a few seconds away. Without thinking, Aldridge pulled on Moorman again and lifted him just enough to clear the chair. With all the force she could muster, she backed away from the track with Moorman in her arms. In the next instant, the train, at only slightly diminished speed, struck the wheelchair, destroying it, before stopping well beyond the crossing.

Lying on the ground, a few feet from the tracks, alive and only slightly bruised, were Ashley Aldridge and Earl Moorman. She had never met him before in her life, yet now she had saved his life with no time to spare. A person who had witnessed the incident from the other side of the tracks said it was like something out of a movie.

For her incredible bravery that day, Aldridge was awarded the Carnegie Medal for extraordinary heroism from the Carnegie Hero Fund Commission. News of her amazing rescue was broadcast from Chicago to the United Kingdom and received coverage in *National Geographic* magazine. She also received a plaque from the Illinois Commerce Commission, and Senator Dick Durbin of Illinois called Aldridge a hero on the U.S. Senate floor. But she would have no greater admirer than Moorman, who would be forever grateful for her actions that day. For Aldridge, the experience had both a positive and negative impact on her life. She said it took her nearly a year to be able to walk over that crossing after it happened. And when she went on walks with her kids during the summer, she said it was almost impossible for her to go over the tracks. Despite all of that, the moment changed her life for the better.

"It makes me look at everything differently now," Aldridge said in a *State-Journal Register* article after the incident. "I was young and kind of did whatever when I was a teenager. I've slowed down a lot now that I've got kids and everything. I'm very overprotective of everybody now because you never know when something's going to happen," she said. Nobody knew that better than Earl Moorman. FILE NO: 87706

C. H. 6589

On December 29, 1980, **WILLIAM C. BRISBANE** scaled the side of a burning San Francisco apartment building to save a woman trapped on an eighth-floor balcony.

About 8 a.m., a smoky fire broke out in the apartment of 23-year-old Annika Backlund, forcing her to flee to the balcony of a neighboring apartment, where she became trapped and was close to panic.

Brisbane, a 32-year-old transit worker, was in his apartment half a block away when he became aware of the fire and Backlund's plight. Although he did not know the young woman, Brisbane thought he could help. He started climbing the building by standing on the railing of one balcony, then pulling himself up to the next. Repeating that method, he climbed until he was on the balcony immediately below Backlund.

He then reached up to Backlund and guided her down to his side, and the two escaped through the seventh-floor apartment. Both were taken to a hospital, where they were treated for minor injuries and smoke inhalation. FILE NO: 57555

C. H. 8431

On April 19, 2000, **LYLE D. BAADE**, a 66-year-old retired construction worker and heart-transplant recipient, single-handedly tackled a man armed with three pistols and an assault rifle.

That afternoon, Baade and his wife had been attending a home-owner's association meeting of a retirement community near Phoenix, Arizona. At a little after 2 p.m., the couple was leaving the meeting in the recreation center for Baade's doctor's appointment for his annual heart check-up.

As they were exiting the room, they encountered a man, 66, entering the room. He blocked their way and told them to go back inside. When Baade protested, the man shoved him into the room. Although he did not recognize him as a former resident of the community, Baade did see the .22-caliber pistol in his right hand.

Baade and his wife retreated into the room and to the end of a 25-foot-long partition that separated the foyer from the main space. The man went the other way. As Baade shouted, "He has a gun," the man started firing into the group of more than 40 attendees, shouting, "I'm going to kill you all." Two women and two men were hit in the first volley. The man then put down the empty pistol and picked up a loaded AR-15 assault rifle that he had put in the room several minutes before encountering Baade.

Baade reacted quickly. He later recalled that, despite his age and infirmities, he knew he could get to the assailant before the assailant could turn the gun on him. Crossing the length of the partition, Baade hit the heavier man at full force, knocking the rifle from his hands. Both men fell to the floor, with Baade on top, and then they struggled for control of the rifle.

The assailant managed to pull the trigger and fire off one round, which struck a man in the foot, but Baade was able to prevent him from shooting more. Three other men then pounced on the gunman and, despite discovering that he had two more 9-mm pistols on him, were able to keep him pinned until the police arrived.

The two women died of their injuries, but the men recovered. Baade suffered scratches and contusions, but his heart proved to be up to his courage. FILE NO: 74499

14 January 1938
RELIABLE WOOD HEEL CO.
NASHUA, NEW HAMPSHIRE

RALPH KELLEY was 16 years old on January 14, 1938, when he helped two women escape from a fire at the Reliable Wood Heel Company in Nashua, New Hampshire.

Having graduated from high school the previous June, Kelley was employed as a floor boy at the plant that manufactured celluloid-covered heels for shoes. Near quitting time that cold winter afternoon, Kelley was working on the ground floor of the two-story facility, his third day on the job. A fire broke out among highly flammable materials and waste, and quickly mushroomed out along the ceiling toward the building's only staircase. All the workers on the second floor managed to escape, except for Margaret Dow, 31, and her sister Ethel Carter, 28, who was panicked by the flames.

Without hesitation, Kelley ran to the top of the staircase and took one of the women by the wrist. He turned to lead them back down but saw that flames had reached the staircase. Instead, he, Dow, and Carter ran across the room to a window that overlooked the snow-covered ground 17 feet below, and opened it. With flames reaching the second floor by then and quickly spreading, Carter, Dow, and finally Kelley climbed through the opening and dropped to the ground. The two women sustained minor injuries from their ordeal and quickly recovered. Kelley, however, had fractured two vertebrae in the fall. Hospitalized for five months, the teenager was permanently paralyzed from the waist down.

In addition to receiving a Carnegie Medal for his heroic act, Kelley was awarded a monthly grant from the Fund to help compensate for his injuries. He received that grant for 35 years. Over the decades since the fire, Kelley has also corresponded actively with the Commission and has nominated numerous others for consideration as medal recipients.

FILE NO: 38184

C. H. 3176

C. H. 10282

Christopher Lee Taylor, 36, forklift operator, of Greenville, Ohio, was driving through a local neighborhood on October 31, 2020, when he saw flames on a nearby home's second floor. Taylor ran to a side door of the home and called out into the house. From inside, he heard David Miles, 30, moaning. Doubled over to keep his head below the smoke, Taylor entered the home, making his way through thick smoke and intense heat to a stairway where he found Miles, then unconscious, near the top. Flames were spreading toward the stairs as Taylor picked up Miles and carried him out of the house. FILE NO: 91387

C. H. 10266, 10267 ☦

An October 3, 2020, fishing outing in Huntersville, North Carolina, turned tragic after a two-year-old boy entered the swift-flowing Catawba River. With the boy on the outing was his mother and her partner, 34-year-old cable installer **D'Angelo Cordero Jenkins**, of Rock Hill, South Carolina. Jenkins immediately jumped in, fully clothed, after the boy and reached him in the river, but then had difficulty swimming with the boy. Hearing the mother's calls for help, **Michael Byers**, a 65-year-old retired business operator of Lexington, North Carolina, entered the river fully clothed, and swam to Jenkins and the boy. He grasped the boy's arm and took him from Jenkins, towing him to the boat ramp where the boy safely exited the water. Byers was nearly exhausted and could not return to assist Jenkins, who was floating in the river. The boy was treated overnight at a hospital; Jenkins drowned. FILE NO: 91393, 91657

C. H. 10246 ☦

After hearing screams and shots fired from inside his daughter's home, **John D. Colter**, a 66-year-old pharmacist of Fenton, Missouri, ran inside the home and tackled his daughter's estranged husband, 45, who had entered on January 23, 2020, lay in wait, and then shot at Kristine M. Kempf, striking her in the leg and ankle. Colter wrestled with the assailant for control of the gun on the hallway floor, where Kempf also attempted to seize the weapon. Colter called for Kempf to leave and get help. She ran to a neighbor's home. The man fatally shot Colter and fled; authorities located him in another state eight days later, and, before they could arrest him, he shot himself dead. Kempf was hospitalized for treatment of her wounds. Colter died at the scene. FILE NO: 91479

(Top) Christopher Lee Taylor was dressed as a superhero for Halloween when he saw flames in a nearby Greenville, Ohio, home and acted. He entered the house and found David Miles, who was unconscious at the top of the stairs leading to the second floor. Flames were spreading toward the stairs, and Taylor carried Miles out of the house.

(Left) John D. Colter

After smoke filled his Bronx, New York, 16-story apartment building in the early hours of June 9, 2019, 19-year-old student **Lucas Y. Silverio Mendoza** and his family descended the building's stairs, he and his cousin assisting his grandmother who had mobility issues. Around floor 14, the family passed three-year-old Yasleen Moreno, who was crying and alone in the stairwell. Instructing his cousin to continue helping his grandmother down the stairs, Silverio Mendoza turned back, returned to the 14th floor landing, and reached for Yasleen. Before he could get to her, flames and smoke exploded through a trash compactor chute door, buckling nearby walls; blowing open several nearby doors, including the one to the stairwell; and filling the area with flames and smoke. The explosion badly burned Silverio Mendoza and Yasleen, separating them, and blowing Silverio Mendoza down a full flight of stairs where he hit his head on a concrete wall. The cousin retrieved Silverio Mendoza and, along with others, helped him from the building. Yasleen was later found on the 12th floor by a firefighter, who carried her to safety. Both Silverio Mendoza and Yasleen died later due to their injuries sustained in the blast. FILE NO: 90578

C. H. 10229

A San Diego police officer used a dog leash to rappel down a 30-foot cliff and then entered the Pacific Ocean to save a man and his two daughters from drowning on June 13, 2020. Before sunrise, the 47-year-old man was the driver of a truck that left the road at the top of the cliff and entered the ocean. The man had left the partially submerged and overturned vehicle and was holding his two-year-old twin daughters in the water beside the truck, as Officer **Jonathan Wiese**, 43, analyzed the scene. He removed his shirt, ballistic vest, and duty belt, wrapped the 100-foot leash twice around his chest, and other officers at the scene lowered Wiese to the base of the cliff, where he removed the leash and entered the water. Wiese swam to the man, who was larger than him, grasped him, and pushed him and the girls to the base of the cliff. One of the girls was unresponsive, and he secured her to a backpack; officers at the top of the cliff hoisted her, and then her sister, to safety; they were later hospitalized with serious injuries. The father was removed from the cliff by helicopter. Wiese eventually used a surfboard to paddle about 200 feet to a point where he could exit the ocean. FILE NO: 91167

C. H. 10217

(FACING PAGE, TOP) JONATHAN WIESE (BOTTOM) THE WRECKAGE OF A PICKUP TRUCK THAT ENTERED THE OCEAN FROM THE TOP OF A 30-FOOT CLIFF. POLICE OFFICER JONATHAN WIESE RAPPELLED DOWN THE CLIFF, ENTERED THE OCEAN, AND BROUGHT TWO YOUNG GIRLS AND THEIR 47-YEAR-OLD FATHER TO SAFETY.

C. H. 10201

After a man wielding a pump-action shotgun shot through the locked, front door of an Annapolis, Maryland, newspaper office and shot a sales assistant, severely wounding her, he proceeded toward the back of the office. Eleven employees were working June 28, 2018, and several people took cover under their desks. Sixty-five-year-old reporter **WENDY WINTERS** of Edgewater, Maryland, grabbed a plastic garbage bin and recycling bin and left her desk area and charged toward the gunman, telling him to stop. The assailant shot Winters in the chest and then proceeded deeper into the office where he fatally shot three others. Two others fled, and although the assailant shot at one, he missed. The assailant hid under a desk until police arrived. Four others hid under their desks for the duration of the ordeal. Winters and the sales assistant died from their gunshot wounds. FILE NO: 89946

C. H. 10185

A retired clerk from North Highlands, California, **FUSAKO M. PETRUS**, 86, was walking with her 61-year-old friend at dawn April 26, 2017, on a North Highlands school track when an 18-year-old man approached the friend, struck her in the face repeatedly, and, after they went to the ground, held her down, groped her, and attempted to rape her. As the woman fended off the man, Petrus approached them, brandishing a large stick. Petrus struck the assailant and told him to leave her friend alone. The assailant shifted his attention to Petrus, beating her to death, while the 61-year-old woman fled the scene to get help. The man was later arrested and at the time of the investigation was still awaiting trial. FILE NO: 89154

C. H. 10167

On September 9, 2018, Terri L. Bradley, 63, was stabbed by a man armed with a kitchen knife while crossing the street in an Atlanta neighborhood. **WINSTON S. DOUGLAS**, 52, of Hapeville, Georgia, was driving a transit bus when he witnessed the attack and immediately stopped the bus. He called for the assailant to stop, but the man continued to attack Bradley. Douglas grabbed a four-foot length of fence post from a nearby construction site and advanced to the assailant while swinging the post, striking the assailant at least once in the ribs. The assailant attempted to strike Douglas with the knife and then thrust the knife at Bradley again. The blade of the knife broke off, and the assailant fled as Douglas chased him. Another man working nearby tackled the assailant. Douglas joined the other man and the two struggled to subdue him. Douglas and the other man were ultimately able to restrain the assailant and hold him until police arrived. The assailant was arrested and charged with various offenses, including aggravated assault. Bradley was hospitalized for several days for treatment of her stab wounds, and she recovered. FILE NO: 90069

While on a family vacation, **KATHERINE M. WENSZELL** sustained a severed toe, multiple fractures, internal contusions, and a concussion after being hit and dragged 50 feet by an Atlanta subway train after saving her 57-year-old mother from the same fate. On August 19, 2018, Susan A. Wenszell was standing on a subway station platform when a man pushed her off the platform onto a track as a train approached. The younger Wenszell, a 28-year-old Milwaukee school teacher, jumped off the platform and unsuccessfully attempted to remove her mother from the path of the train. As the train bore down on them, Wenszell positioned her mother in the middle of the track so the train would pass over her. She also attempted to lay between the rails, but the train struck her and dragged her. Susan suffered a broken arm, concussion, back injury, and contusions to her body from being pushed onto the track, but she was not struck by the train. Wenszell, who was unconscious by the time the train came to a stop, was removed from the track by rescue personnel and underwent several surgeries for her injuries. FILE NO: 90059

C. H. 10143

Retired laborer **STEVEN W. FITZPATRICK**, of Marysville, Washington, responded to his neighbor's burning mobile home on April 18, 2018. With fire extinguishers, Fitzpatrick entered the home's living room through the front door. Fitzpatrick crawled to 88-year-old Theodore Shockley, who was unconscious on the living room floor near a flaming couch. Fitzpatrick used a fire extinguisher near Shockley to suppress flames, then grabbed Shockley and moved him toward the front door. Forced to retreat by the blistering heat, Fitzpatrick exited the home briefly and then returned to Shockley. With difficulty, he moved Shockley to the threshold of the front door, where another man grasped Shockley and pulled him from the home. Fitzpatrick exited the house, which was shortly engulfed by flames. Shockley sustained smoke inhalation and extensive burns; he died later that day. Fitzpatrick sustained burns to his head, forearm, and hand, for which he received hospital treatment. He recovered. FILE NO: 90047

C. H. 10120

(Top, Left) Fusako M. Petrus, (right) Winston S. Douglas
(Bottom, Left) Steven W. Fitzpatrick, (right) Brent Rudy Edwards

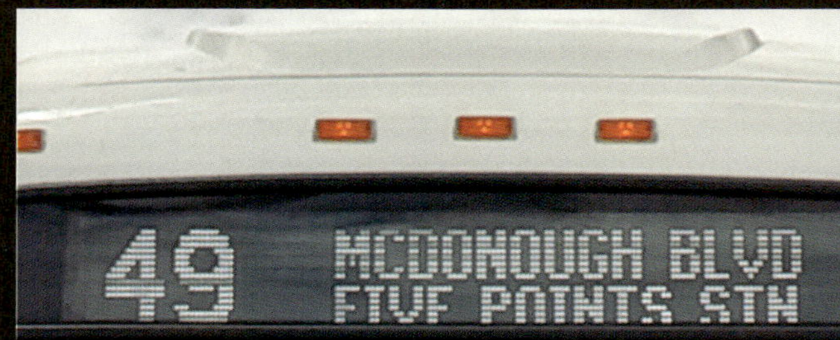

49 MCDONOUGH BLVD
FIVE POINTS STN

After a July 30, 2018, accident near Olympia, Washington, 29-year-old administrative assistant **HEATHER ZABROWSKI** of Olympia responded to a burning sport utility vehicle that had come to rest in a ditch. Despite flames burning beneath the vehicle and dry grass around the vehicle aflame, Zabrowski opened the driver's door and saw 67-year-old Alan E. Rathbun slumped over the steering wheel. She extended her upper body inside the passenger compartment and reached across Rathbun to unlatch his seat belt. She then turned Rathbun to face her and pulled him from the vehicle to the ground. Too heavy for her to lift, Zabrowski called to others nearby for help. Zabrowski and a man who responded aided Rathbun to safety. Flames grew to engulf the rear of the vehicle and spread to its interior. Rathbun was not burned. FILE NO: 90033

C. H. 10115

A high school teacher saved students and staff from a school shooter on September 20, 2017, in Mattoon, Illinois. Students were at lunch in a high school cafeteria when a 14-year-old boy showed several students the .40-caliber, semiautomatic pistol he had brought to school. One student informed teacher **ANGELA LYNN MCQUEEN**, 40, of Mattoon, and as she approached, the boy began to fire the gun toward other students. McQueen lunged for the gun and forced the assailant's hand upward toward the ceiling as he continued to fire. McQueen kept the gun pointed to the ceiling until the gun was emptied, and then disarmed him as a school resource officer arrived to handcuff him. One student was hit with a bullet and recovered. McQueen suffered minor hearing loss in both ears and other injuries. The remaining students and staff escaped the cafeteria unharmed. FILE NO: 89410

C. H. 10099

A 64-year-old retired teacher saved a woman from being struck by a train on October 10, 2017, in Brookhaven, New York. Janice C. Esposito, 43, was driving a van when it collided with another vehicle and came to rest straddling a nearby railroad track. **PETER C. DI PINTO, SR.**, heard the crash from his nearby home and responded. He ran to the driver's door of the van, which was smashed, and told a dazed Esposito that she needed to exit. Suddenly the crossing's gates descended and lights flashed, warning them of the approaching commuter train, traveling at 65 miles per hour. Di Pinto ran to the passenger side of the van, opened the front door, reached

C. H. 10072

in, and grasped Esposito. Di Pinto pulled her through the door and moved her off the track to safety behind a signal box. The train, which had slightly slowed, struck the van about six seconds after Di Pinto had removed Esposito. They both survived. FILE NO: 89440

27 May 2017
ROW HOUSE
PHILADELPHIA, PENNSYLVANIA

C. H. 10045

Seventeen-year-old **Brent Rudy Edwards** rescued his toddler nephew, Bryce Noel, from a burning home on May 27, 2017, in Philadelphia, Pennsylvania. After fire broke out in a row house, adults inside evacuated four young children from the home. His mother roused Brent from sleep, and he followed his family outside, where his mother realized that Bryce, 23 months, was still inside. Despite thick, black smoke that had filled the first floor, Brent re-entered the house to search for his nephew. Hearing the toddler cough, Brent crawled inside the house 12 feet to him, clutched him to his chest, and ran toward the light at the front door. Once outside, he handed Bryce to his mother and collapsed, losing consciousness. Arriving paramedics revived him, and he and Bryce were taken to the hospital for treatment of smoke inhalation. They recovered. Bryce was not burned. FILE NO: 89303

18 April 2017
SUBURBAN NEIGHBORHOOD
TURLOCK, CALIFORNIA

C. H. 10029

A 47-year-old receptionist, **Ana Maria Ramirez**, was driving in Turlock, California, when she witnessed 12-year-old Jose J. Ramos being attacked by two pit bull dogs on April 18, 2017. Jose was attacked by the 65-pound dogs while walking his family's dog on a leash in his suburban neighborhood. During the attack, Jose and his dog were bitten, and he was unable to release his grip on his dog's leash. Ramirez stopped at the scene and, concerned that Jose would be pulled to the ground in the struggle to control and protect his dog, Ramirez blew the car's horn. She exited the car, approached, and shouted at the pit bulls. One dog, a female, moved away, but the male continued its attack on Jose and his dog. Ramirez returned to her car and, retrieving part of a child's booster seat, approached the male pit bull, and struck it. The dog bit her wrist and forearm and held on. Ramirez struck the dog again with the booster seat, and the dog released her. Both pit bulls fled the scene. Jose was treated for a bite wound to his finger, contusions, and lacerations. He recovered. Ramirez was treated for a bite wound to her wrist and forearm and lacerations to her arm. She also recovered. FILE NO: 89178

Next-door neighbor **MICHAEL E. SURRELL, SR.**, 64, a disabled truck driver, entered a burning Allentown, Pennsylvania, home to save the eight-year-old girl inside. On May 4, 2017, Tiara was on the second floor of a three-story row house after fire broke out in a bedroom on the home's second floor. Surrell, learning that Tiara remained inside, entered through the front door and climbed the stairway but was soon repulsed by dense smoke and heat and forced to retreat outside. Undeterred, Surrell re-entered the house, climbed the stairs to the second floor, and went to his hands and knees. Surrell heard Tiara moan, and despite intense heat and dense smoke that precluded visibility, crawled toward the sound of her voice, finding her on her back several feet from the top of the stairs. Surrell stood up and placed Tiara over his shoulder, then carried her down to the first floor and out onto the porch. Tiara, unresponsive, was given rescue breaths by Surrell, and was revived. Tiara was hospitalized for smoke inhalation; she recovered. Surrell was hospitalized for a burn to his larynx and smoke inhalation. At the time of the investigation, he had not yet fully recovered. FILE NO: 89147

A 65-year-old woman was in the driver's seat of a car that was parked March 7, 2016, at a self-service car wash in Colorado Springs, Colorado, when her estranged husband in the front, passenger seat suddenly punched her in the face and stabbed her in the abdomen with a pocket-knife. As the woman cried out for help and struggled with the assailant, **ROSS A. JOHNSON**, 52, maintenance man of Colorado Springs, heard her cries and approached the car where he saw the assailant stabbing her. At the open front, passenger door, Johnson shouted forcefully for the assailant to stop, prompting him to cease his attack and exit the vehicle. As the wounded woman exited the car through the open door, the assailant, who had remained at the door, grabbed her and stabbed her three more times before Johnson, several feet away, could intervene. After the woman collapsed outside the vehicle, Johnson pushed away the assailant, who had placed the knife down nearby. Johnson knelt beside her, putting himself between her and the assailant to prevent further injury to her. Johnson comforted the injured woman until police arrived shortly thereafter. Police arrested the assailant without incident. The woman spent eight weeks hospitalized and in rehabilitation and suffered partial paralysis from her wounds. FILE NO: 89566

C. H. 10026

C. H. 10007

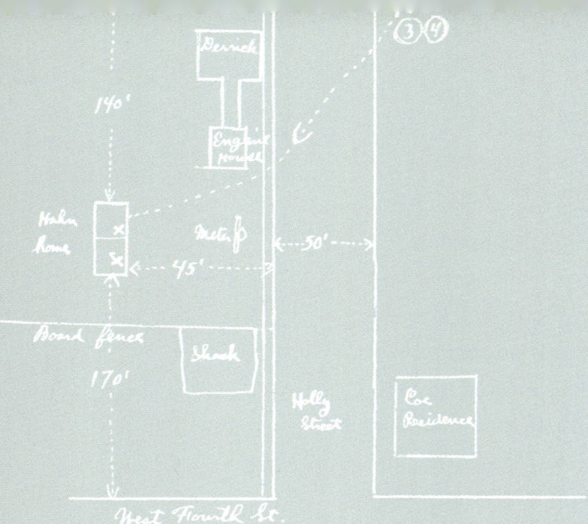

6 February 1923
HAHN RESIDENCE
BURKBURNETT, TEXAS

C. H. 1865

On February 6, 1923, 30-year-old **Charles L. Coe** died while trying to rescue two small children from their burning home in Burkburnett, Texas.

Three-year-old Arnold Hahn and his one-year-old brother, David, were sleeping in the bedroom of their parents' small, single-story dwelling when a fire broke out. The flames spread rapidly through the flimsily constructed structure, its walls lined with heavy paper.

Coe, a neighbor and a father of three daughters, was among several men who responded to the fire. Even though smoke and flames were already leaking from cracks in the building's outer walls, Coe and one of the other men raced in. Making their way through the dense smoke, they checked the bedroom but were unable to find the two children.

Seeing flames starting to sheet over the partition walls, the other man realized they would soon be engulfed and grabbed Coe to warn him. Refusing to leave, Coe jerked away and turned back toward the bed. The other man ran from the house, but, even though his hands and face were scorched, he punched a hole through a panel of a door that led into the bedroom. Almost immediately, the older Hahn child was thrust through the opening, followed by an intense burst of flame.

Unfortunately, before the fire could be extinguished, sections of the house's roof and walls collapsed. Coe and the baby, who was in his arms, were later found burned to death just inside the doorway through which the hero had entered the house. He was posthumously awarded a Carnegie Medal, and his widow received a monthly grant from the Hero Fund for many years. Although badly burned, Arnold eventually recovered. Coe was the last individual to be awarded a gold Carnegie Medal.

FILE NO: 23074

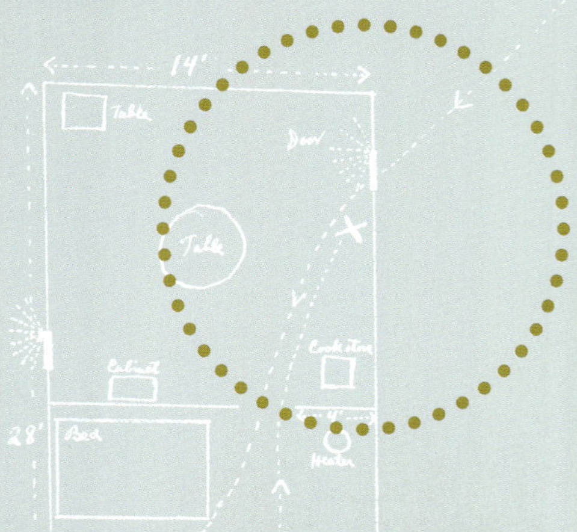

Upper sketch-- General view of Hahn house and surroundings
Lower sketch-- Hahn house in detail.
RX'X--Course of Coe to the children and with them
M--Point at which Donaho deserted Coe
X'--Point at which Coe delivered Arnold to safety
X--Point at which Coe's body was found with David's.

CHARLES L. COE, DRILLER,
AND DAUGHTER FRANCES.
THIS PHOTO WAS TAKEN
ABOUT 1920. FRANCES WAS
BORN IN 1916.

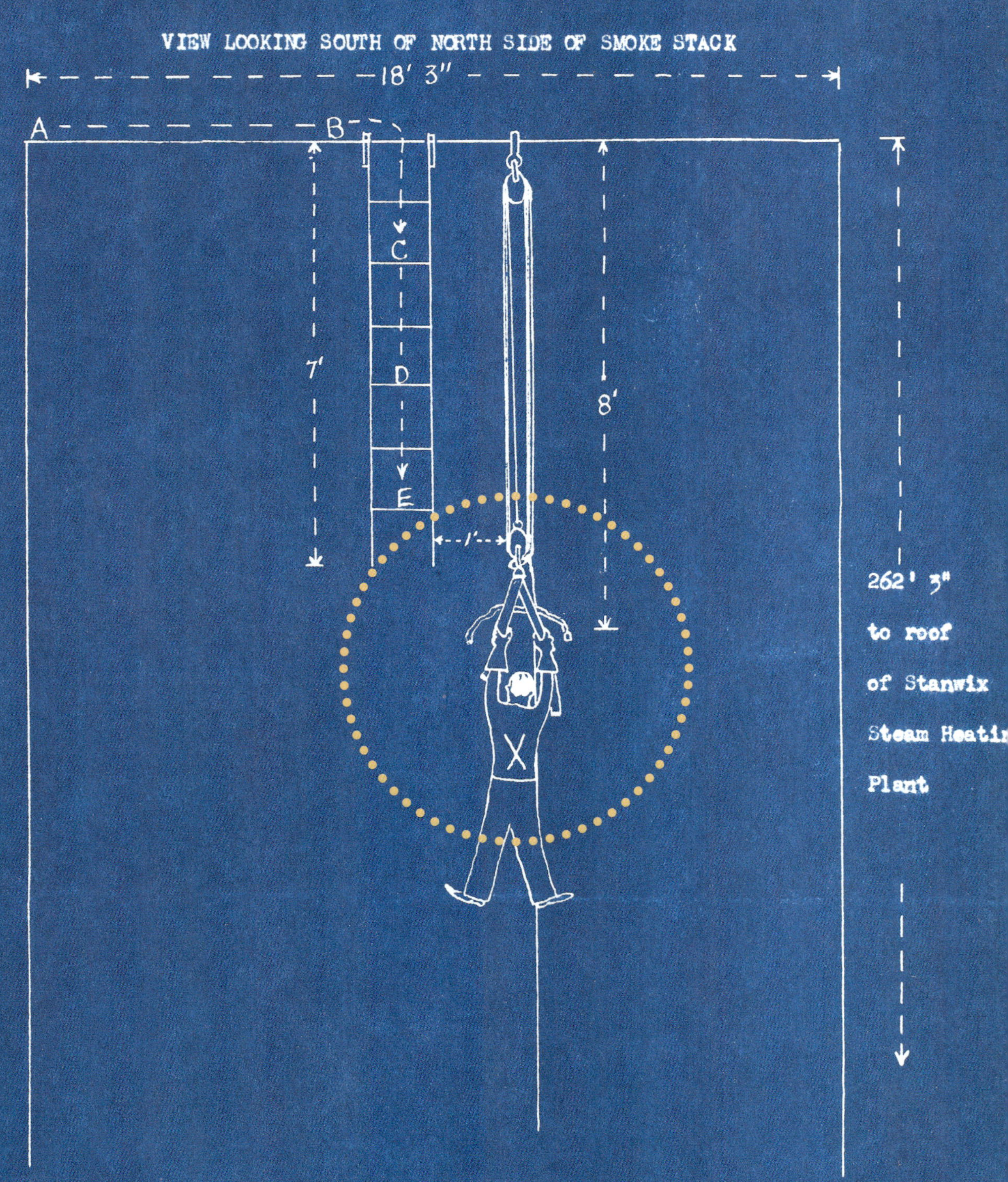

CASE OF P. ROSCOE CHAPMAN, FILE NO. 41057
VIEW LOOKING SOUTH OF NORTH SIDE OF SMOKE STACK
18' 3"
A
B
C
D
E
7'
8'
1'
X
262' 3"
to roof
of Stanwix
Steam Heatin
Plant
X   - position of Samuel L. Hopkins
ABCDE - course of P. Roscoe Chapman to position on ladder
E   - position of Chapman's right foot
D   - rung over which Chapman hooked his left leg
C   - rung to which Chapman clung with left hand

Forty-nine-year-old **Rosco Chapman** earned his Carnegie Medal on May 15, 1947, when he saved a co-worker from a fatal fall.

Chapman and Samuel Hopkins were painting a smoke stack that rose 260 feet from the roof of the Stanwix Steam Heating Plant in downtown Pittsburgh. The two men had just climbed to the top of the 18-foot-diameter, steel-clad, brick-lined stack following their lunch break. They normally worked from boatswain's chairs hanging from a block and tackle attached to the top of the stack, but when Hopkins climbed down the short, temporary ladder from the chimney's top and swung into his chair, a strap snapped and his seat dropped away. Even though one of his work gloves had wet paint on it, Hopkins managed to grab the ends of the broken strap and hang on, dangling eight feet below the top of the stack.

Chapman, who had been straddling the top of the stack, immediately circled around to the work ladder and climbed down. Bracing one foot on its lowest rung, he hooked his other leg over a higher rung, and, hanging on to a third rung with his left hand, managed to reach down with his right hand and grab Hopkins's left wrist. Chapman then let go of the ladder and managed to remove Hopkins's work glove, enabling the dangling man to get a better grip on the strap end. Then, by shifting and lifting, Chapman was able to haul Hopkins up so he could get a grip on the ladder and climb to safety.

Though he suffered from shock and a strained back, Hopkins eventually recovered completely, thankful that Rosco Chapman had what it takes to be a hero. FILE NO: 41037

On March 31, 1977, **David G. Jackson**, 19, stepped into the path of danger to save a co-worker from a falling piece of steel.

Jackson and Jerry Duncan, 26, were working on a new vertical shaft of a zinc mine in Gordonsville, Tennessee. The partially constructed, 1,470-foot-deep shaft was 16 feet in diameter.

Both men were working on a platform at a level over a thousand feet below the top of the shaft, when a sheet of corrugated steel suspended at the shaft's opening broke from its supporting cable. Jackson, a driller, heard the metal plummeting down the shaft just as Duncan stepped into its path. The young man reacted instantly and lunged toward Duncan to push him out of the way, but just as he reached his co-worker, the falling sheet of metal hit both men.

While Jackson's push probably saved his life, Duncan's right arm was severed at the shoulder. Both of Jackson's arms were severed near the elbows, but they were able to be surgically replaced. FILE NO: 55716

C. H. 3533

(FACING PAGE) COMMISSION INVESTIGATOR'S SKETCH SHOWING COURSE OF ROSCO CHAPMAN'S RESCUE.

C. H. 6290

On October 6, 1965, **Michael V. Ulrich**, 15, crawled into a tight cave crevice three times to extricate a trapped schoolboy.

The previous morning, Morris Baetzold was exploring a side fissure off the main passage of Wild Cat Cave, near Hinckley, Ohio. The 15-year-old boy had wriggled about 25 feet into the narrow slit when he toppled over and became wedged between the cave walls, which at that point were about nine inches apart and four and a half feet high.

Stuck and unable to move, Baetzold called for help. A number of attempts were made to reach him, but all were unsuccessful because no one could fit into the tight opening. News of the boy's predicament was made public, and Ulrich's father thought one of his sons might be able to help. Baetzold had been trapped for 24 hours when the Ulrichs arrived on the scene.

After being briefed about the situation, Ulrich's 12-year-old brother tried first to reach Baetzold but was unable to go very far. Ulrich, an Eagle Scout, then volunteered. With two ropes tied around him and taking the ends of two others, he squirmed into the tight opening.

At about two-thirds of the distance to the trapped boy, the passage became so narrow that Ulrich had to turn on his side and wriggle along parallel to the downward sloping floor, supporting himself on his right arm, until he reached Baetzold's feet. Then, working with only his left hand extended over his head, Ulrich managed to knot a rope to a strap he had maneuvered around one of the boy's legs. Then he backed out to where he could stand.

When rescuers pulling on the rope were still unable to budge Baetzold, Ulrich crawled back in and rearranged the strap so that it was around both the boy's legs. Then, looping the second rope around a clamp that he strapped to a small outcropping above Baetzold and attaching the end to the boy's legs, Ulrich backed out again. This time, rescuers managed to lift and free Baetzold's hips and right arm, but his chest remained tightly wedged.

Ulrich wormed back in a third time and, working with Baetzold, was able to get another rope around his upper body. Then Ulrich backed out again. Baetzold was covered with a slippery solution, and greased boards were slid in under him. Then, lifted slightly by the rope around his chest, he was slowly drawn out of the crevice to a place where he could stand. Though debilitated by his ordeal, Baetzold recovered without consequence. Ulrich, although exhausted and sore from his three forays into the crevasse, each of which had taken half an hour, suffered no serious injuries.

FILE NO: 48334

On November 7, 1960, two employees at an H. J. Heinz Company food plant in Pittsburgh, Pennsylvania, **STEPHAN JAGUSCZAK** and **PETER P. SMOLEY**, died attempting to save a co-worker from suffocation inside a railroad tank car.

C. H. 4373, 4374

Joseph Buttice, a 34-year-old factory hand, had climbed down through the small, circular hatch of the tank, in which tomato paste had been shipped. Although the 19,880-gallon tank had been emptied of most of its contents, several inches of paste remained in the bottom, along with nitrogen used as a preservative during shipping. Just after Buttice reached the bottom of the ladder, he was overcome and collapsed backwards into the soupy paste. His supervisor, at the top of the ladder, immediately climbed off the car and ran to a nearby building to report the accident. Jagusczak, a 34-year-old cook's helper, was among several men in the building, and he ran back to the accident scene with the supervisor.

While the supervisor got an air hose, Jagusczak climbed up on the tank car, squeezed through the hatch, and started down the ladder. The supervisor called out a warning, but though Jagusczak hesitated an instant, he continued climbing down. The supervisor scrambled to the top of the tank car and looked into the hatch in time to see Jagusczak also slump, face forward, into the paste.

The supervisor inserted the hose into the tank and began feeding in fresh air. Other men arrived. One supervisor put on an air mask, but was unable to squeeze through the hatch, which was only 20 inches in diameter. Then Smoley, a 25-year-old preparation helper, put on a mask and, after being instructed to leave if he felt affected by the gas, climbed down the ladder. At the bottom, he was only able to turn Jagusczak's head so it was out of the paste before he himself was overcome, collapsing across Buttice.

A man from the plant's safety department arrived and, donning an air mask, climbed down, secured by a rope around his waist and carrying a second. He was able to get the second rope around Smoley and Buttice, and each was hauled out of the tank. A fireman entered the tank for the rescue of Jagusczak.

Although Buttice had been in the tank car the longest, he was resuscitated and, though hospitalized for a time, eventually recovered. However, neither Smoley nor Jagusczak could be revived. In addition to accepting a posthumously awarded Carnegie Medal for their son's heroic act, Smoley's parents were granted money to help defray his funeral expenses. The Commission also awarded Jagusczak's widow a monthly grant, which she continued to receive until her death in 2009. FILE NOS: 45288, 45287

12 February 1927
LAKE CHAMPLAIN
ESSEX, NEW YORK

On February 12, 1927, **WINFERD L. HATHAWAY** braved the frigid waters of Lake Champlain to rescue five fishermen stranded on an ice floe.

That cold Saturday morning, Albert Reynolds, 61, Henry Mero, 56, Leslie Mero, 20, John Pedro, 27, Clarence Sayword, 12, and James Moore, 15, were fishing in three sheds built several hundred feet out on the frozen lake near Essex, New York. A stiff wind of 40 mph was blowing, and even though the air temperature was 10 degrees Fahrenheit, it caused the ice field to heave and break. The five, sensing danger, started for shore by jumping from one ice floe to another, but soon were stranded on a slab 400 feet square, which began to heave in the wind-driven waves.

Hathaway, a 19-year-old farm boy who had recently been laid off from a local paper mill, was at his parents' home by the lake. He saw the ice breaking up and noticed the five small forms in the distance. Realizing the trouble they were in, he dragged a light canoe out across the shore ice and paddled across a 300-foot stretch of choppy water that had opened in the broad floe. Alternating paddling the canoe and pulling it across ice, and twice slipping into the water to his waist, Hathaway took 45 minutes to reach the men, huddled on the dwindling slab.

Then, since the ice conditions on the opposite shore were better, Hathaway and the others used the canoe to ferry themselves from floe to floe for two miles to safety. They then walked several miles along the lake's east shore where they found solid ice, and then crossed to the west shore. None of the five was seriously injured, saved by Hathaway's quick thinking and skillful courage. FILE NO: 28961

4 April 1917
ATLANTIC OCEAN ICE FIELD
BONAVISTA, NEWFOUNDLAND

On April 4, 1917, five men braved pack ice in the Atlantic Ocean to save seal hunters stranded on a drifting ice field off the northeast tip of Newfoundland.

At 4 a.m. that day, John Marsh, Philip Way, 57, and Way's 42-year-old nephew Robert started a hike of several miles out on the field of packed ice along the Atlantic coast to hunt seals. The wind shifted, causing the sea to heave and break up the ice. The three men became stranded on separate ice cakes that were tossed in waves up to six feet high as the field drifted from shore. Before long, Marsh fell from his cake and drowned. The two Ways clung to separate cakes, which threatened to break apart. When they were spotted, they were a half-mile apart and more than two miles from shore, drifting across the mouth of Bonavista Bay.

Sixty-three-year-old **HEZEKIAH ABBOTT**, a local fisherman, was the first to respond. He organized a boat to go out and try to find a way through the ice to rescue the two stranded men. Four local fishermen, including two brothers, **DAVID ABBOTT**, 58, and **HENRY J. ABBOTT**, 42 (who were not related to Hezekiah), along with **DANIEL BUTLER**, 57, and his nephew, **ISAAC J. BUTLER**, 38, joined him. All volunteered even though none of them could swim and several other men had refused to go.

The five of them loaded a day's rations into a 20-foot-long work skiff and entered the mist-bound ice field. They made slow, arduous progress through the slurry of slushy ice, using oars where they could and pushing larger cakes aside with gaffs where the field was more tightly packed. At times, the men climbed out of the boat onto larger cakes and pulled the boat along.

After more than an hour, the rescue party finally reached the older Way and took him aboard. A half-hour later, they got to his nephew. Then the boat was turned back toward shore, but they made slower progress because the ice had now become more tightly packed. Two hours later, they emerged from the ice field about three miles from where they had entered, all hands safe. A motorboat towed them to shore, where a crowd of hundreds greeted them. Other than being tired by their efforts and stress, none of the men was injured. FILE NOS: 18029, 18030, 18031, 18032, 18033

On December 25, 1906, two young men went to the aid of a skating companion who had fallen through weak ice, and then another young man went to their rescue when they fell in.

Three of the men, all deaf and mute, were students at the Kansas State School for the Deaf who had gone skating that sunny Christmas afternoon on nearby New Lake. About 2:30 in the afternoon, one of them, Ernest Albright, 21, was about 100 feet from shore when he broke through the ice and began floundering in eight-foot-deep water.

Another student, **ROLLO EASTMAN**, 19, immediately went to Albright's aid. He tried to pull him out by hand, but the ice crumbled under Eastman and he tumbled into the water as well. The same thing happened when **THOMAS HERRMAN**, 21, tried to extend a short board toward Albright.

EARL A. AMES, 20, was standing on the bank when he saw what had happened. Borrowing a pair of skates and grabbing the reins from a horse standing nearby and tying them into a strap about 20 feet long, Ames skated some 600 feet to the floundering trio. He tossed one end of the strap to Albright and, after several attempts, managed to pull him out of the water and then dragged him to shore, even though his feet broke through the weak crust. Ames skated back to the hole and threw the strap toward Eastman and then Herrman, but they were already exhausted. Neither could grab hold of the rope, and both sank into the icy water and drowned.

FILE NOS: 1524, 1525, 1475

C. H. 207, 206

C. H. 205

7 September 1913

SUSANVILLE HOSPITAL

SUSANVILLE, CALIFORNIA

C. H. 959

On the cool morning of September 7, 1913, a father and son were residing in adjacent rooms of California's Susanville Hospital. William D. Minckler, Sr., a 62-year-old civil engineer, was suffering from palindromic rheumatism, which caused inflammation and made it difficult to walk. His son, William D. Minckler, Jr., 25, a civil engineer's assistant, had been in a motorcycle accident and was experiencing a severe concussion that caused delusions and outbursts of violence. He had been in the hospital for six weeks and was not expected to live.

LILLIAN M. COBURN, 42, matron of the hospital, requested an orderly fill and light the coal oil stove in the elder Minckler's room while she prepared to give him a bath.

She stepped out of the room located in the northwest corner of the hospital's one-story wing to gather towels from a linen closet and warm water from the bathroom.

During this brief absence, Coburn heard a popping noise. When she turned back to Minckler's room, she saw flames erupting from the top of the door. The stove, containing about one gallon of oil, had exploded and caught fire. Flames quickly spread throughout the hospital's pine structure, and there were no fire extinguishers available to provide relief. Hero Fund Special Agent M.H. Floto presented these details about the hospital's structure and specific risk factors Coburn faced, so Hero Fund officials who would review Coburn's qualifications for the Carnegie Medal had no doubt of the dangers she faced.

Minckler, lethargic from the medicine he had been given, remained asleep. In the room adjacent to the east, his son, William, was oblivious to the peril. It was clear that father and son were in danger of being burned to death.

In addition to the Mincklers, there were at least 15 other patients in the building, including four or five who were considered by staff to be practically helpless.

J.H. Platt, a patient who was faring well, shared a room with the younger William and had been keeping an eye on him while Coburn tended to other duties. He exited to the hallway where Coburn had just witnessed the eruption of flames.

"What can I do?" Platt inquired, wringing his hands.

"Save yourself," Coburn directed. Platt ran for safety.

In the regulation linen uniform of a trained nurse, Coburn, who was assiduously familiar with the hospital, ran into Minckler's room. Flames covered the walls and ceiling, and the hospital bedding was ablaze. Fire licked Minckler's head and had spread to his head and shoulders.

Coburn pulled Minckler from his bed, put a bath towel over his head, and walked him into the hall. She pushed him ahead of her until they reached William's door. Here, she instructed him to stay close to the wall and pushed him in the direction of safety.

By now, fire had spread to the west end of the hall. Flames and upper segments of the walls burned easily as they were full of a cotton material for insulation and covered with wallpaper. Heavy smoke permeated the hallway. A draft from an open transom window pushed the flames east.

Coburn entered William's room. He lay in his hospital bed as flames were beginning to encroach the upper portion of the west wall. Coburn quickly lifted William in her arms. She attempted to push him out through the first-floor window, but in his concussed state, William kicked and struggled, and Coburn was thrown to the floor. She toiled for a few more minutes before deciding on another method. Using a bath towel, she twisted it around William's neck and dragged him into the hall.

Here, Coburn found Minckler had not gone to safety and was still standing along the north wall, dazed and mumbling to himself. Smoke weighed down on them ominously and the draft pushed flames to the ceiling of William's room. As conditions worsened, the two other nurses on duty removed patients out through windows.

"Keep your mouth closed," Coburn instructed a murmuring Minckler, before she pushed him forward with one arm and dragged William with the other.

A sharp pain pinged Coburn's neck, shoulders, and arms—her clothes had caught fire. Battling the excruciating sensations, and struggling to maintain control of the disillusioned men, Coburn remained steadfast in her conviction to get her patients to safety. She continued toward the kitchen, but the screen door offering exit was locked. Undeterred, Coburn maintained her hold on the father and son, making her way to the dining room and then out to a screened porch. A man who was never identified met Coburn at the door and threw a coat around her shoulders to extinguish the fire burning on her uniform.

About this time, Coburn became aware that her hair was also burning. She had been wearing a celluloid comb, a decorative hair piece made of synthetic materials prone to combustion, and it had ignited.

Coburn's injuries included third-degree and minor burns on her neck, shoulders, arms, left ear, and a portion of her cheeks, and smoke inhalation. Case investigator Floto noted that she had undergone continuous treatment after the incident.

There was no doubt Coburn risked her life to an extraordinary degree to save the Mincklers, and well beyond her professional responsibility, as Floto's report to the Commission clearly proved.

Coburn was awarded the silver Carnegie medal and a $1,100 grant. From 1914 through 1919, the Hero Fund supported Coburn and her son with beneficiary payments. FILE NO: 12126

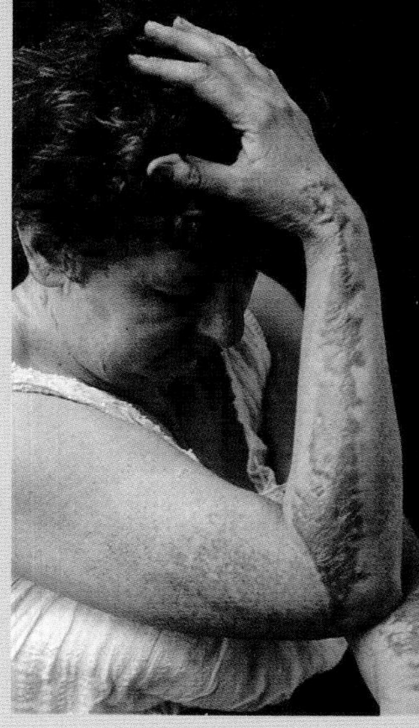

C. H. 9973

On July 10, 2015, police officer Tammy K. Walter, 50, was punched by a man in a public waiting room of a Topeka, Kansas, police station, which caused her to fall to the floor. The assailant stood over her and punched and kicked her repeatedly. Alerted by Walter's screams, **TERRYANN E. THOMAS**, 46, an inventory specialist that served patrons in that waiting room, left her secured area to go to Walter's aid. She yanked at the assailant from behind, pulling him away from Walter, but she released her grasp when the assailant began punching her. He then resumed his attack on Walter, and Thomas pulled him away again. When an elevator door in the room opened, the assailant grasped Thomas and pulled her toward the elevator. In the doorway of the elevator, Thomas struggled against the assailant, falling to her hands and knees on the floor and pulling the assailant back into the room with her. He then kicked her in the head and chest. Thomas rose and ran to a door, opened it, and shouted for help. Responding officers took the man to the floor and into custody. Walter and Thomas were taken to the hospital where they were treated for injuries, Thomas recovering in about two months. FILE NO: 88969

C. H. 9121

Badly injured, Catherine A. Moffat, 37, and Andrea L. Higgins, 38, remained strapped in their seats after the sport utility vehicle in which they were traveling overturned in an August 1, 2006, highway accident in Central Elgin, Ontario, and caught fire at its front end. At a nearby residence, **DANIEL WILLIAM BAILEY**, a 43-year-old off-duty police officer, heard the accident and ran to the scene. He attempted to free Higgins from the wreckage but found she was pinned by it. Bailey then approached the driver's side of the vehicle, reached inside, and cut Moffat's seat belt with his pocketknife. After he and others took her to safety, Bailey returned to the wreckage. Despite growing and spreading flames, which by then entered the vehicle's passenger compartment, he reached inside and cut Higgins's seat belt, worked her free of the wreckage, and helped remove her to safety. Flames shortly engulfed the vehicle. Both women were taken to the hospital, where Moffat died of her injuries. Higgins was detained for treatment of her injuries, which included severe burns. Bailey also required hospital treatment, for minor burns to both forearms, from which he recovered. FILE NO: 79557

Early in the morning of August 3, 2006, Kaili M. Heronema, 7; Amanda R. Humphreys, 17; and their grandfather, Arden L. Humphreys, 78, were found clinging to the bow of a boat that had swamped and partially sank about 14 hours earlier while the party was on a fishing outing on Fontenelle Reservoir near La Barge, Wyoming. They were in deep, cold water about 450 feet from the closest bank when found by Deputy Sheriff **CLIFFORD R. BOYD**, 30, who had been dispatched to search for them. Although he was recovering from recent ear surgery, Boyd, knowing it would take time for a rescue team to arrive at the remote location, swam to the boat. Grasping Kaili, he towed her ashore and placed her in his vehicle to warm. Another deputy arrived, with empty plastic containers, and Boyd, using one of them as a flotation device, swam to the boat again. With both Amanda and him holding on to the container, Boyd swam Amanda to shore, and she joined Kaili in his vehicle. Again, using the container, Boyd swam a third time to the boat. Helping Humphreys hold the container, he swam to wadable water, towing Humphreys, then was helped by the other deputy in removing Humphreys from the reservoir. Humphreys and his granddaughters were taken to the hospital for treatment of hypothermia and dehydration, and they recovered. Boyd was nearly exhausted, and he developed ill effect in his affected ear that required medical treatment. FILE NO: 79615

C. H. 9093

During a dust storm with high winds, Ann B. Byrne and her husband, William A. Byrne, both 87, were trapped inside their car after a March 10, 2005, accident in Martin, South Dakota, in which the car left the roadway, entered a ditch, and caught fire at its rear end. Ann Byrne was unable to open the passenger door, and her husband was rendered unconscious in the accident. As she pounded on the window and shouted for help, motorists **ROGER W. MYERS**, 57, carpenter, and a co-worker, **KENNETH LEE THOMPSON**, 35, maintenance worker, stopped at the scene. While Thompson called for help, Myers approached the burning car and attempted to open its doors. Unsuccessful, he returned to his vehicle for a fire extinguisher. Following the call, Thompson also responded to the car and attempted to open its doors. He then removed the window of the passenger door, assisted Ann Byrne from the car, and carried her to safety. Learning that William Byrne was still in the vehicle, Myers and Thompson returned to it. Thompson used the fire extinguisher against the flames, which by then had reached the backseat area, and he opened the passenger door. He and Myers partially entered the car, grasped the man,

C. H. 9078, 9079

and then they pulled him through the passenger door and carried him to safety. Flames shortly engulfed the car's interior. The couple was hospitalized for treatment of their injuries. Myers and Thompson also received hospital treatment for minor burns and smoke inhalation; they recovered. FILE NO: 79446, 79445

C. H. 9065

Duane Damron, 71, leaped into action to save Curtis A. Nemetz from being struck by a shifting mobile home in Gulfport, Mississippi, on December 12, 2005. Nemetz and retired athletic coach Damron were part of a group of volunteers installing a mobile home. Nemetz was sitting on the ground near the home; his back was against a chain-link fence and his legs were underneath the unit. The mobile home shifted from its supports toward the fence. As Nemetz scurried to his feet, Damron lunged toward him from a kneeling position around the corner of the unit. With his right hand, Damron grasped Nemetz and pulled him from between the fence and the shifting home. That end of the unit dropped to the ground against the fence, pinning Damron by the left hand. He pulled the badly injured hand free. Damron was taken to the hospital, where he remained two months for treatment, including three surgeries. Two of his fingers were amputated. FILE NO: 79043

C. H. 8958

One-year-old Evan J. Moore was in his crib in a bedroom of his family's single-story house in Swiftwater, Pennsylvania, on December 7, 2004, when a fire broke out in a nearby bedroom and filled the house with dense smoke. Alerted to the fire, neighbors, including **Maria Christine Ericson**, 42, human resources director, responded to the scene. Ericson climbed a ladder at the window to Evan's room, then broke out the window and entered the house. Heat was intense in the bedroom, and dense smoke kept her from seeing. Walking with outstretched hands, Ericson located the crib, then found Evan. She picked him up, took him to the window, and handed him outside to safety, then she climbed through the window to safety. Flames spread inside the house and claimed the lives of his two sisters, but Evan was not injured. Ericson suffered minor smoke inhalation and a scrape to her right hand. She recovered without seeking medical attention. FILE NO: 78187

Rochelle M. Rose, 28, and her son Thomas L. Giles, 4, were in a bedroom of their Regina, Saskatchewan, one-story house when a man armed with a steak knife broke down the front door, entered, and, threatening to kill Rose, proceeded to the bedroom. The assailant had just broken into other houses on that block on June 19, 2003, and neighbors, including **JOHN GLENN DUBOIS**, 43, who was disabled, witnessed the break-in at Rose's house. Obtaining a wooden broom handle from his next-door home, Dubois entered Rose's house, where he found that the assailant was holding the door to the bedroom closed. Dubois forced his way into the bedroom and struggled with the assailant, disarming him of the knife. As Rose and Thomas fled the house, Dubois pinned the assailant to the floor with the broom handle, the assailant continuously struggling against him. Police officers responded shortly and with difficulty handcuffed the assailant. Neither Dubois nor Rose or Thomas was injured. FILE NO: 77009

C. H. 8927

A 16-year-old boy entered a restroom of the East Greenbrush, New York, high school he attended, then emerged brandishing a loaded 12-gauge shotgun on February 9, 2004. He fired two shots at students in the hall but missed, and the students fled to safety. In a classroom in that wing of the building, **JOHN P. SAWCHUK**, 41, assistant principal, heard the gunshots and, followed by teacher **MICHAEL BENNETT**, 36, proceeded through the hall to investigate. Turning a corner, they saw the armed assailant about 20 feet away. Sawchuk immediately ran to him, grabbed him, and started to struggle for control of the gun. The assailant fired again, striking Bennett in the leg as he approached. Sawchuk convinced the assailant to release the gun, which Sawchuk then handed over to another teacher. He took the assailant into a nearby office and detained him there until police arrived and arrested him. Bennett required hospital treatment for his wound. Sawchuk was not injured. FILE NO: 77487, 77522

C. H. 8916, 8917

A 47-year-old woman was the passenger of an automobile being driven on a Houston, Texas, beltway when the car was struck by a 300-pound tire that had detached from a tractor-trailer traveling on the same highway on November 14, 2003. The driver of the car was killed instantly, and the car continued forward, out of control, with a female passenger inside.

C. H. 8875

It veered in and out of the inner emergency lane, striking the concrete median barrier repeatedly. Another motorist, **Christopher Cranford**, 18, a plumber, was traveling behind the car and witnessed the accident, then, passing, saw the woman struggling to control the car. Cranford drove his half-ton pickup truck into the emergency lane at a point about 30 feet ahead of the car and removed his foot from the accelerator. After having traveled out of control for a half-mile, the car, then going about 45 miles per hour, struck the back of the pickup, pushing it forward 10 feet. Cranford applied his vehicle's brakes and took both vehicles to a stop. The woman was not badly injured. Cranford sustained back pain and soreness, and he recovered within a week. FILE NO: 77301

C. H. 8864

On April 11, 2001, a 58-year-old man who was attempting suicide was at an Elora, Ontario, outlook atop a 70-foot-high promontory at the convergence of the Grand and Irvine rivers. Beyond the 30-inch-high wall that rimmed the outlook was a narrow ledge that formed the far end of the promontory. On duty, **Belinda Lee Rose**, 29, a police officer, was called to the scene. On her arrival, the man, who had secured a rope to his neck, dived headfirst partially over the wall. The man landed with his lower legs atop the wall and his upper body caught by branches on the outside of the wall. Although he outweighed her by 120 pounds, Rose grasped the man's lower legs and held on to him. The man struggled against Rose and heaved himself forward, taking Rose with him, her feet coming off the landing. She lay atop the man, holding him to the wall. She screamed for help, and another officer arrived within minutes and pulled Rose and the man back to the safety of the landing. Both were taken to the hospital, where the man was treated for injury to his back. Rose required treatment for contusions and abrasions, and she recovered. FILE NO: 76539

C. H. 8836

While attempting to close the door to a den of a tiger cage at the Sacramento, California, zoo where he was employed, Chad Summers, 30, was attacked by a 320-pound tiger that had rushed the door on March 23, 2003. Wounded, he went to the floor, where the tiger began to maul him. Starting her third day as a volunteer at the zoo, **Hannah Lynn Goorsky**, 23, was standing nearby and witnessed the attack. She grabbed a shovel, approached the tiger, and struck it on the head repeatedly with the shovel. The tiger retreated into its den, and Goorsky secured the door. Summers was hospitalized for treatment of numerous bite wounds. He recovered and returned to work at the zoo. Goorsky was not injured. FILE NO: 77059

Hannah Lynn Goorsky

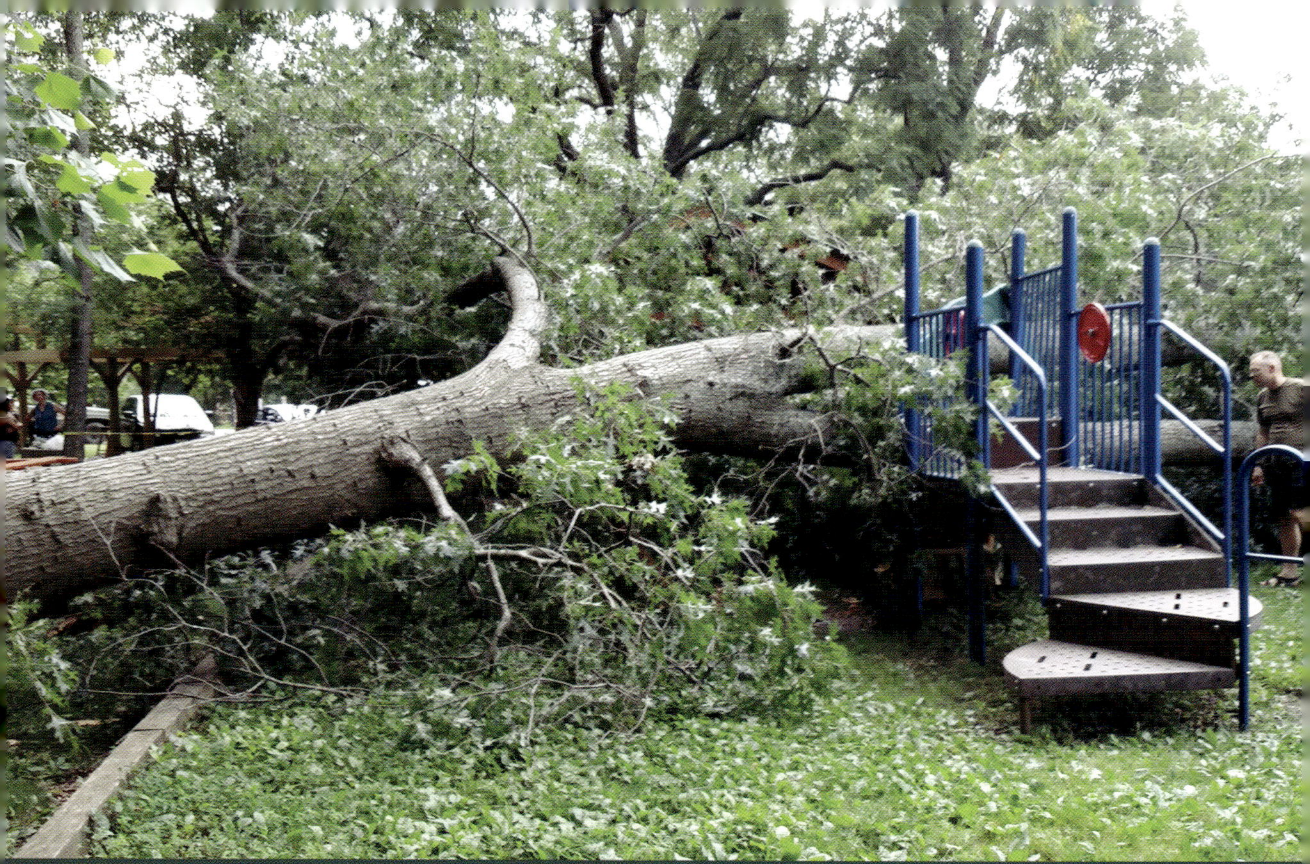

The 80-foot-long, fallen tree limb that landed on play equipment from which John Paul Hollyfield had removed 6-year-old Ashley S. Gruwell moments earlier.

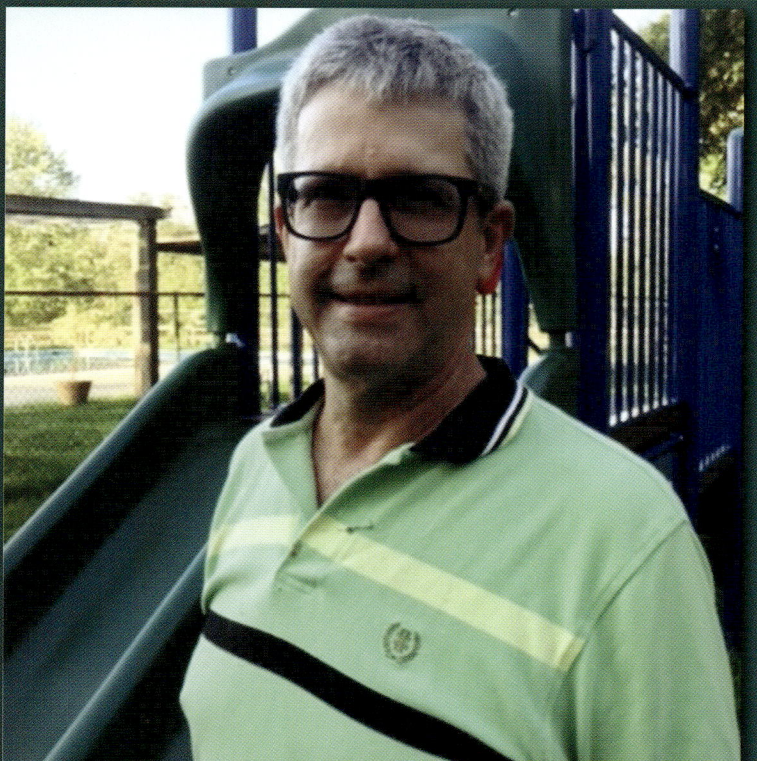

John Paul Hollyfield

At work on an equipment upgrade, Jon Stanger, 35, was overcome and lay unconscious at the bottom of an underground sump, which was above a gasoline storage tank on the premises of an Escondido, California, convenience store on February 11, 2003. Atmosphere in the sump was deficient in oxygen, and gasoline fumes there were at an explosive level. A customer in the store, **RICHARD P. MOTEN**, 50, a plumber, was alerted to the situation. He immediately responded to the sump's ground-level opening, from where he saw Stanger and detected fumes. Moten then dropped about six feet to the bottom of the confined space and grasped Stanger. He found a foothold about two feet above the sump's floor and used that as he hoisted Stanger up to others at ground level. They pulled Stanger from the sump, then aided Moten out. Stanger was revived at the scene but taken to the hospital for observation. Moten was given oxygen at the scene then also was taken to the hospital for observation. They recovered. FILE NO: 76706

C. H. 8804

A 13-year-old girl intervened when she saw a six-year-old being attacked by a 75-pound dog on January 29, 2003. As the dog mauled Caleb J. Orland, **KERILYN BELLE CRAWFORD** entered the Navasota, Texas, yard, jumped from the porch to the ground, and approached Caleb. She grasped the dog by its collar and struck it on the head. The dog released its grasp on Caleb, who then fled the yard at Kerilyn's direction. Kerilyn returned Caleb to his nearby home. He was taken to the hospital, where he was detained a week for treatment to his bite wounds, including surgery and well over 100 sutures. Kerilyn suffered a bruise to her arm; she recovered in about a week. FILE NO: 76654

C. H. 8774

During a July 9, 2015, cookout on the wooded Moyaone Reserve in Accokeek, Maryland, Ashley S. Gruwell, six, was seated at the top of a slide about 10 feet beneath an 80-foot-long limb of an old-growth tree, the base of which was about 20 feet away. At the trunk, the limb was at least three feet in diameter. An attendee, 56-year-old teacher **JOHN PAUL HOLLYFIELD** heard the limb cracking from the tree and concluded that its collapse was imminent. While Hollyfield and others yelled for guests nearby to disperse, Ashley remained on the slide. Hollyfield ran about 30 feet to the slide where he grabbed Ashley and led her to the ground. Hollyfield then led her to safety in the vicinity of the pavilion. Within seconds, the limb fell across the top of the slide, destroying it, while also damaging other structures at the scene. FILE NO: 88656

C. H. 9962

C. H. 9935

Anthony H. Ortiz, 27, was the passenger in a sport utility vehicle that in a June 8, 2016, accident left a Manteca, California, highway, went down a steep embankment, and stopped upright, straddling a set of two railroad tracks. Another motorist, 35-year-old hospice nurse **Stephanie Melinda Marino** witnessed the accident, and stopping at the scene, ran down the embankment to the vehicle. Going to the vehicle's passenger side, she helped Ortiz, who was injured, stand outside it. A commuter train was approaching at about 70 miles per hour and was about a quarter mile away when its engineer saw the vehicle. He immediately applied the train's emergency brakes and sounded its horn, which first alerted Marino to the train's approach. In the seconds that it took for the train to reach the scene, Marino grabbed Ortiz, who was larger than she, and pulled him by an arm and his shirt toward the rear of the vehicle. She stepped off the tracks but maintained her grip on Ortiz as the train struck the vehicle at somewhat of a diminished speed and knocked it about 10 feet away. Marino and Ortiz fell to the ground, debris from the impact striking them. The train came to a stop about 2,000 feet beyond the point of impact. Ortiz required hospitalization for treatment of his injuries, and Marino recovered from bruising to her knees and cuts to her arms and hands. FILE NO: 88362

C. H. 9933

While playing on August 27, 2016, a two-year-old boy fell through the small, ground-level hatch of an underground septic tank on a residential property in Dublin, Ohio, and ended up submerged in sewage about four feet deep. Neighbors who responded to the scene could not reach him in the eight-foot-deep tank. Alerted to the situation by her mother, 13-year-old **Madison L. Williams** lay on her stomach and, positioning her arms over her head, entered the 12-inch-wide opening to her thighs while others secured her by the legs. She skimmed the surface of the sewage with her hands searching for the boy for several moments before she saw his foot. Madison grasped the boy's foot and shouted at the others to be pulled out. As she and the boy were being lifted from the tank, the boy's free foot became stuck under the inside lip of the hatch. On Madison's instruction, she was lowered somewhat, and repositioned the boy. Those on the ground then pulled her and the boy completely free of the opening. The boy was not breathing but was then revived, and he fully recovered after hospital treatment. Madison required medical treatment for damage to her left wrist that required a brace for two months and physical therapy. She also recovered. FILE NO: 88542

(Top) Stephanie Melinda Marino

(Bottom) Keoni Bowthorpe

(TOP) CALVIN BRADLEY STEIN, DAYS AFTER BEING TRAMPLED BY RUNAWAY PONIES IN RESCUE ACT.

(BOTTOM) CALVIN BRADLEY STEIN WITH HIS OWN TEAM OF PONIES.

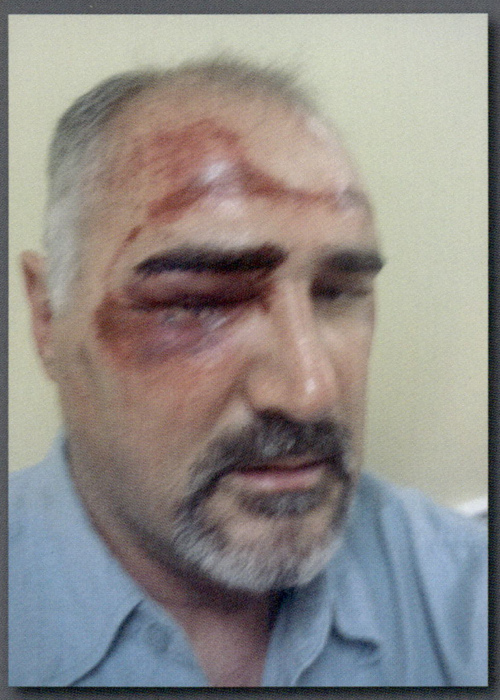

At a Tweed, Ontario, fair held July 9, 2016, three-year-old Rylee Vilneff was standing inside the track at a fairground when a team of two ponies, each weighing about 600 pounds, broke free and, harnessed together, ran away at full speed. Seeing that, **Calvin Bradley Stein**, 51, a utility worker who was also inside the track, moved toward a position to intercept them, but they changed course and headed directly toward Rylee. Stein then ran about 55 feet to the girl and scooped her into his hands to throw her clear of the path of the runaways. She landed about four feet away. The ponies struck Stein, knocking him to the ground, and dragged him a distance before coming to a stop. Stein was taken to the hospital, where he was treated for a concussion, facial fractures, and lacerations, which required suturing. Rylee was also taken to the hospital, but she suffered only minor injuries. She recovered. FILE NO: 88402

C. H. 9909

Colin W. Cook, 25, was surfing on October 9, 2015, in the Pacific Ocean off Haleiwa, Hawaii, when he was attacked by a shark. At a point about 600 feet from shore the tiger shark, about 11 feet long, bit him, severing his left leg above the knee and inflicting a severe hand injury. Standing on a paddleboard in the water about 500 feet away, filmmaker **Keoni Bowthorpe**, 33, witnessed the attack. He immediately headed to Cook, who by then had gotten back onto his board in the bloodied water. As he neared Cook, Bowthorpe saw that the shark was still in the immediate vicinity. When the shark approached them, Bowthorpe thrust one end of his paddle against it to push it away. Cook moved to Bowthorpe's board but ended up in the water. Bowthorpe then lay prone atop the board and pulled Cook onto his back. With Cook holding on to him as best he could, Bowthorpe paddled about 1,300 feet to shore, having to stop a few times to secure Cook. In wadable water, another man helped pull Bowthorpe and Cook to the beach. Bowthorpe and others then carried Cook to the highway, from where he was taken to the hospital. Cook remained there for treatment of severe injuries and was later fitted with a prosthetic leg. FILE NO: 87776

C. H. 9877

C. H. 9821

On October 8, 2014, a minivan continued to roll in reverse after its 84-year-old driver left the vehicle following a minor accident on a residential street in Aurora, Illinois. The driver reentered the vehicle and it, still in reverse, accelerated quickly and erratically off the street and through the front yards of two properties. Standing at another property across the street, carpenter **Dennis C. Hunke II**, 51, witnessed the accident and ran to the open driver's door of the minivan as it was moving back onto the roadway. Running alongside the vehicle, he attempted to enter it in what witnesses concluded was an attempt to hit the brake pedal. The van accelerated, and the inside of the driver's door struck Hunke, knocking him to the pavement, where he was badly injured. The van came to a stop on the opposite side of the street. Hunke was taken to the hospital, where he died two days later of blunt force trauma. The driver was not injured. FILE NO: 86919

C. H. 9783

Erin A. Greene, 30, was walking home from a Halloween party in the dark through a Churchill, Manitoba, residential neighborhood on November 1, 2013, when a 275-pound, male polar bear approached and attacked her, taking her to the ground and biting her about the head. From his house nearby, **William Ayotte**, 69, a retired water treatment plant operator, heard Greene's screams. He opened his front door and saw the bear thrashing Greene about. Taking a snow shovel with him, Ayotte advanced to Greene and the bear and struck the bear once, hard, about the face. The bear released Greene, who then fled to safety inside Ayotte's house. As Ayotte retreated, the bear took him to the ground and began to maul him. Neighbors attempted without success to scare the bear away until one of them approached in his pickup truck. The bear then left the scene. Ayotte and Greene were taken to the hospital, where Greene was detained a day for treatment of numerous bite and claw wounds. Ayotte was detained a week for treatment, including surgery of extensive lacerations, and a nearly severed ear. He fully recovered. FILE NO: 86909

11 August 2013
INTERSTATE HIGHWAY
MERIDIAN, IDAHO

On August 11, 2013, an elderly man was driving a sport utility vehicle the wrong way on a Meridian, Idaho, interstate highway. Driving on the same highway, **ALAN CAVENER**, 54, an off-duty police officer from another municipality, came upon the scene and saw other motorists swerving around the vehicle. He drove to a point ahead of the vehicle and parked on his lane's inner shoulder. Exiting his car, Cavener climbed over a concrete barrier and ran across three lanes of traffic to meet the man's vehicle, which was approaching at a speed of less than five miles per hour. When he shouted at the man to stop, the man rolled down the driver's window but continued. Running alongside the car, Cavener reached through the opened window and grasped the steering wheel. After continuing for about 75 feet, Cavener saw a break in the oncoming traffic and steered the vehicle off the highway to safety on the shoulder. FILE NO: 86642

C. H. 9774

20 January 2014
COMMUTER TRAIN STATION
SANTA CRUZ, CALIFORNIA

On January 20, 2014, a man went to a point between the rails of a track at a commuter train station in Santa Clara, California. An express train traveling at 70 miles per hour approached the station on that track. A commuter, **PHILIP SCHOLZ**, 35, a technology marketer, was standing on the platform not far away. Scholz sprinted toward the man, advancing to a point at the edge of the platform opposite him as the man moved toward the platform. Scholz extended his arms around the man as the train, then in emergency braking, bore down on them. Both men were struck by the train. Scholz died at the scene, but the man, though suffering significant injury, survived. FILE NO: 86319

C. H. 9748

24 November 2013
OAKLAND COLISEUM
OAKLAND, CALIFORNIA

After a November 24, 2013, event, a 20-year-old woman sat on an outside ledge atop the highest deck of an Oakland, California, stadium, drawing attention from those on the concrete concourse 67 feet below. One of them, **DONNIE NAVIDAD**, a 61-year-old government employee, moved to a point directly beneath the woman as she started to fall. He bent at the knees and stretched out his arms to catch her. Navidad grasped the 100-pound woman as she struck him, knocking him to the pavement. The woman required hospitalization for treatment of severe injuries, and Navidad was treated at the emergency room for contusions to an arm and shoulder. He fully recovered. FILE NO: 86205

C. H. 9705

C. H. 9929 ✢

It was early on a frigid February morning in Norristown, Pennsylvania, when 58-year-old Sanford Harling, Jr., awoke. He reached for his walker; it was the only way he could get around since his hip replacement surgery a month earlier. Slowly and carefully, Harling made his way out of the bedroom where he and his wife, Dana, slept and headed toward the bathroom.

Sound asleep down the hall in another bedroom was his 12-year-old son **SANFORD HARLING III**. The family called him "Man Man." He was an energetic, athletic kid with a big personality who loved spending time with his friends, his family, but most of all, his dad.

As Harling ambled down the second-floor hallway, he briefly glanced down the stairs. The first floor of his three-story duplex was on fire. Flames were moving swiftly across the floor, consuming furniture, walls, and everything else in its path. He realized the fire had progressed to a point where he could never make it down the stairs, in his condition, to try and stop it. It was about to block the stairwell and trap him and his family upstairs. He frantically shouted for his family to wake up and get out of the house.

As he went to another bedroom to attempt exiting from a second-story window, Harling's wife, daughter, and son Sanford descended the stairs and fled through a back door. Sanford's older brother left the home through a third-floor window.

Surrounded by thick black smoke and flames, Harling did not know if his family had left the house safely. As the fire tore up the stairs, he dragged himself toward another window.

Outside, Sanford huddled with his family in the cold and watched in horror as the fire engulfed his home while firefighters and other emergency personnel arrived on the scene. He desperately searched for any sign of his father who was trapped inside. He shouted to anyone who would listen that his dad was still in the house.

Still struggling upstairs, Harling quickly surveyed the windows on the second floor and recalled where each of them led. He had to find the one that would give him the greatest chance of survival since he was still recovering from surgery. He made his way to the window that overlooked a grassy part of the yard—his best shot at a softer landing.

Meanwhile, Sanford continued to stay vigilant as he watched the house, looking for something, anything, that would indicate his dad was okay.

Inside, reeling from the pain of his hip surgery and feeling the heat of the fast-approaching fire, Harling reached the window. Since he could not lift his leg, he pulled his body out onto the ledge.

Outside, in the chaotic wailing of fire engine sirens, Sanford couldn't wait any longer. He escaped the grip of his family and sped toward the growing inferno of the house, ignoring his mother's desperate pleas for him to come back.

In a final push to save himself, Harling threw himself out of his burning house.

In a final rush to save his dad, Sanford went back into his burning house.

Sanford Harling, Jr., loving husband and father of three, landed with a crunching thud on the ground two stories below, fracturing his back, ribs, and femur. He was alive.

Sanford Harling III, loving son and brother, his whole future ahead of him, did not survive. Firefighters found him under the dining room table with second- and third-degree burns over 100 percent of his body.

Sanford Harling III

The pain his father experienced after his fall from the second floor of his duplex and the ensuing 10 surgeries and three months he spent in the hospital was nothing compared to the pain he felt in his heart after learning of the fate of his beloved son.

In that single tragic moment, Man Man was never more of a man. He loved his father, looked up to him, emulated him. Fire was not going to stop him from saving him. Witnesses recalled that the last word he uttered before going back into the house was, "Dad!"

"I don't know any other kid who would have taken that chance to run into a house with flames burning to save his father's life or his mother's life," said his father.

Eric P. Zahren, then executive director of the Hero Fund, presented the Carnegie Medal to Sanford's parents, Dana Henderson and Sanford Harling, Jr., in a special ceremony held May 2, 2017, during a Norristown Council meeting.

"When you think of courage, what do you think of? I think of four words: fearless, heroism, bravery, and boldness. These four words describe Sanford for he exemplifies the meaning of courage," said Council President Valerie Scott Cooper. "His selfless courage is an example of family love."

Harling, still haunted by the pain of losing his son, tearfully said, "We feel really honored to be able to receive this award in honor of Sanford. This is something that will remain in our hearts. Our son was already labeled a hero, but now he's officially a hero in history." FILE NO: 88049

C. H. 9688

Stuart E. DeLand, 93, remained in the driver's seat of his automobile after an August 15, 2013, accident in which it left a roadway, entered Bradley Brook Reservoir in Eaton, New York, and sank in water about 12 feet deep. High schooler **ALEXANDER LIAS TRAVIS**, 17, was a passenger in a vehicle that stopped at the scene. He immediately ran to the bank of the reservoir, removed his shoes, and entered the water. After swimming about 35 feet to the driver's side of DeLand's car, the front end of which was submerged, he attempted, without success, to open the driver's door. He was successful in opening the rear door on that side of the car, and water then rushing inside forced him into the backseat area. Alexander reached over the center console and released DeLand's seat belt but was unable to pull him from his seat. He exited the vehicle and pulled on the window of the driver's door until it broke out. Reaching inside the submerging car through the window opening, he grasped DeLand and pulled him headfirst out of the car. They both submerged, but Alexander took DeLand back to the surface. He then swam DeLand to the bank, where he had help in removing him from the water. DeLand required hospitalization, and Alexander sustained lacerations on his hands, from which he recovered. FILE NO: 86002

C. H. 9663

Amy Wong, 31, was fly-fishing August 6, 2011, in the Cheakamus River near Whistler, British Columbia, when she lost her footing, fell, and was moved downstream, her hip waders filling with water. Her friend, 34-year-old software engineer **JUSTIN TAK CHAN**, was fishing closer to the bank. Also wearing hip waders, he immediately jumped into the deeper pool of water between him and Wong, swam across it, and made his way to her. Chan cradled Wong but did not regain his footing as both were carried downstream. Chan was found an hour later at a point about 2,000 feet downstream. He had drowned. Wong was not found. FILE NO: 84279

Alan Cavener

Michael Wayne Pirie

C. H. 9636

On April 9, 2013, a nine-year-old boy entered the Merced River just above Vernal Falls in Yosemite National Park, California, and was carried downstream by the swift current toward the brink of the falls. From another party on the bank at the scene, 16-year-old **ALEC JUSTIN SMITH** immediately ran to the river, jumping over a three-foot-high railing. At the water line, he lay on the smooth granite bank, which was slick, and, holding by one arm to a knob in the rock, extended his body partially into the 36-degree water at a point about 20 feet from the falls. With his other hand he grasped the boy when the boy came within reach. Alec pulled the boy onto the bank, where another man then helped to secure them as they regained their footing. FILE NO: 85641

C. H. 9630

When John A. Crandon, 43, entered a Cato, New York, pasture to tend one of his cows on August 19, 2012, his 1,100-pound Jersey bull charged and attacked him, taking him to the ground and ramming him in the chest repeatedly with its head. Unable to escape, he screamed for help. A 23-year-old carpenter, **BRIAN D. LOZIER**, was about 1,200 feet away and heard Crandon's screams. Calling 911, he ran to a wire fence along the edge of the pasture, picked up a few rocks and threw them at the bull, but to no effect. Lozier then grasped a nearby four-foot length of two-by-four board, stepped over strands of the fence, and approached Crandon and the bull, then about 10 feet away. He threw the board at the bull, striking it on the back. The bull left Crandon and went to the barn, and Crandon crawled from the pasture, Lozier joining him to drag him farther away. Crandon required hospitalization for treatment of significant injuries. FILE NO: 85363

C. H. 9602

Grant S. Lockenbach, 20, and **MICHAEL WAYNE PIRIE**, 18, were among a group of college students exploring Ellison's Cave in LaFayette, Georgia, on February 12, 2011. A backpack containing personal items and gear was lost to the bottom of a pit, 125 feet deep, inside the cave. Lockenbach lowered himself by rope to retrieve the bag, but, encountering difficulty, he shouted for help, and several members of the party left to alert rescue personnel. With Lockenbach continuing to shout for help, Pirie donned a harness and descended into the pit on another line. For several minutes he and Lockenbach remained in communication with those students at the top of the pit, despite the noise of a nearby waterfall dropping into the pit. Eventually their voices were silenced, Lockenbach's first. Rescue personnel arrived at the scene, descended into the pit, and found Lockenbach and Pirie suspended by one of the lines in the spray of the waterfall. They had died of harness-hang syndrome and hypothermia. FILE NO: 84896

Margaret E. Mullet, a 54-year-old, Lincoln, Nebraska, pharmacist, was behind the counter at the store where she worked on May 29, 2011, when a masked man, armed with a gun and knife, climbed over the counter and threatened her. A customer in the store, 29-year-old telephone technician **BRANDON M. WEMHOFF**, responded to the pharmacy, climbed over the counter, and confronted the assailant. A struggle between the two men broke out, with the assailant momentarily pinning Wemhoff against a counter. Wemhoff then overpowered the assailant and disarmed him, taking him to the floor and pinning him there until police arrived shortly thereafter and arrested him. Mullet was unharmed. FILE NO: 84768

C. H. 9593

On the night of December 14, 2010, a 53-year-old woman was found suspended from a New Brunswick, New Jersey, railroad trestle about 25 feet above a paved street in what was reported to be a suicide attempt. Police, including **GARY YURKOVIC, JR.**, 27, responded. From the deck of the trestle, officers reached through a hole in the chain-link fence along the edge of the trestle and grasped the woman. In their struggle to keep her from falling, they experienced difficulty maintaining their holds in the 20-degree air temperature. Fearing that the officers were about to lose their grip of the woman, Yurkovic climbed over the fence and lowered himself to a two-inch-wide ledge. Holding to the fence with one hand, Yurkovic reached down and grasped a sleeve of the woman's jacket with the other. She was uncooperative as Yurkovic held her against the trestle for several minutes. During that time, another of the officers climbed to the top of the fence, reached over, and secured Yurkovic by his clothing. Firefighters responding in a bucket truck lowered the woman and Yurkovic to the ground. Both were taken to the hospital, where Yurkovic was treated for hypothermia. He recovered. FILE NO: 84057

C. H. 9561

19 January 1956
GAY NINETIES NIGHTCLUB
CLEVELAND, OHIO

C. H. 4059

(FACING PAGE)
PHOTOGRAPH OF
DOROTHY KOCHS IN AN
ARTICLE SHE WROTE ABOUT
HER HEROIC ACT FOR
THE JULY 1956 ISSUE OF
FRONT PAGE DETECTIVE.

On January 19, 1956, **DOROTHY KOCHS**, an exotic dancer who performed under the name of Tina Lamont, saved two policemen from being shot by a robber in the Gay Nineties, a Cleveland nightclub.

The 32-year-old single mother of a 3-year-old daughter was sitting at the bar after the club had closed when a patron, also at the bar, pulled out a gun and demanded money from the club's two managers. Unknown to the gunman, however, the club's porter had slipped out and found two officers who were on duty nearby.

Their pistols drawn, the policemen entered the club, but the gunman turned and took direct aim at them. Kochs reacted instantly. Taking several steps toward the gunman, she grabbed his arm and pulled down, just as both he and the officers fired. The gunman's bullet went into the floor. Four shots fired by the policemen struck and killed the gunman instantly, but a fifth hit Kochs in the spine. She survived, but was paralyzed for life from the waist down. "In a split second," Kochs said some months later, "fate handed me a lifelong challenge. I may not win, but I like challenges."

In addition to being awarded a Carnegie Medal for her bravery, Kochs received a cash award, which she used to purchase a small boarding house. That and a monthly grant from the Commission helped Kochs to support herself until she died in 1981. FILE NO: 43838

13 December 1932
CAPITOL BUILDING
WASHINGTON, D.C.

C. H. 2690

On December 13, 1932, **MELVIN J. MAAS**, 35, a U.S. House of Representatives member from Minnesota, confronted a distraught man brandishing a loaded pistol in the Capitol Building in Washington, D.C.

Shortly after 4 p.m. that afternoon, the House was in session, with Maas and some 125 other members present. Another 75 people in the gallery watched the proceedings. Suddenly, a 25-year-old department store clerk appeared at the gallery rail, waving a pistol and demanding to speak.

Many of those present ran for the exit doors; others took cover behind furniture. But Maas, who at first started to exit the chamber with the possible intent of going to the gallery to disarm the man, walked with his arms slightly raised to a point below the balcony where the man stood. Then, despite the fact that the assailant pointed the revolver at him, Maas quietly reasoned with the man until he dropped the weapon into his hands. At that point, two armed policemen arrested the man and led him away. FILE NO: 32730

ELSIE H. McEVOY, a 28-year-old housewife in the town of Hinton, Alberta, saved a young neighbor boy from being mauled by a cougar.

C. H. 4553

On the afternoon of March 16, 1962, six-year-old Brian Kilbreath was playing with other children in a sparsely wooded area near their homes in Hinton on the eastern slopes of Canada's Rocky Mountains when a young cougar attacked. Knocking Kilbreath to the ground, the cat began biting him on the face and neck. Two of the other boys ran to the nearest house for help. Despite the fact that she was recovering from recent surgery, the slightly built McEvoy, herself the mother of two, responded to the boys and ran into the woods.

Although winded, McEvoy grabbed a dead branch and began striking the cougar on the head until the branch broke. Then she stooped and grabbed the cougar's head by the scruff and smacked it on the snout with the stub that remained. The cat rose and turned, but when McEvoy pushed, it slumped to the ground. Picking up Kilbreath, she carried him toward an armed party of neighbors looking for them.

(FACING PAGE)
ELSIE H. McEVOY
WITH THE PELT OF
THE COUGAR THAT
ATTACKED BRIAN KILBREATH
(ALSO PICTURED).

While the injured boy was taken to the hospital, McEvoy led the neighbors back to the scene of the attack. They found the cougar nearby, its skull fractured by McEvoy's blows and, to be sure, it was shot three times.

Though critically injured and requiring more than 100 stitches on his face and neck, Kilbreath survived. McEvoy suffered no serious wounds and had recovered the following morning. In addition to being honored with a Carnegie Medal, her act earned letters of acclamation from both the Prime Minister of Canada and former vice president of the United States Richard Nixon. FILE NO: 45957

On October 3, 1927, **LEWIS A. KEE**, 56, prevented a quick-tempered husband from murdering his wife and her aunt.

C. H. 2314

Leona Cordrey, 24, and her 36-year-old husband had been having marital difficulties. She had filed for divorce four days before, and her husband was under an order to remove his belongings from the couple's farmhouse within the next week. Fearing her husband's wrath, Mrs. Cordrey had asked her aunt to stay with her. She had also asked Kee, a neighbor, to stay at the farm and help with the chores until her husband left. Kee and Cordrey, who were friends, were sharing a bedroom in the farmhouse.

At about 4:30 in the morning, Kee was awakened by screams and hurried through the farmhouse, fearing that Cordrey was striking his wife. Cordrey, meanwhile, had just attacked his wife with a hatchet, fracturing her skull, and had struck the aunt, also on the head. Kee found Mrs. Cordrey outside the screened door of a sleeping porch, her husband nearby, hatchet raised, about to strike again.

Kee opened the door between them, preventing Cordrey from taking another swing at his wife, but the younger man stepped around the open door and hit Kee with the hammer edge of the hatchet, knocking him to his hands and knees. Mrs. Cordrey escaped through the porch and out of the house. Cordrey continued to hit Kee with the hatchet, now with the sharp edge, but Kee finally managed to grab hold of the hatchet's handle.

Cordrey wrestled free, grabbed a shotgun, and ran out of the house in pursuit of his fleeing wife and the aunt. He took a shot and hit the aunt, but she and Mrs. Cordrey continued running for half a mile to a neighbor's home. Cordrey, who at some time had set fire to the house, fled to a garage, where a short time later he killed himself with a revolver.

Though seriously injured, both women eventually recovered. Kee, who had difficulty escaping from the burning house, suffered five fractures to his skull, and sustained several other severe injuries, including a deep cut on his right shoulder. FILE NO: 27810

28 June 2001
LAKE DELTA SPILLWAY
ROME, NEW YORK

C. H. 8601, 8602

On June 28, 2001, **ROBERT B. KEANE** and **DAVID M. CIRASUOLO** came to the aid of five people in a boat about to be swept over a 60-foot-high spillway.

Late that warm summer afternoon, three adults and two children were on a 17-foot boat, cruising on Lake Delta, near Rome, New York. At 6:38, they were in the vicinity of the spillway over which the lake flowed into the Mohawk River when the boat's motor failed. Despite repeated attempts to restart the engine and efforts to paddle the boat, it drifted toward the precipice.

Cirasuolo, 34, was fishing with Keane, 27, in the latter's 18-foot boat about a quarter of a mile away when he noticed what was happening. The two men responded immediately, but by the time they reached the stricken vessel, it was dangerously close to the lip of the spillway.

The boat's occupants slipped into the water, from which Cirasuolo plucked the children. Keane maneuvered his craft close enough to rescue two of the adults who had remained near the stalled boat, which now was pinned against the lip of the spillway. Twice they bumped the helpless vessel, but it did not dislodge. They managed to get two victims aboard, but then their boat also lodged against the spillway. Fortunately, by then another boat had arrived. The remaining adult in the water swam a line to it from Keane's boat, and it was towed away from the dam, where its engine was started. Everyone was taken to safety. FILE NOS: 75449, 75450

On August 6, 1919, **HERBERT A. FRIEDLICH** saved a young climber from a fatal fall in Glacier Park, Montana.

C. H. 1726

Friedlich, a 26-year-old, Harvard-trained lawyer was among a group of horse riders enjoying park trails at the base of a mountain known as Pinnacle Wall.

Earlier that day, Raymond Kraft, a 21-year-old clerk, had set out on a risky adventure, a solo climb of the mountain. He had made his way 350 feet up along the edge of a glacial seam on its flank. When he tried to traverse the 30-foot-wide strip of ice, Kraft slipped, sliding 75 feet and breaking three bones in his ankle. Painfully, he had lowered himself down along narrow ledges until he reached a point from which he could go no farther. Below him was a nearly vertical slope of bare rock that plunged for 150 feet.

Although he had never met Kraft, Friedlich responded to the call for a rescuer. With great care, he slowly made his way some 250 feet up Pinnacle Wall toward Kraft. At two places, he had to lean back for handholds on the steep slope and swing his feet out to climb higher. Finally, Friedlich reached the stricken climber and slowly helped him down to safety. Kraft recovered, and, other than being shaken by the two-and-a-half-hour rescue, Friedlich suffered no injuries. FILE NO: 19833

On January 16, 1907, **ALEXANDER FRASER**, 46, entered the engine room of a powerhouse soon after the steam chest of an engine exploded, releasing a torrent of scalding steam at 85 pounds of pressure, to search for a co-worker he thought remained inside.

C. H. 541

The accident occurred at 4:30 that afternoon at the Allston, Massachusetts, facility of the Boston Elevated Railway Company.

People on the scene feared that a stationary engineer, Frank Stenberg, was trapped inside, but he had escaped unseen out another exit. When Fraser, who tended the boiler in the plant, was told of Stenberg's perceived plight, he immediately entered the steam-saturated room, with no regard for his own safety, to search for the missing man. Badly scalded when he finally emerged about five minutes later, Fraser was later taken to a hospital, where he died the next morning of external and internal burns.

In addition to accepting a posthumous Carnegie Medal for her husband's bravery, Fraser's widow received a monthly death benefit for both herself and her daughter for many years. FILE NO: 6318

C. H. 7080

It was the night of February 19, 1986, when **Andrew Wray Mathieson** of suburban Pittsburgh acted heroically to save a woman's life.

The Pittsburgh Penguins had just finished a National Hockey League game with the Winnipeg Jets. Mathieson, 57, and his wife were among the 12,558 fans in attendance, as were Mathieson's secretary, Jane Celender, 39, and another woman in their party. The foursome was standing at the Mathiesons' car in the hockey arena's parking lot when they were approached by Celender's estranged husband, a large man at more than six feet tall and 250 pounds.

After Celender refused her husband's order to get into his nearby car, the man produced a loaded .38-caliber handgun and, from a distance of 10 feet, fired at her. She was not struck, but the round hit her purse and remained lodged there. She started to run for refuge behind a van parked 50 feet away.

Mathieson recognized the assailant and pleaded with him: "Jim, don't do this." He then approached the gunman, but the gunman turned toward Mathieson and shot him at point-blank range. Although the bullet struck Mathieson in the upper right chest, he continued toward the assailant and took him to the pavement, where he struggled to hold him by the legs. The gunman fired again, striking Mathieson a second time, then stood.

Mrs. Mathieson, meanwhile, had secured the other woman's safety and began to approach her wounded husband. The gunman fired twice more, striking her once, also in the right chest, and Mathieson, for the third time. Mrs. Mathieson continued toward her husband as the assailant returned to his car, got inside, and inflicted a fatal gunshot wound. Both Mathieson and his wife required hospitalization for their wounds, Mathieson's treatment including surgery to remove a part of his right lung.

Mathieson's obituary in the *Pittsburgh Post-Gazette* 15 years later was a lengthy one. It had to be, to cover the list of accomplishments and affiliations represented in the 72-year life of this quiet, industrious powerhouse, who was widely known and universally respected as financial advisor, corporate director, and foundation executive. His "confidence in himself was no greater than the trust others could place in him," the obituary read. Never was that more evident than on the night of his heroic act.

Celender paid tribute to her late boss: "He always tried to do what he could to make a difference and make someone's life better." She is living proof of that. FILE NO: 60937

On January 22, 1926, **GROVER C. BREWER**, a 41-year-old clergyman in Sherman, Texas, saved three children from a rabid dog.

After leaving his office late in the morning, Sherman happened to see a dog with foamy saliva at its mouth snap at a child. Thinking the dog might be rabid, he got out of his car and followed it several blocks when he encountered a policeman, also in pursuit of the animal. Brewer returned to his office.

An hour later, Brewer went out again. While driving, he spotted the same dog, this time in an alley approaching a street where three children were. When Brewer got out of his car and motioned for the children to stay back, the dog turned toward them. Brewer then started to remove his overcoat to try to capture the dog, but the animal jumped up and struck him on the breast with both paws. As Brewer grabbed it by the throat, the dog snapped and bit him on the left wrist.

Brewer struggled with the writhing, 50-pound animal, at one point banging its head against the wall of a garage. Another man then arrived and both held the dog for several minutes until the dog catcher arrived with a rope. The dog catcher then left to get his gun, returned in a few minutes, and shot and killed the dog. Brewer removed the dog's head and sent it for tests, which confirmed that it had been rabid. Subsequently, Brewer underwent a series of shots for rabies, but he suffered no other ill effects from the encounter. FILE NO: 26339

On September 14, 1908, **G. JAMES SHAW**, 40, foreman at an elevator manufacturing company in Goderich, Ontario, risked his life and limbs to save a fellow worker.

A few minutes before noon that day, Harry Videan, a 36-year-old plant laborer, was working at a car-pulling machine when his left wrist became caught in the winding rope and drum of the machine. In response to Videan's cries for help, Shaw ran to the machine's leather power belt and, with his hands, tried to pull it off the pulley around which it turned at a speed of 4,000 feet per minute. Unsuccessful on his first attempt, Shaw grabbed the belt again, and held on as it pulled him toward the pulley. Just as his arm reached the pulley, the belt slipped off.

Although Videan was badly mangled, he eventually recovered. Shaw suffered no serious injury from the rescue. FILE NO: 3652

(ABOVE)
CAPTAIN CASTO

(FACING PAGE) THE
RESCUE BY CAPTAIN
MARK CASTO AND THE
CREW OF THE *ALBERTA*
WAS WIDELY REPORTED,
PARTICULARLY ALONG THE
EAST COAST. THE MEDAL
WAS PRESENTED TO CASTO
BY THE CLOVER CLUB OF
PHILADELPHIA.

14 January 1906
FREIGHTER S.S. CHEROKEE
BRIGANTINE SHOALS

On Sunday morning, January 14, 1906, seven volunteer sailors braved an Atlantic storm to save 54 people stranded on a storm-tossed freighter.

Two afternoons earlier, the S.S. *Cherokee* had become disoriented in foggy weather and gone aground on the Brigantine Shoals, a shelf of submerged sandbanks five miles offshore northeast of Atlantic City, New Jersey. The 2,556-ton, 264-foot-long *Cherokee* had been steaming north from San Domingo with a crew of 46, 10 passengers, and a mixed cargo. Though a rescue boat offered to evacuate the ship, everyone chose to stay aboard, assuming the *Cherokee* would be pulled into open water. That attempt had to be abandoned when gale force winds blew in. By Sunday morning, after two sea-battered days on the shoals, the ship was starting to take on water, and concern grew for the safety of her passengers and crew.

Captain **MARK CASTO**, 36, was skipper of the *Alberta*, a local 58-foot, 10-ton, two-masted fishing smack. Aware of the *Cherokee*'s plight since it first went aground, Casto decided to act at 9 a.m. that Sunday when he heard a message that 11 feet of water was in the *Cherokee*'s hold. He contacted his crew, fishermen **NELS GREGERSEN**, 26, **FREDERICK BOUCHIE**, 47, **MARIUS NELSEN**, 25, **JOSEPH M. SHUTE**, 30, and **AXAL HOLMQUIST**, 26, and the ship cook **LEWIS J. JOHNSON**, 25, and proposed attempting a rescue. Despite the apparent risks, all six men volunteered to come along.

They provisioned the *Alberta* and cast off under dark clouds at about 10 a.m. After maneuvering to within 200 feet of the *Cherokee*, one of the *Alberta*'s dories was smashed during a launch attempt, and a second dory, with Casto, Gregersen, and Bouchie in it, was broken apart when it hit the side of the *Cherokee*. The three men, with two others, then rowed back to the *Alberta* in one of the *Cherokee*'s lifeboats, which had to be abandoned once the men reached the *Alberta*, leaving them with no lifeboats. Casto, though, had brought a line with him from the *Cherokee*, and tied it to the *Alberta*.

By means of the line, the two boats were pulled closer to each other, and another line was then attached to a small lifeboat on the *Cherokee*. It took 12 trips of the lifeboat to take everyone off the foundering freighter. Casto then raised anchor and sailed to shore without the aid of power since the ship's engine had been disabled.

Captain Casto was awarded a gold Carnegie Medal, the first awarded by the Commission. A silver medal was awarded to each member of the crew.

FILE NOS: 796, 797, 798, 799, 800, 801, 802

Brave Commander of Little Fishing Schooner
Brought Into the Inlet at Atlantic City
Passengers, Seamen and Life-Saving
Crews Who Were in Danger of
Being Swept Into the Ocean

of the fishing schooner. The passengers landed were United States Consul William Handy, of Trinidad, who was forced to abandon his papers in which there were records of the revolution on the island, and his clothing; Ensign H. MacL. Walker, of the United States Navy, who has been detached from service with the Yankee and is to do special duty at Washington; Robert H. Pearson, N. Train and Joseph Schwartz, New York, and Edward Laporte, merchant; Elias Amarais, and their two small daughters.

Exhausted from their sleepless vigil every moment of which they expect...

eight hours, and she has filled through the water leaking from deck crevices and open doorways. Her hatches remained firm. She, however, has been driven a mile and a half within 24 hours on the shoals where a wrecking tug cannot reach her. She is doomed to remain a new victim of the treacherous shoals.

The wreck and the rescue from which the viewpoint comes on the boardwalk and the simple story of who risked their lives may be the first it means a star 20,000 ... out where the waves are sweeping around ship fore and aft without rest. It means an excitement ... that there ... dinner, no ... driving ...

C. H. 5756

On October 14, 1970, **JOSEPH C. WIEST**, 35, crossed a pit of hot slag to help a fallen co-worker.

At about 4 a.m. that day, Frank Simmer was on a small platform over a three-sided concrete pit where molten slag was gathered. Suddenly, the platform gave way, tumbling the 57-year-old man 27 feet into a corner of the pit. Although that corner of the pit was free of slag, Simmer was seriously injured by the fall.

Wiest, a floor helper on duty that morning, ran to the pit's open end, which was blocked by a thick layer of slag. Although its interior was at least 500 degrees, the cooling slag had already crusted over, but its surface temperature was still about 212 degrees. Trusting that the crust would support him and that his thick-soled shoes would protect him, Wiest stepped onto the slag and quickly covered the 25 feet to where Simmer lay.

Despite the pit's intense heat, Wiest hoisted the fallen man to his shoulders and started back. He was almost safely across when he slipped and fell on the hot slag crust, still holding Simmer. Then another workman stepped onto the slag and helped Wiest back to his feet so he could carry Simmer the rest of the way. Both men were taken to the hospital, where Simmer died three days later of shock and burns. Although also treated for burns, Wiest recovered without permanent injury.

This rescue provided the title to a book on the Commission, A Walk on the Crust of Hell, *by Jack Markowitz. (Stephen Greene Press, Brattleboro, Vt.; 1973)* FILE NO: 51759

C. H. 1213

C. H. 1214

C. H. 1215

On March 27, 1916, **JAMES E. DOUGHERTY**, **EDWARD DAVIS**, and **ROGER W. WELLS** all entered an industrial kettle to aid stricken co-workers.

The accident occurred at a chemical company plant in Heidelberg, Pennsylvania. At 2:30 that morning, Charles Galbreath, 18, climbed into an empty benzene kettle that had to be cleaned before work at the plant could proceed. Normally, he would have worn a protective helmet, but the man who was in charge of the helmets had failed to show up on time for work that morning, according to local news coverage. Shortly after Galbreath got to the bottom of the ladder in the eight-foot-deep tank, he was overcome by the fumes and collapsed.

Without taking any precautions, Dougherty, a 21-year-old worker, climbed through the manhole in the top of the kettle and was able to lift Galbreath up within reach of other men, who lifted him out. He revived. By that time, however, Dougherty himself was overcome by the fumes and collapsed back into the kettle.

Then Davis, a 32-year-old pump man, climbed in, a wet handkerchief tied over his mouth and nose. The fumes affected him before he could do anything and he climbed out. Then Wells, a 40-year-old guard in poor physical condition, made an attempt to reach Dougherty. With a rope around his waist and wearing a makeshift facemask, Wells descended the ladder. However, he was unable to do anything to help before he started choking from the fumes and climbed out.

With the rope tied around his waist, Davis made a second attempt. He managed to tie a second rope around Dougherty and then hurried out of the kettle. As he emerged, however, he gasped and fell unconscious. Using the rope, other men hoisted Dougherty out through the manhole.

Dougherty was revived with a pulmotor, although he suffered acid burns and was disabled for a month and a half. Wells, who did not lose consciousness during the incident, was disabled for two weeks with lung congestion. Attempts to revive Davis were unsuccessful, and he was pronounced dead.

Davis left behind his wife, a five-year-old son, and a three-year-old daughter. The Commission provided a monthly grant for his widow for nearly 50 years until her death in 1965. FILE NOS: 16293, 16291, 16474

On January 10, 1918, 13-year-old **R. VERNON CALLAWAY** stood for more than an hour in shoulder-deep, freezing water trying to keep a fellow student from drowning.

During noon recess on that 20-degree day, a group of four boys were skating on the ice that covered flooded lowlands near their school in St. Joe, Idaho. Three of them had so much fun that they decided not to return to school. Some time afterward, one of them, 12-year-old Roland Cyr, fell through a weak spot in the ice into four feet of water. He paddled to keep his head above water while the other boy who was nearby tried unsuccessfully several times to haul him out.

Although a non-swimmer himself, Callaway skated over to help. Lying on the ice with the other boy holding onto his hands, he stretched his leg toward Cyr. The younger boy managed to grab Callaway's foot, but when the third boy tried to pull them out, the ice kept crumbling under them until both Cyr and Callaway slid back into the frigid water.

Although the water was up to his shoulders, Callaway was able to support Cyr while the other boy ran to get help. Several times, Callaway tried to lift Cyr out of the water, but each time the weak ice thwarted his effort. Even after Cyr lost consciousness, Callaway kept his head above the surface of the water. When several men finally arrived and pulled both boys from the water, Callaway was at the point of passing out himself, the sleeve of his coat frozen to the surface of the ice.

Unfortunately, Cyr, who had a weak heart, never regained consciousness. Though treated for three weeks for exposure, Callaway made a complete recovery. FILE NO: 18732

C. H. 1614

C. H. 8590, 8591

C. H. 8592, 8593

On March 25, 2000, three 17-year-old high school students went to the aid of a chaperone of their hiking trip who had been swept by a wave into dangerous surf. Two of them drowned. A local fisherman also risked his life in the rescue attempt.

Barbara Clement, 45, was a parent chaperoning a group of Canadian high school students hiking a remote ocean-side trail near Shelter Cove, California. Around 12:40 that afternoon, as the group was crossing a surge channel on Black Sands Beach, Clement was surprised by a wave and was knocked off her feet. While struggling with her backpack, she was pulled down the beach by the rush of the backwash.

DAVID M. ELTON and **BRODIE MACDONALD** immediately dropped their packs and ran to help Clement, who was struggling to regain her footing. The two boys reached the woman and were helping her to her feet when a large wave broke over them. Its backwash sucked all three deeper into the roiling surf.

The third student, **JORDAN D. NIXON**, and the 37-year-old leader of the expedition both dropped their packs and ran to help, but they too were sucked up by the surging, 48-degree water and dragged seaward by the strong current.

A call was made to the Coast Guard, which sent out a distress call, and several local fishermen responded in their boats. One spotted Nixon floundering in the water beyond the breakers and was able to rescue him. Meanwhile, another fisherman, **DONALD J. SACK**, 46, had piloted his 18-foot boat more than six miles to reach the area. Sack came across Clement, also floating outside the breakers. He pulled out her limp body and passed it to another boat. Then Sack saw the group's leader still struggling some 60 feet from shore, but well inside the 12-foot breakers. At considerable risk, Sack maneuvered his boat into the turbulent waters to a point where he could get the man's attention. Throwing him a line, Sack towed the nearly unconscious man through the breakers. Then holding him against the boat's side, he carefully steered it to calmer waters where another fisherman boarded his boat and they pulled the man aboard.

Nixon and the leader were evacuated to a hospital and were treated for near drowning and hypothermia, but both were released the following day. Sack twisted his right knee but also recovered. Along with Clement, Elton and MacDonald drowned. Despite an intensive search, the two students' bodies were not discovered until several days had passed.

FILE NOS: 74353, 74354, 74917, 75085

CHARLES N. WRIGHT, assisted by **WILLIAM L. DILLARD**, saved a fallen climber from the edge of a 2,000-foot precipice.

C. H. 840, 841

It was warm and dry on Sunday afternoon, May 14, 1911. R. Augustus Baty had walked with some friends to the top of Whiteside Mountain, near Highlands, North Carolina. At a point known as Fool's Rock, he either slipped or intentionally stepped over the edge and tumbled 150 feet down a nearly vertical slope. He would have plummeted to certain death over the sheer cliff at the bottom of the slope, but he became entangled in a small rhododendron bush growing just two inches from the edge. Battered by the fall and unconscious, Baty lay lodged there with an arm and a leg dangling over the edge of the cliff.

Wright, a 38-year-old storeowner in Highlands, and Dillard, a 33-year-old liveryman, had also been hiking, with their wives, on Whiteside. Alerted to Baty's predicament, the two men descended an embankment 15 feet to the top of the slope. Then they slowly zigzagged down and across its rocky face, using inch-long indentations and protrusions for hand and foot holds, attempting to reach an intermittent line of rhododendrons growing along the slope's lower lip.

Partway down, Dillard lost his nerve, but Wright coaxed him several steps to a place of relative safety. When Wright's wife saw what he was doing, she began screaming, which nearly unnerved him as well. After a moment, however, he regained his composure and continued down until he reached a bush just above where Baty lay. Then Wright slowly lowered his feet to the narrow ledge just 24 inches from the brink, reached down, and grabbed the collar of Baty's jacket.

Feeling a hand on his collar, Baty jerked suddenly, which so alarmed Wright that he nearly lost his grip. Ordering Baty to be still, Wright was able to pull the stricken man back a bit from the brink. He then reached up, grabbed a bush, and wrapped his legs around its base, which allowed him to drag the now delirious Baty farther up. Dillard, meanwhile, had shed his shoes for more secure footing and, in stocking feet, had inched to Wright and Baty. Then the three men crept 15 feet along the ledge to where another man had descended with a bucket of water with which Wright and Dillard applied crude first-aid treatment to Baty. The rescuers, now numbering three, took Baty back up and across the slope to within 15 feet of the top, and he was hoisted by rope to safety, the rescuers following. The rescue had taken two and a half hours, but all three men recovered without serious injury. FILE NOS: 7327, 7328

C. H. 7440

Over six days in 1989, **DAVID M. NYMAN**, a 31-year-old civil engineer, braved Alaskan snowstorms to save his stricken climbing partner.

On the sunny morning of April 19, Nyman and James Sweeney, 33, were climbing a deep vertical gorge on Mt. Johnson near Ruth's Glacier in Denali National Park when Sweeney was swept away by an avalanche, fracturing and dislocating a hip.

With great difficulty, Nyman managed to lower his partner to a place where they could spend the night in the avalanche-prone area. The next morning, Nyman left Sweeney and skied more than seven miles to a lodge down the glacier. Two of the people staying at the lodge went out to rescue Sweeney, but they were unable to find him and were not equipped to continue searching in the dark.

The following day, when Nyman learned that his friend had not been found, he skied back to Sweeney, knowing that help had been or would be alerted. But another avalanche struck, trapping the men on the mountain. For two days, the climbers remained stranded. Nyman kept moving Sweeney and their camp to dodge avalanches, several of which partially buried them.

On the 25th, with their supplies nearly gone, Nyman decided he had to get Sweeney to safety by himself and began tracking a path through fresh snow that drifted up to four feet deep. Covering several hundred yards at a time, he would then go back to Sweeney and drag him forward. In that way, they progressed almost a mile, descending some 1,200 feet down the mountain, braving several more avalanches, one of which carried them into a deep crevasse. Finally, on April 26, they were spotted by a helicopter and were rescued.

It took Sweeney twelve weeks to recover from his ordeal. Nyman was treated for frostbite and dehydration. FILE NO: 64291

(FACING PAGE, TOP) MT. JOHNSON AND "ELEVATOR SHAFT" WHERE ACCIDENT OCCURRED.
(BOTTOM) ROUTE OF DAVID M. NYMAN AND JAMES SWEENEY.

(RIGHT) SWEENEY, IN BED, AND NYMAN AT PROVIDENCE HOSPITAL, ANCHORAGE, ALASKA

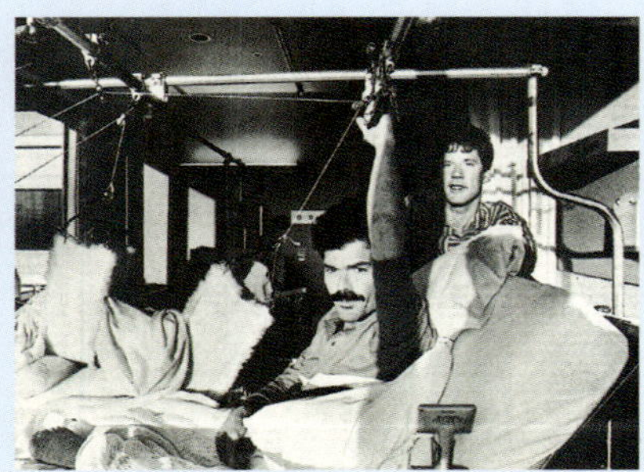

Elevator Shaft
1
2
3
4
5
6
7
1 Sweeney fall/avalanche
2 Sweeney Nyman bivy on April 19
2 Sweeney bivy night of April 20
3 Nyman and Sweeney tent of April 21 and 22
4 Nyman and Sweeny bivy of April 23
5 Nyman and Sweeney snow cave of April 24
6 Sweeney and Nyman bivy of April 25
7 Crevasse fall of April 26

the audience—none of us knew about it. The minute he stepped inside the door, one of the females jumped

Here is author Joe Arcaris at work. At the time this story took place, Joe worked at Clyde Beatty's Jungle in Florida.

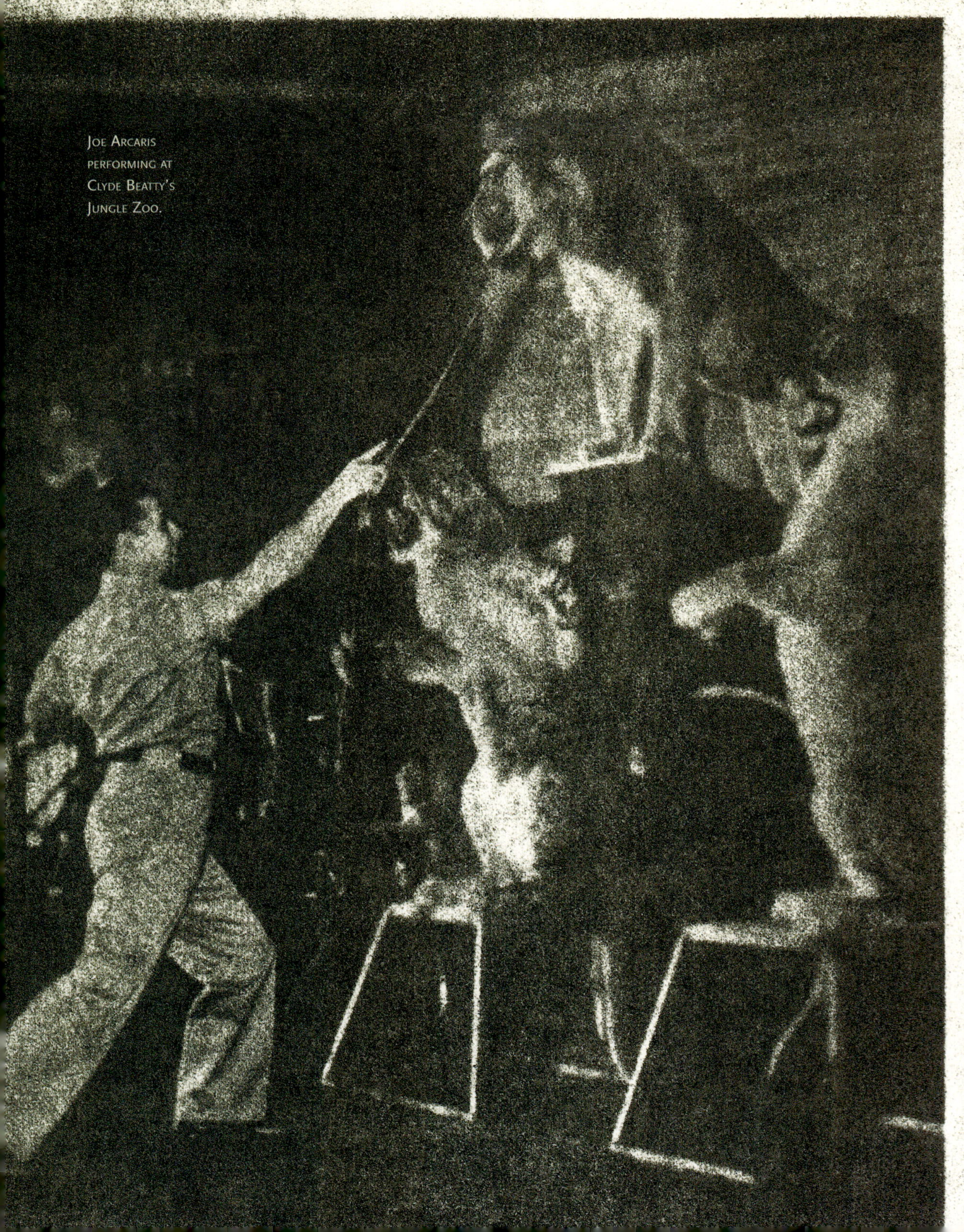

JOSEPH ARCARIS saved a man by facing down five lions on February 9, 1940.

Arcaris, age 31, had been hired to be an animal trainer at Clyde Beatty's Jungle Zoo in Fort Lauderdale, Florida. He was dressing after a show when he heard shouting. Chester Czaja, a 24-year-old circus animal caregiver, had entered an enclosure not knowing it held five untrained lions. The big cats attacked Czaja, knocked him down, and dragged him across the enclosure.

Arcaris arrived shortly afterward. Although an animal trainer, he had never been inside the enclosure or worked with these particular lions. Nonetheless, the slightly built Arcaris grabbed a six-foot length of 2-by-2-inch lumber left by construction workers and went to help the blood-covered victim, who, unconscious, was now being bitten by three of the carnivores.

Arcaris drove off two of them but broke his wooden weapon while violently beating the third. That lion then dragged Czaja into a niche, where it was joined by one of the others. Arcaris followed the beast to the niche and beat it until it ran off. Then the brave man moved several steps into the niche and confronted the final attacker, striking it on the head with what was left of his stick until the beast finally dropped Czaja and moved a few feet away. To prevent the animal from attacking again, Arcaris walked toward it and struck a final blow, then flourished his club until the lion backed away. Then other workers outside the enclosure drove the five lions into holding cages by firing blank cartridges.

Though seriously wounded, Czaja eventually recovered. The uninjured Arcaris felt that he had done nothing extraordinary. "A man can hardly be considered a hero," he later explained, "if he does something without thinking. If I had been thinking that day, I might never have done what I did." FILE NO: 38229

Early in the morning of July 27, 2001, **ERIC FORTIER**, a 32-year-old orthodontist, rescued two friends who were being mauled by a polar bear.

Fortier was on a six-day canoe trip with his longtime friend Alain Parenteau, 31, and their girlfriends, Anne Dumouchel, 33, and Patricia Doyon, 25. The four were camping along the Soper River in a remote region on the southern tip of Baffin Island in the Canadian territory of Nunavut. The two couples were sleeping in separate tents about 30 feet apart. It was daylight at 3:30 a.m. when Fortier was awakened by something pushing against his foot. Dumouchel then saw the outline of a bear against the roof of the tent, and both began to shout to scare the bear away and warn their friends.

C. H. 3165

C. H. 8753

The bear, estimated to weigh about 350 pounds, then moved to the other tent and slashed open its top with a paw. When Parenteau and Doyon scrambled out through the door flap, the bear swatted Parenteau on the left hip, and then moved off after Doyon. Parenteau gave chase and tried to distract the bear, but it turned on him, and knocked him to the ground with its paws, cutting him on the head, neck, shoulder, trunk, and leg.

Fortier and Dumouchel climbed out of their tent and saw Parenteau on his back kicking at the bear, with Doyon several feet away throwing stones at the animal. Fortier's only weapon was a folding pocketknife with a three-and-a-half-inch blade. He used it to cut a tent line that was tied to a rock measuring about 18 inches by six inches.

Picking up the rock, Fortier ran to within six feet of the bear and threw it, hitting the animal on the shoulder. The bear turned toward Doyon, who tried to run but slipped and fell. The bear quickly caught up with the young woman and began to maul her. Fortier and Dumouchel threw more rocks at the bear and distracted it long enough to allow Doyon to flee. But as the bear followed her, she fell, and again the bear began to paw her, slashing her clothing and skin. Armed with only the knife, Fortier ran to the bear and stabbed three times up under its neck, the final thrust drawing blood. The animal ceased its attack on Doyon, rambled away behind some large rocks by the water's edge, and disappeared. The attack had lasted less than five minutes.

The party, however, was still many miles from safety, with both Parenteau and Doyon bleeding from multiple wounds. After assessing the injuries, they quickly threw their gear into the canoes to paddle to the planned take-out point. After a short distance, it became clear that Parenteau and Doyon were too weak to paddle, so the two canoes were lashed together, and Fortier and Dumouchel did the work.

When they reached the landing place two hours later, Fortier ran and walked for another hour to a small village, where he was able to get help. Parenteau and Doyon were eventually taken by helicopter to a hospital, where both were treated and released, Doyon the next day, and Parenteau two days later. Neither Fortier nor Dumouchel suffered any injuries.

FILE NO: 76426

27 June 1954
LEAF RIVER
MERRILL, MISSISSIPPI

C. H. 3973

On June 27, 1954, **CHARLES B. VINES**, a 22-year-old former Marine who had been blinded by a bursting mortar shell two years earlier in the Korean War, saved two women from drowning in a Mississippi river.

Anne Ball, 18, and her cousin Barbara Wood, 15, were wading with Vines and his friend, James Peacock, on a submerged sandbar in the Leaf River near Merrill, when both women stepped into deep water and went under. They surfaced 10 feet away, struggling for air. Ball grabbed for

Peacock, who was swimming nearby, but submerged him. When one of his legs cramped, he swam to the sandbar alone.

Vines, the only other person around, heard Wood's screams and immediately swam to her. Holding on to his shoulder, the young girl directed him to Ball, who by now was struggling wildly to keep her head above water. Vines towed both women back across the current toward the sandbar, but when they got near, Wood let go, intending to swim the rest of the way herself. Instead, she was caught by the current and carried downstream.

Vines got Ball to the sandbar and then started swimming after Wood, who was then 200 feet away and being carried into the Pascagoula River. Because he was unable to see, Vines had to change his course repeatedly while he swam, following Wood's screams and directions shouted by Peacock on the sandbar. Swimming 350 feet, he caught up with Wood and towed her back to the bank, where she lost consciousness.

Both women were briefly hospitalized, but they recovered completely. Although Vines was exhausted from his efforts and nauseated from the river water he had swallowed, the blind ex-Marine was fine when he had a chance to rest. FILE NO: 43200

20 August 1928
LONG ISLAND SOUND
FISHERS ISLAND, NEW YORK

On August 20, 1928, **ERNEST F. DAVIS**, a 64-year-old fisherman, saved his grandnephew from being pulled down into the 200-foot-deep water of Long Island Sound.

About 3 p.m., Davis and the 17-year-old boy, Robert Lane, were working together on a slow-moving motorboat setting lobster pots into the choppy sound near Fishers Island, New York. When Lane was casting the pots on one line, he swung a coil of rope over his head. Stooping then to grab another coil, the line dropped, looped around his neck, and was pulled tight instantly by the weight of three 50-pound already-sinking pots. He screamed just as he was jerked off his feet and dragged to the boat's stern. In an instant, he was hauled overboard.

Davis, hearing the boy's yell and thinking the line was around Lane's ankle, started to wrap it around a cleat, but quickly realized it was around his neck. He let go of the line and immediately grabbed a double-edged knife and jumped into the water. He reached Lane just below the surface and was able to slash the line between him and the boat. Then, reaching around Lane's neck, again Davis with one slash cut the length of rope from which the three pots hung. Both men surfaced, and, after catching his breath, Lane was able to reboard the circling boat. Though nearly exhausted by his effort and burdened by the weight of oilskin overalls and high, rubber boots, Davis managed to tread water until Lane brought the boat about and helped him aboard. FILE NO: 28714

C. H. 2331

C. H. 4466

Joseph J. Granahan, a 30-year-old waiter, entered a collapsing New York City tenement to save an elderly woman who was calling for help from the fourth floor.

It was just after 11 p.m. on November 17, 1960. Granahan was relaxing in a nearby bar when he saw clouds of plaster dust outside and thought there was a fire. A nearby building had been recently demolished, but the foundation of the adjacent apartment building hadn't been shored up. Now the five-story brick building was caving into the excavation. It was already separating from the building next to it when Granahan arrived. All residents were accounted for except 83-year-old Helen Giles, who had been asleep in her fourth-floor apartment and was awakened by plaster falling onto her head.

Although Granahan had never been in the building and did not know anyone who lived there, he kicked out the glass panel of the now jammed front door, climbed through the opening, and started up the stairway through a cloud of crumbling plaster and dust. On the second floor, he had to kick through another glass door panel. He proceeded to the third floor, shouting a warning at each apartment he passed.

When Granahan reached the fourth floor, the lights went out, the entire structure groaned and creaked, and visibility was less than a foot. Still, he was able to locate Giles in the hallway and lead her to the stairs. Picking up the frail woman, he carried her down the three flights, the final one as the staircase was pulling away from the wall. He had to lift Giles through the two blocked doorways. Less than four minutes after he brought her out, the building collapsed into a 20-foot-high pile of rubble. Though dazed and bruised, neither was seriously injured.

Granahan received a Silver Medal, the highest award made to an individual in 35 years. He was later able to recount his story for a national television audience, when he appeared as a guest on *To Tell The Truth*.

FILE NO: 45298

C. H. 2411, 2412

On September 4, 1927, two fishermen, **Carl Seidner**, 28, and **James W. Brooks**, 25, rowed through pounding surf of the Pacific Ocean to rescue a family whose fishing boat had capsized.

The Peters family, Kirby, 36, Maude, 45, and Floyd, 13, had been among several groups net fishing that evening from small boats in the mouth of the Klamath River near Requa, California. However, when the tide shifted, creating a strong outflow, they were unable to reel in their net or cut the line that attached it to the boat. The tide dragged their boat toward the ocean. Unbalanced by the net, the craft capsized in the breakers, flinging all three into the water. The father and son managed to find their way back to the boat and hang on, but Mrs. Peters, crying for help, was carried away and drowned.

Witnessing the situation from shore, Seidner and Brooks launched a small fishing boat into the surf. After being twice flung back by breakers cresting at seven feet, the two men managed to row into open water. Searching in the darkness, they finally reached the capsized boat about a quarter of a mile from shore. After hauling in the two, and while waiting for a signal from shore that conditions were favorable for a run through the breakers, they searched the roiling waves unsuccessfully for Mrs. Peters. Then Seidner and Brooks rowed the boat stern-first back toward shore, maneuvering it skillfully through the breakers and riding in on a large wave.

FILE NOS: 27992, 27991

10 September 1942
INTERNATIONAL FIBRE BOARD, LTD.
GATINEAU, QUEBEC

An accident on September 10, 1942, at International Fibre Board, Ltd.'s, wood processing plant in Gatineau, Quebec, gave rise to eight acts of heroism.

Arthur Nerbonne and **Douglas Read** were working in an underground concrete tank where the sludge from wood pulping operations was collected when both men were engulfed in a noxious buildup of hydrogen sulfide, an irritating and highly poisonous gas. Read managed to get to the exit ladder and climb out, but Nerbonne collapsed face forward into the 18 inches of foul broth. Read called for help and immediately re-entered the tank. He managed to drag Nerbonne to the ladder and cradle his head above the pulp before he also passed out, only 30 seconds after re-entering.

Maurice Dorion was the next volunteer to enter the gas-filled tank. After repositioning the men, he felt himself beginning to faint and climbed out. **Wilfred Racine** took a deep breath and went down the ladder. He managed to raise Read's head out of the liquid, and get Nerbonne into a seated position. **Joseph Jackson** then descended and tied a rope around Read's chest. Succumbing to the effects of the gas, Racine released Nerbonne and ascended the ladder, at midpoint passing **Lucien Charron**, who had decided to enter the pit. Charron got Nerbonne's head up but, feeling dizzy, sat against the wall of the tank, where he became semiconscious. Men at the top tried to pull Read out, but he slipped out of the rope and dropped limply back into the sludge. After Jackson left the tank, **Phillipe Turcotte** went in, retied the rope around Read, and helped hoist him out, escaping himself. **Lucien Verreault** was able to go down and get a rope around Nerbonne before collapsing himself, despite the use of an air hose that had been lowered by then. **David Moreau** managed to go into the tank, get ropes around Charron and Verreault, and help lift them out.

All of the men who had been overcome were revived with no long-term ill effects. FILE NOS: 39737, 39777, 39774, 39772, 39775, 39773, 39778, 39776

C. H. 3294, 3295, 3296, 3297, 3298, 3299, 3300, 3301

C. H. 7935

On August 30, 1994, **JOHN ESPADA**, a 35-year-old carpenter, climbed to the top of a Ferris wheel to save two trapped children.

Shortly after noon that summer day, the amusement park in Scotch Plains was bustling. All 16 benches on the 53-foot-high Ferris wheel were occupied. When the wheel jerked to a stop to allow one group to get off, the restraining bar on the highest seat popped open, tumbling the three children in it forward. Six-year-old Evan Manganiello fell out and dropped to the pavement below. His brother Tyler, seven, and six-year-old Brittany Pezzillo managed to catch hold of structural members and hold on.

Espada was visiting the park with his wife and two-year-old son. When he heard about the two stranded children, he ran to the Ferris wheel and soon realized that none of the young park employees would be able to get up quickly enough to rescue them. A good climber and not afraid of heights, Espada spidered his way up the structure to the two children. First he grabbed Pezzillo, then Manganiello and, pulling them on to a supporting beam, hugged both of them close until a park employee arrived with a safety harness.

The two children were lifted back into their seat, and the wheel turned so they could be removed at ground level uninjured but for minor cuts and bruises. Espada also came down safe but sore. Though he suffered a fractured skull, the younger Manganiello did survive his fall. FILE NO: 69068

C. H. 723

On January 18, 1908, 12-year-old **W. ROY STOKES** died attempting to save three young girls who had fallen through thin ice.

At about 9 a.m. on that day, the Kenly sisters, Sarah, 13, Lorena, 12, and Charlotte, 8, were walking on one end of a frozen reservoir between two coke yards near their home in the village of Coral, Indiana County, Pennsylvania, when the two-inch-thick ice collapsed under them, and the three girls, all non-swimmers, fell into nine-foot-deep freezing water.

Stokes, who was skating near the other end of the reservoir some 400 feet away, became aware of what had happened. Immediately he sped toward where the girls had gone in, even though he was aware the ice in that area was not safe. Lying face down on the surface, he managed to pull Lorena from the water. However, when they tried to reach the other girls, both slipped back into the water. All four bodies were discovered a half hour later. They all had drowned.

In addition to accepting a Carnegie Medal in honor of his son's brave act, Stokes's father received a $1,000 death benefit, a portion of which was used to buy a house for his family. FILE NO: 8981

PHOTO   Figuring Ferris wheel.

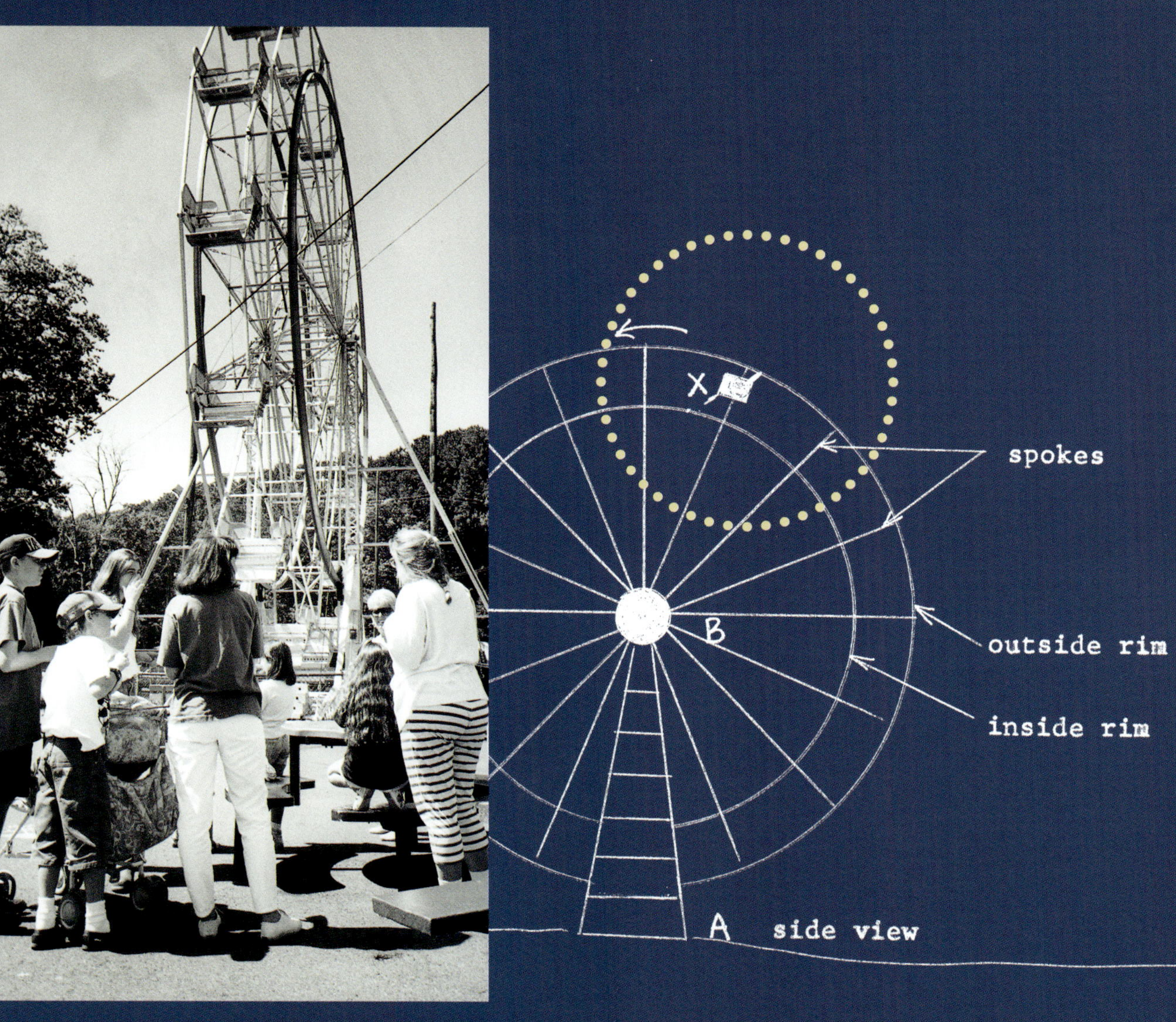

X - Location of Tyler Manganiello and Brittany A. Pezzillo as they clung to a Ferris wheel after being thrown from their seat

ABX- Course John Espada climbed to the children

X - Point where Espada grasped children and secured them to the wheel for several minutes

X - Point at which Espada and another man positioned children back into their seat

XA - Course of Espada and children to ground as wheel was turned

The extension ladder Forest W. McNeir climbed.

On February 12, 1910, **FOREST W. McNEIR**, a 34-year-old contractor and architect, saved a city fireman from death.

It was about 7:15 that cool, fair Texas evening, but things were hot for Charles Rogers, a Houston fireman. A fire was burning in a three-story brick building that housed a hardware company, in which it was suspected that a quantity of explosives was stored.

Rogers was fighting the blaze from an aerial ladder, when the cable supporting the ladder extension came in contact with a live electrical wire and was burned into two. The extension plunged, catching Rogers's foot between it and the top rung of the stationary ladder. The stricken fireman dangled 35 feet above the ground near a window from which smoke and flames erupted, which frequently engulfed him. Even worse, the live wire was still in contact with the truck, and the current was shocking Rogers.

As soon as the accident occurred, two firemen tried to climb to rescue Rogers, but were knocked away from the truck by an electrical jolt. McNeir arrived on the scene and, even though the firemen had been warned away, jumped up on the ladder and, carefully grasping only its wooden rungs, climbed up toward Rogers, planning to cut off his trapped leg at the knee. However, when McNeir reached up and touched the snagged fireman, he received a shock that sent him flying backwards. As he fell to the ground, he hit the ladder, jarring it enough to allow Rogers to release his foot and slide to the ground.

McNeir was knocked unconscious when he fell, and was taken to the hospital where he was treated for scalp wounds and burns on his hands and face, but he eventually recovered. FILE NO: 5019

On July 30, 1996, **MARIE-EVE RENAUD**, a 22-year-old college student, rescued a motorist from being killed by falling debris.

About 2:25 that afternoon, Gerard Gravel, 50, was the driver of a car stopped at a traffic light beneath a railroad overpass that was being rebuilt in downtown Montreal. Above Gravel, a dump-truck driver backed onto the walkway portion of the overpass, which was not intended for vehicular traffic. The loaded truck weighed more than 25 tons, and its rear wheels crushed through the deck, sending large slabs of concrete down onto Gravel's car and trapping him inside. The truck's load of stone and sand spilled partially out and through the hole in the overpass and onto the car.

Renaud was driving close by and witnessed what happened. She jumped from her car and ran to help. Despite the continuing flow of debris, she eventually managed to pull open the driver's door and help Gravel crawl out. Both were able to flee to safety without suffering serious injury.

FILE NO: 72218

C. H. 4853

ADDIE S. McCORMICK, a hotel switchboard operator, lost her life on July 30, 1964, when she remained at her post to warn guests about a fire.

McCormick had worked the switchboard at the Beacon Arms Hotel in Ottawa, Ontario, for six years, but had been a telephone operator on and off for 48 of her 64 years. She was in the switchboard room at the back of the 12-story hotel's first-floor office when a fire broke out in a storage closet and spread into the foyer. As dense smoke billowed into the main floor, the fire alarm was sounded. The hotel's accountant was in the office and instructed employees to get out, but McCormick stayed at the switchboard.

The first call she placed was to report the fire and summon help. Next she answered calls from at least two of the employees and approximately 60 guests believed to be in the hotel at the time. Then McCormick began phoning guest rooms to notify people of the fire and instruct them to use the stairs rather than the elevator. At least one guest reported getting a call from McCormick, and a maid heard phones ringing in rooms on two floors as she fled down the steps.

Before he left the office, the accountant looked into the phone room and saw McCormick still at her post. Again he told her to leave, and she answered, "I'm coming." By then, flames had nearly engulfed the foyer. The accountant ran out of the building, but, two minutes later, when McCormick didn't appear, he tried to get back in, only to discover the foyer filled with flames, blocking McCormick's only escape route.

Ten minutes after McCormick phoned in the alarm, firefighters arrived and quickly extinguished the flames. McCormick's body was discovered on the floor in front of the switchboard. FILE NO: 47405

C. H. 6713

On June 13, 1982, 14-year-old **CAROLYN B. HARTSOCK** braved a flame-filled hallway three times to save a younger sister and brother.

At 4:30 that morning, the seven members of the Hartsock family were asleep in their two-story home in the town of Castlewood in Virginia's southwest corner, when a lightning strike is believed to have started a fire. Mr. and Mrs. Hartsock were in the downstairs bedroom, 16-year-old David was in one upstairs bedroom, while Carolyn, Loretta, 13, Norma, 12, and Johnny, 9, were in the other upstairs bedroom. David woke to the smell of smoke in the hallway and escaped out a window and alerted his parents. The other children awoke to discover flames filling the upstairs hallway. Loretta dashed down the stairs, while Carolyn roused Norma and pushed her through the flames to the top of the stairway.

Then, with her nightclothes on fire, Carolyn went back to the bedroom to get Johnny, who suffered from cerebral palsy. Wrapping her brother in a blanket, she carried him through the flaming hallway to the stairs, where Norma still stood, too frightened to move. Urging Norma to flee, Carolyn went partway down the stairway to hold back flaming strips of wallpaper so her sister could run down past her and out of the house.

Carolyn then went back up to Johnny and pushed him through the flames before going down the stairs herself. Her father met her at the bottom of the stairway and took her outside, where her mother fell on her to extinguish her burning clothing.

Norma and Johnny were burned badly, but both recovered. Carolyn also survived, but the third-degree burns she received over 85 percent of her body have left her permanently scarred. FILE NO: 58548

On March 9, 1917, 14-year-old **LILY BLANKS CLARKE** saved her nine-year-old sister and two other children from drowning in Lake Beulah in Monroe, Louisiana.

Clarke's sister was with Emma Biedenharn and Leland Petagna, both 14, in a small boat about 260 feet from shore. When the boat took on a little water, Clarke's sister became frightened and jumped into the eight-foot-deep lake. When she did, the boat capsized, tumbling the other two children into the water. Poor swimmers, all three began paddling to shore, but after a short distance Petagna stopped, having found something on the bottom that allowed him to stand and keep his head above water.

Clarke, who had been watching from the shore, happened to be a good swimmer. Realizing she was the only other person in the immediate area, she pulled off her sweater and shoes, waded in, and swam toward the tiring girls, meeting them about 125 feet from shore. With one holding on to each of her shoulders, she started towing them toward safety, but covered only 15 feet in this fashion. After taking her sister 10 feet farther, Clarke returned to Biedenharn and, with difficulty, towed her to wadable water while the sister swam ashore on her own.

Then without stopping for a rest, Clarke swam 240 feet back to the upturned boat and shoved it toward Petagna, who was about 10 feet away. With him clinging to the boat, she propelled it to wadable water, where men assisted them to the bank, Clarke semi-conscious by then. The three children had been saved, and, although exhausted, Clarke recovered quickly.

FILE NO: 17765

C. H. 1477

C. H. 1438, 1439

On February 5, 1915, two men from Wadsworth, Ohio, risked their lives to save a five-year-old girl who had dashed into the path of an approaching train.

Though he had only one arm, 29-year-old **PETER J. BACSO** was the crossing watchman where railroad tracks ran through the small town just west of Akron. Bacso was already stopping pedestrians from crossing ahead of the train that was rolling through at 40 mph, but young Lois Shelly was in a hurry. She darted past Bacso and onto the tracks, but she stumbled to her knees between the rails of the track. The engineer of the train, which was then 260 feet away, immediately applied the brakes.

Bacso reacted quickly. He turned and dashed to the girl, the train then only 30 feet away, grabbed her skirts with his hand, and snatched her to safety just as the train thundered past. **CHARLES KUNKLER**, who had been standing a few feet closer to the train than Bacso when Shelly fell, also responded. The 45-year-old Kunkler dashed in front of the train and reached Shelly an instant after Bacso. None of the three was injured.

FILE NOS: 16399, 16133

C. H. 1060, 1062

C. H. 1061, 1063

On March 7, 1913, four mariners from Baltimore returned to a burning freighter containing a cargo of dynamite to rescue two stranded seamen.

WILLIAM E. VAN DYKE, 35, was captain of the *Atlantic*, a tugboat that worked in and around Baltimore harbor with a crew of three, **HENRY M. DIGGS**, 35, **WILLIAM W. MARSHALL**, 39, and **LOUIS H. COMEGYS**, 33. That day the tug was moored in the Patapsco River tending a barge from which several dozen stevedores were transferring 300 tons of dynamite into the hold of the steamer *Alum Chine*. The dynamite was to be used for blasting work at the Panama Canal.

When a fire broke out in the ship's hold, and with everyone aware of the explosive nature of the cargo, a general panic ensued. A number of stevedores crowded into a launch and fled. More than 20 others climbed onto the *Atlantic*, and Van Dyke quickly steered the tug away. However, when the tug had gone about 450 feet, two men were seen on the bow of the *Alum Chine* signaling for help.

After conferring briefly with Marshall, his engineer, Van Dyke concluded that they had to rescue the trapped men. Ignoring the pleas of several stevedores who begged him not to return, the captain turned his tug and headed full speed back to the burning vessel.

Dense black smoke billowed from the *Alum Chine*'s open hatchways, and flames rose from its deck. The two men had climbed down the ship's anchor chain, and when Van Dyke brought the *Atlantic*'s bow underneath them, they dropped onto its deck. Van Dyke backed the tug away as quickly as possible, but when it had gone only 75 feet the dynamite exploded. The detonation completely destroyed the *Alum Chine*. Flying debris killed people on shore two miles away.

The cataclysmic force leveled the *Atlantic*'s pilothouse, instantly killing Van Dyke and Diggs, six stevedores, and one of the two rescued men. Though badly injured, Marshall and Comegys, the other rescued man, and all the other stevedores survived. FILE NOS: 10333, 10334, 10335, 10336

19 October 1964
ANCHORAGE HARBOR
ANCHORAGE, ALASKA

C. H. 4994, 4995, 4996

A collision between two fuel tankers near the harbor of Anchorage, Alaska, on October 19, 1964, gave tugboat captain JACK C. ANDERSON, JR., his wife, LOIS, and their 17-year-old son, JOHN, a chance to demonstrate skill and bravery.

The *Sirrah* and *Santa Maria* were each loaded with millions of gallons of liquid fuels when they collided in an ocean inlet about one mile from the Anchorage city docks. Aviation fuel gushing from a hole torn in the *Santa Maria* quickly ignited and engulfed her stern in flames, along with the bow of the *Sirrah* and one of the two tugboats that had been accompanying the second ship.

Anderson, 41, was owner and pilot of the stricken tug. Lois, 39, was helping him. John was piloting the other tugboat. The elder Anderson radioed his son to stand by the *Sirrah* while they went to help those on the *Santa Maria*. While Jack extinguished the flames on the tug, Lois steered the craft toward the *Santa Maria*, which was drifting on the tide, leaving a wide trail of fire 30 feet high in her wake.

The younger Anderson positioned his tug against the *Sirrah* on the side opposite the flames. Crewmen, fearing an explosion, climbed down an emergency ladder to the tug's deck. But when the *Sirrah*'s captain announced that the fire was under control, the crew re-boarded the stricken tanker. John then steered his tug to help his parents at the *Santa Maria*, which, by then, was engulfed for 175 feet along one side by flames that reached 80 feet above the water.

The older Anderson brought his vessel alongside the *Santa Maria*, manipulating its propellers to keep water-borne flames from igniting the tugboat. When the captain of the burning tanker gave the order to abandon ship, 31 crewmen jumped down onto the tug's deck. The captain and seven other crewmembers launched a lifeboat from the *Santa Maria*'s opposite side and were in short order met and rescued by John, who had arrived with his tug. When it was discovered that one crewmember was unaccounted for, John piloted the tug in a circle around the burning tanker, but to no avail.

The tugboats conveyed all the rescued crewmembers to shore. The fire on the *Santa Maria* was not extinguished until the following day.

FILE NOS: 47535, 47847, 47557

C. H. 1020

On March 26, 1912, **Henry T. Mathews**, a 12-year-old delivery boy, volunteered to be lowered 28 feet into an abandoned well to rescue a young boy.

Three-year-old Benjamin Grant was with his nursemaid at the house his uncle rented in Dothan, Alabama, waiting for his father to pick him up after work. Playing in the backyard, the boy crawled under the porch and fell feet first into an abandoned well there. The woman heard his cries and ran for help. Men came and quickly located the young boy, but because the pipe casing was only 13 inches in diameter, none of the men could fit into the hole.

A call went out for someone small enough to help, including a special message to one boy who had a reputation as being particularly daring. All of them refused.

However, when Mathews, who was working in a store that afternoon, heard about the situation, he went immediately to the Grant house and offered his help. At that point, the child had been in the hole for more than an hour, and rescuers feared he could not survive much longer. A rope was tied securely around Mathews, and he was lowered head first into the tight casing. He grabbed Grant's upraised hands and was hoisted with him for a few feet, but then the child slipped from his grasp.

Mathews was pulled up to get a breath of fresh air and then lowered back into the hole, this time with a looped rope. Unfortunately, Grant was still wearing a broad-brimmed hat, which made it impossible for Mathews to get the rope around him. So he removed the hat from the young boy's head and asked to be raised to the surface again. When he was lowered a third time, Mathews managed to get the rope under Grant's shoulders. Both boys were then hoisted to the surface. Neither was injured during the ordeal.

Mathews was modest about what he had done. When a collection was taken up for him at the scene, he tried to run away. In addition to a Carnegie Medal, the Commission awarded Mathews $2,000 to be used for his future education. FILE NO: 8301

HENRY T. MATHEWS
AND BENJAMIN GRANT

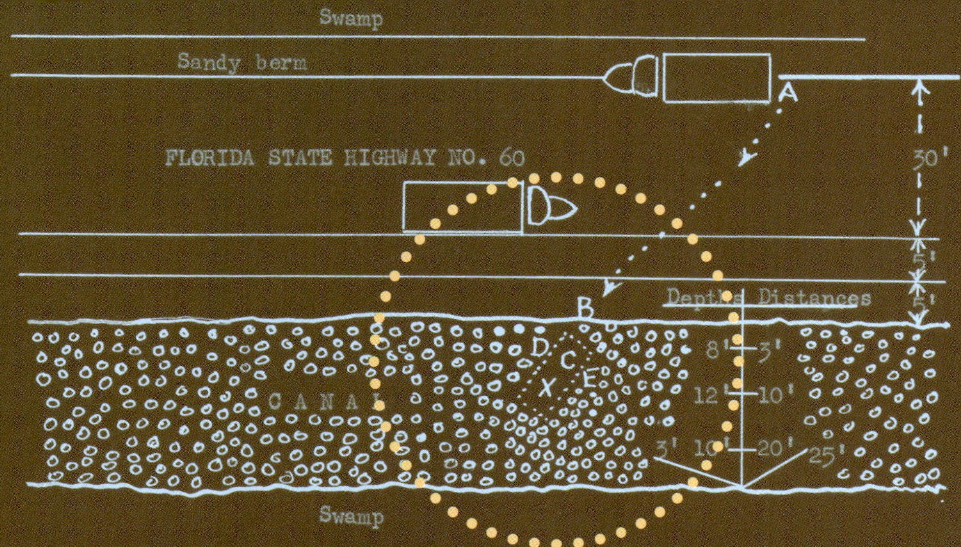

AUTOMOBILE THAT FIGURED

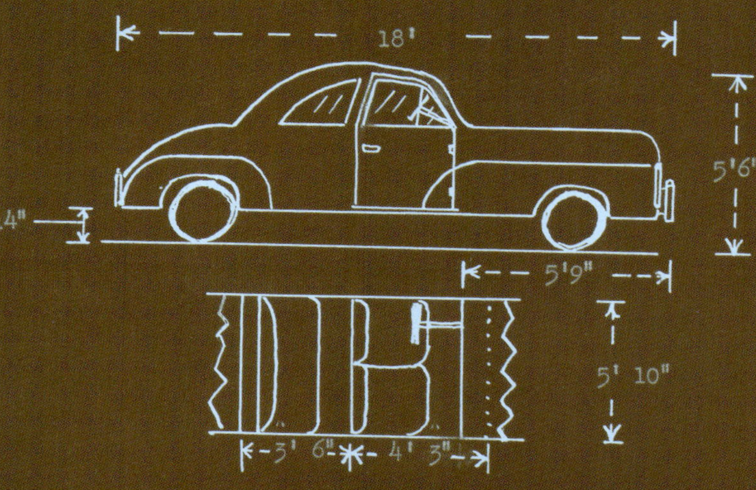

X - position in submerged coach of Carol Baisden

AB - course of Theodore Henderson, Sr., to bottom of N bank of canal

ENLARGEMENT SHOWING ACTION AT SUNKEN AUTOMOBILE

BC - course Henderson waded and swam to C where he stood briefly on sinking vehicle
CD - course Henderson lowered himself at NW side of car
D - where Henderson's left hand became caught between door and frame
DCB - course of Henderson to bank after freeing himself
BC - course Henderson returned to sunken vehicle with tire-iron
C - position of Henderson standing on car as alligator surfaced about 10' W of him
CE - course Henderson lowered himself to rear SE window and broke it with tire-iron
E - where Henderson probed through broken window but did not touch Miss Baisden
EC - course of Henderson to point at C for air.
XD - course Henderson pulled Miss Baisden from auto.

CD - course of Henderson to NW door.
DCB - course Henderson towed her to bank

THEODORE HENDERSON, SR., braved alligators and water snakes to save a young girl trapped in her car at the bottom of a muddy, 12-foot-deep canal near Yeehaw, Florida, a few miles from Vero Beach.

C. H. 3942

The sky was overcast at mid-afternoon on August 17, 1953. Henderson, a 39-year-old truck driver and father of five, was standing with his 10-year-old son and three other men, fixing a flat tire by the side of the highway, when Carol Baisden, 19, drove by. She lost control of her two-door sedan, which skidded on the damp road, plunged over the bank of the roadside canal, and landed on its roof in the dank water, which was inhabited by alligators and poisonous snakes.

Henderson ran to the canal in time to see the car's tires slip beneath the hyacinth leaves on the water's surface. Aware of an eight-foot-long alligator swimming in the canal, he immediately plunged in fully clothed and swam to where the car had sunk. Taking a breath, he groped down to one of the doors and pulled it open a few inches. But the sinking vehicle shifted and the door slammed shut, catching two of Henderson's fingers and dragging him to the bottom. Bracing his feet against the side of the vehicle, he pulled free, but one finger was broken and the nail and tip of the other was torn off. Despite his injuries, he surfaced and swam to the bank.

Even then, Henderson didn't give up. Grabbing a tire-iron, he swam back to the car. The alligator appeared at the surface of the water about 10 feet from one side of the car, so Henderson dove down on the other side and smashed the vehicle's left rear window. Reaching inside, he could not find Baisden, who was unconscious. He surfaced, crossed over the upturned vehicle, took a deep breath of air, and again submerged. This time he was able to open the door of the car, whose interior was now filled with water. Wriggling inside to his waist, he found Baisden and pulled her out. Rising to the surface, he called for help, but since the three bystanders were not willing to enter the canal, Henderson towed the woman to the bank himself. Both required medical attention but recovered within a few weeks without complications.

FILE NO: 42943

Early in the morning of January 16, 2000, **GERALD BOWLES** got out of his car on Interstate 20 in Jackson, Mississippi, to try to help an accident victim.

C. H. 8541

At about 12:30 a.m., a 35-year-old man lost control of his sport utility vehicle, and it flipped over, ejecting him onto the outside lane of the highway, where he was then struck by at least two other cars.

Bowles, a 67-year-old clothing store salesman, was driving toward the accident scene when he saw the man lying on the highway. Bowles pulled his car toward the left shoulder and parked across the highway's outside lane about 35 feet before the man, in an attempt to shield him from traffic. Putting on his car's emergency flashers, Bowles climbed out to get a flashlight from his trunk. He had just opened the trunk when an approaching car hit him.

Thrown into the air by the impact, Bowles landed on the windshield of his car, which was pushed into the median strip. Shortly afterward, a local police officer arrived on the scene and called for an ambulance. The accident victim was pronounced dead at the scene.

Bowles sustained multiple fractures and other injuries that required extensive hospitalization, during which he underwent amputation of both lower legs. Bowles later wrote to the Commission, "I have no remorse, I don't look back, I keep my eyes forward." FILE NO: 74697

C. H. 8648

On June 22, 2001, **CHRISTOPHER DUPLESSIS**, a 14-year-old student from Maine, pulled an unconscious race car driver from his burning vehicle.

For several years, Duplessis and his father, Richard, 51, had been volunteer "corner workers" at the Mount Washington Hill Climb, an annual event where drivers race their vehicles on an eight-mile course up New Hampshire's most famous mountain.

About 8 a.m. that day, during a practice run, they were positioned about a mile and a half up the course from the start. Edward Romney, 37, was driving his 130-horsepower Legend race car at 70 mph when he lost control, ran off the road, and struck a tree about 200 yards short of where Christopher and his father stood.

Hearing the crash and an explosion, the older Duplessis told his son to grab a fire extinguisher, and the two of them ran to the site and found the car almost totally covered in flames. While the father tried unsuccessfully to extinguish the flames, the son went to the driver-side door of the windowless vehicle, which had popped open from the impact.

Afraid that Romney might burn to death, the young man reached in and, despite the intense heat and threat of explosion, started to pull him from the burning vehicle. However, although Romney had released part of a safety belt restraining his torso, one of his arms was still held by a wrist restraint. Duplessis continued tugging, bracing his feet against the car's frame, until the melting restraint finally gave way and he was able to pull the stricken man free. Then, with his father's help, Duplessis dragged Romney away to safety.

Romney was treated for second-degree burns, several broken bones, and a concussion, but he eventually recovered. Duplessis was not injured. FILE NO: 75651

On May 4, 1933, **DAVID H. JONES**, 39, and **BENJAMIN F. MAJOR**, 45, risked their lives to save a fellow worker from an explosion.

Jones and Major were part of a 10-man crew igniting fuses of dynamite sticks set to blast apart huge boulders of ore spread across a flat area on the side of a copper pit in Jerome, Arizona. One charge exploded prematurely, throwing one of the miners, 44-year-old John Stout, to the ground. A three-feet-in-diameter slab of a boulder broke off, fell on his legs, and pinned him.

Six of the men fled, taking with them another man who was seriously injured by a flying rock, but Jones and Major responded to Stout's call for help. They briefly tried to free the trapped miner, but when that proved impossible, both men began to frantically pull fuses from nearby sticks of dynamite. Thirty-five sticks had been set within a 30-foot radius, and they each managed to pull 10 fuses. Realizing time was running out, Jones ran to get a pry bar, and Major flung himself down next to Stout to protect him from flying debris.

The dynamite started exploding, and within 30 seconds 15 explosions occurred. The concussion threw Jones to the ground, and rock shards rained down. The other men in the crew then returned and quickly freed Stout. Jones sustained slight burns on his hands while pulling the fuses, but otherwise none of the three suffered serious injury. FILE NOS: 33702, 33703

On March 15, 1928, **SEMKO SAWCZYUK**, a 36-year-old boiler washer in a Sydney, Nova Scotia, steel plant, died attempting to save a co-worker.

Sawczyuk was working with Alexander McNeil, 24. The two men were cleaning a boiler, near to which there was a shaft revolving at a speed of 50 to 60 revolutions per minute. There were no witnesses to the accident, but it was the opinion of plant officials that the three-foot-long wrench McNeil was using to tighten bolts slipped, causing him to lose his balance and fall back on the shaft. The first person on the scene, McNeil's brother, saw McNeil being whirled around the shaft. Sawczyuk was lying several feet away, seriously injured. He had grabbed for McNeil, and the shaft crushed his arm and tore off his hand.

Several minutes later, after the machine had been turned off, McNeil was pulled from it, but he was dead. Sawczyuk died four days later of his injuries, leaving behind a wife and four children. His widow received monthly benefits from the Hero Fund for more than 45 years.

FILE NO: 28126

C. H. 9468

An infant, Bobbi Stott, was in a playpen in the master bedroom of her family's mobile home in Belfair, Washington, when fire broke out on the structure's front porch on August 22, 2010. Her mother escaped with three other children. When flames blocked her re-entry for Bobbi, she tried to gain access to the bedroom through one of its windows. **ROBIN ADAIR**, 22, and her boyfriend were driving in the area when they saw the fire. Adair joined Bobbi's mother at the window and, after removing its screen, climbed up to the window with help from the mother and entered the bedroom. Smoke inside extended almost to the floor and obscured visibility, but Adair made her way to the playpen in the far corner of the room. She picked Bobbi up and, covering her with a blanket, turned back toward the window. Momentarily blinded by the smoke, she followed her boyfriend's voice to the window and handed Bobbi outside. Aided by the others, Adair then climbed through the window and dropped to the ground. Flames grew to destroy much of the structure. Bobbi was not injured, but Adair sought medical treatment for back pain. FILE NO: 83455

C. H. 9447

On July 16, 2010, while helping to secure a helicopter to a flatbed trailer on the tarmac of a Salt Lake City, Utah, airport, Thanish Kalis, 46, was struck by the helicopter during its maneuvering. He fell to the pavement, the helicopter crashing next to the trailer and leaking fuel. **RANDELL RANSON**, 39, an aircraft mechanic, was at a hangar nearby and witnessed the accident. He immediately ran to Kalis, removed a piece of wreckage from Kalis, and grasped him by the arms to move him. The fuel ignited explosively, throwing Ranson 10 feet back and setting fire to the helicopter wreckage. Others responding with fire extinguishers fought the flames and removed Kalis. He died at the scene. Ranson was hospitalized overnight for treatment of burns, up to second-degree, to his legs, left forearm, and face. FILE NO: 83360

C. H. 9398

On August 23, 2009, an unmanned, 23-foot boat continued to travel off the Pompano Beach, Florida, coast of the Atlantic Ocean after its occupants jumped overboard. Its course took it along a line of mooring balls just offshore in an area frequented by divers and other boaters. **JULIE FITZPATRICK**, a 37-year-old consultant, was in a 15-foot boat in the vicinity with her husband when their attention was directed to the runaway boat.

They followed in their vessel, intending to warn anyone who might have been in its path. As they closed in on the runaway, which was traveling at undiminished speed, they realized there was insufficient time to warn those at boats moored ahead. After Fitzpatrick's husband took their boat alongside the runaway, Fitzpatrick jumped over the side and dived into the runaway boat. Regaining her footing, she stopped the craft and then returned it to shore. Fitzpatrick sustained a bruised hip, and she recovered. FILE NO: 82718

Five children, ranging in age from 2 to 10, were secured to their seats in a minivan that was parked and left running in front of a Watauga, Texas, store on June 16, 2009. The vehicle rolled backward toward a busy, six-lane highway. **JAMES CALLAHAN**, 48, a car dealer, was in the store and saw the minivan moving. He immediately ran from the store and approached the driver's side of the vehicle. He opened the driver's door and placed his right leg and foot inside the minivan to apply the brake, but he became caught by the front left tire of the vehicle and was taken to the pavement and dragged as the minivan turned away from the highway. The minivan ran over Callahan's left leg and arm, narrowly missing his head, before it stopped. The children were not injured. Callahan was hospitalized for treatment, including surgery of a fracture to his left leg, cuts and abrasions. FILE NO: 82418

C. H. 9382

Erik M. Lageroos, 26, was cross-country skiing January 11, 2009, on snow- and ice-covered Candlewood Lake in Danbury, Connecticut, when he broke through thin ice at a point about 500 feet from the closest bank. He was able to hoist himself back onto the ice, where he called for help. **RORY AHEARN**, 57, who lived nearby, saw Lageroos on the ice and reported the accident. He went to the edge of the lake and pushed an aluminum rowboat out to Lageroos. With Lageroos holding to a line at the bow of the boat, Ahearn started to return to the bank, pulling the boat. When they were about 100 feet from the bank, Ahearn broke through the ice, striking his head on the boat. He was able to get his legs back onto the ice, but with difficulty, as he maintained his hold of the boat. Firefighters arrived shortly thereafter. They secured a line to Ahearn and pulled him to the bank and then secured Lageroos and pulled him through open water to safety. Both men required hospital treatment for hypothermia, and Ahearn for a laceration to his forehead. They recovered. FILE NO: 81921

C. H. 9330

Rory Ahearn

On July 17, 2008, A teenaged girl wading along the bank of the North Saskatchewan River in Edmonton, Alberta, entered water beyond her depth and was carried downstream by a swift current. She tired in her attempts to return to the bank. **Krista D. Girvan**, a 25-year-old nursing student, was walking along the bank nearby when she heard cries for help and then saw the girl in the river. Telling others nearby to call for help, Girvan ran along the bank after the girl. When she saw that the girl struggled to stay afloat, Girvan removed her shoes, entered the river, and swam to the girl. She grasped her, and despite her training as a lifeguard, struggled against the current as she towed her to the bank, the current taking them several hundred feet downstream. Rescue personnel aided them from the water and provided treatment. FILE NO: 81721

C. H. 9326

James J. Frings, Sr., 70, lay in the living room of his one-story house in Jacksonville, Oregon, on November 15, 2008, after a fire broke out in the structure. His next-door neighbor, **Jacob T. Carr**, 33, a vascular technologist, responded to the front door of the burning house and opened it to intense heat, dense smoke, and ammunition that was detonating in the spreading flames. Carr called out repeatedly to Frings and then saw his hand at a point about 10 feet from the door. He crawled to Frings, grasped him about the forearm, and retracing his steps, dragged Frings to the front door and outside to safety. Frings required hospitalization for burns, up to second-degree, and he recovered. FILE NO: 81782

C. H. 9304

On September 8, 2007, an 83-year-old woman mistakenly drove her car onto one of two railroad tracks at a Glenview, Illinois, crossing, and the car became stuck as a passenger train approached on that track at high speed. High schooler **Thomas Eugene Foust**, 17, was driving nearby. He and others immediately ran to the car as the crossing's gates and bell were activated, indicating the train was approaching. Thomas and his friends urged the woman to exit her car, and as the train bore down, Thomas pulled open the driver's door, reached inside, and unfastened her seat belt. He then pulled the woman from the car, took her 10 feet to a fence that bordered the track bed, and shielded her with his body. Within seconds, the train struck the car and knocked it into the path of another train, which was approaching on the second track. The car was struck again, sending debris flying. The woman was shaken but uninjured. FILE NO: 80678

C. H. 9265

C. H. 9259

CHRISTOPHER A. HOWARD rescued a father and son from an out-of-control tractor-trailer in St. Helens, Oregon, on August 7, 2007. Traveling at about 30 miles per hour on a four-lane highway, Matthew T. Lovo, 32, was driving a truck pulling two loaded trailers when he lost consciousness and fell to the floor of the cab between the two seats. The rig crossed the opposing lanes of traffic as his son Matthew R. Lovo, nine, who was accompanying him, took over the steering wheel and turned off the ignition. Matthew took the truck, which was slowing, back across the highway. Howard, a 36-year-old millwright, was approaching in his vehicle when the tractor-trailer crossed his path and then passed him. Seeing that a boy was attempting to control the rig, Howard immediately left his car on the highway, ran after the truck, and mounted the driver's side of the tractor. He opened the door, partially entered the cab, and stepped hard on the brake pedal, taking the rig to a stop. FILE NO: 81190

C. H. 9232

James J. Juarez, 34, and John S. McAndrews, 37, were among a crew of ski patrollers, on April 6, 2006, recovering a fence buried by snow at a resort on Mammoth Mountain in Mammoth Lakes, California. About 20 feet of snow covered the ground except at a fumarole, or natural vent, through which gasses, particularly carbon dioxide, were released. A cap of snow covered a cave that had formed in the snow above the fumarole, and from the surface the existence of the cave was not evident. Without warning, Juarez and McAndrews broke through the snow covering and fell to the floor of the cave, and within moments they lost consciousness in its toxic atmosphere. Equipped with an oxygen mask, one of their co-workers at the site, **WALTER ROSENTHAL**, 58, entered the hole resulting from the men's fall and slid to the bottom of the cave. He walked to Juarez and McAndrews but then lost consciousness and collapsed. Another co-worker entered the cave in a rescue attempt but was also overcome. Over the course of several minutes, other personnel responding to the scene dug a trench through the snow toward the bottom of the cave and recovered the four victims. The last man to have lost consciousness was revived, but attempts to revive Juarez, McAndrews, and Rosenthal were not successful. FILE NO: 79258

Nineteen-year-old **WILLIAM DEAN BASLER** rescued Kristy A. Dudley, 26, and Stacey L. Taylor, 28, from a runaway carriage in Indianapolis, Indiana, on April 8, 2007. Sightseeing, the friends Dudley and Taylor were passengers inside a closed carriage that was being pulled by a horse on a six-lane, center city street. A van approached from behind and struck the carriage, sending its driver to the pavement. Spooked, the horse continued, at a trot, causing the carriage to lurch. Witnessing the accident, Basler chased the carriage, but when a taxicab stopped beside him, he boarded it and was driven to a point ahead of the runaway carriage. As the carriage approached him, having covered 1,000 feet, Basler climbed onto its side and then forward to its bench, which served as the driver's seat. He seized the reins and pulled, stopping the horse, but the momentum of the carriage prompted the horse to resume running. Basler took the horse and carriage to a stop about 600 feet beyond the point where he had boarded it. Dudley, Taylor, and the carriage driver, who regained consciousness at the scene, were taken by ambulance to the hospital and examined. One month after the incident, Dudley and Taylor were still receiving treatment for injuries sustained in the incident. Basler was not injured. FILE NO: 80214

Twelve-year-old Colton T. G. Reeb was camping with family friends in Clinton, British Columbia, when, on August 1, 2007, a 70-pound cougar attacked him, bringing him to the ground and taking his head into its mouth. A member of his party, **MARC PATTERSON**, 45, a disabled construction worker, was alerted to the attack and responded immediately from nearby. Patterson kicked the cougar in the head repeatedly, but it would not release Colton. Patterson then went to his knees, grasped the cougar by its neck, and applied pressure, causing it to release Colton. Colton fled to safety. Patterson and the cougar struggled on the ground briefly, the cougar then freeing itself. Patterson regained his footing as the cougar, just a few feet away, growled at him. He made gruff noises and waved his arms while backing away from the animal up a hill and to his truck with Colton. He drove Colton to a police station, where he was given first aid and an ambulance was called to the scene. Colton was hospitalized for two weeks for treatment of puncture wounds and lacerations to his head that required nearly 300 sutures. He also needed a blood transfusion and underwent reconstructive surgery to his ears and face. Patterson sustained minor injuries that required no treatment. FILE NO: 80549

C. H. 9211

C. H. 9195

"Evan died a hero, with no second thoughts or hesitation." These are the words of Anjelica Ishima, sister of Evan Patrick Ishima who rushed to the rescue of a man who had submerged in the Cosumnes River in California on May 28, 2020. She said her brother was humble and never sought attention. He was just out to do the right thing. When Ishima was posthumously awarded the Carnegie Medal for his bravery, an emotional Anjelica said, "I have no words . . . I think there's probably nothing more honorable than that," according to a September 14, 2021, report by CBS Sacramento.

Ishima wasn't the only one who risked his life that day trying to save his fellow human being. Gabriel Saechao, a 20-year-old college student from Sacramento, also went into the river to save lives. One of them was his good friend, Tim Nguyen, and the other was Ishima, whom Saechao had never met. Both men exhibited the type of courageous action that made their friends and families proud and caught the attention of the Carnegie Hero Fund. Neither of them set out to be a hero that day, but when the situation called for it, they didn't think twice about what to do.

It was a fatal series of events that brought these two groups of hikers together. They were young, athletic, and loved the outdoors. So what better place to spend a day than the Cosumnes River Preserve, located in El Dorado County about 68 miles west of Sacramento? This bucolic 50,000-acre preserve features nearly 11 miles of scenic trails and is a popular destination for outdoor enthusiasts who love to kayak, nature watch, and hike along its trails. However, the beauty of the preserve belies some of the dangers held within. The river features three forks—North, Middle, and South—that cut through canyons of Northern California. The North Fork is 40 miles long and receives its largest tributary, Camp Creek, at Somerset, the area where the incident occurred. Just below Camp Creek the river flows through the granite narrows of the Cosumnes River Gorge, creating rapids and waterfalls that can make swimming difficult and dangerous.

At around 4 p.m., as the temperature hovered around 100 degrees, these two groups of hikers, independent of each other, had stopped to take a break near the North Fork of the river. The water temperature was 60 degrees and offered a cool respite to the late afternoon heat. Nguyen, 20, was in one of the groups with Saechao. Nguyen entered the river and swam over to an area where the river narrowed and climbed over boulders that led to a waterfall. The water was about four feet deep where he stood. It spilled over the fall and down a seven-foot drop, creating a swirling rush of whitewater in the river below. Nguyen was known for being a strong swimmer, so his friends who had remained on the riverbank took little notice of where he was going. Nguyen worked his way over the big rocks

Evan Patrick Ishima

Gabriel Cedrik Saechao

until he came to the top of the falls. He did not real-
ize that just below the surface of the water, unseen,
was an opening about three feet wide that led to an
underwater chamber under the falls. Nguyen slipped
on the mossy boulders and was pulled down into the
chamber. Despite his prowess in the water, he could
not overcome the force of the current and submerged.

Ishima, a 24-year-old from Florin, California,
was hiking in the other group when he glanced
toward the river that ran alongside the trail. He saw
Nguyen climbing over the boulders at the top of a
falls and then saw him disappear into the foamy swirl.
When the man failed to resurface, Ishima immediately
jumped into the river and made his way over to the
area where he thought he saw him submerge. When
Ishima reached the top of the waterfall, he thrust his
arms down into the water desperately hoping to feel
an arm, a leg, anything that he could grab on to and pull out. He noticed
there was an opening between the boulders, big enough for a human.
Ishima was resourceful, creative, and eager to help. As an aspiring cabinet
maker, he was detailed, good with his hands, and knew how to figure
things out. He quickly thought of another way he could help locate the
man. He lowered his legs into the water, bracing his arms and elbows
between the boulders. This allowed him to reach farther down into the
chamber and feel around for any sign of a person struggling. He was
shouting for others to come help and caught the attention of Nguyen's
group of friends on the river's edge. Others soon arrived and tried to hold
on to Ishima, but the force of the river's pull was too strong. Ishima lost his
grip on the boulders and disappeared into the roiling water.

That's when Saechao sprang into action. Two men had gone under.
One of them was his good friend and the other a stranger who had come
to his aid. There was no time to wait for help. The nearest police station
was nearly 15 miles away. Saechao rushed over to the waterfall opening.
More people arrived and formed a human chain to hold on to Saechao as
he lowered himself into the spot where the men had been seen minutes
earlier. Saechao could feel nothing under the water. He tried harder to no
avail. Suddenly, Saechao lost his grip on the people who were holding to
him and was swept below the surface. Tragically, all three men drowned.
But the heroic actions of Evan Ishima and Gabriel Saechao will never be
forgotten.

For their bravery and sacrifice, Ishima and Saechao were awarded
the Carnegie Medal. These men lived life to the fullest, were loved by
many, and perished doing something that came naturally to them—as
natural as the places where they loved to hike—rushing to help someone
in need. FILE NO: 91144, 91595

24 August 2004
ALLEGHENY LUDLUM STEEL CORPORATION
VANDERGRIFT, PENNSYLVANIA

C. H. 9172

Co-workers John L. Ressani, 48, and **MICHAEL J. CARNEY**, 50, were, on August 24, 2004, changing the two stacked rolls of a temper mill at a Vandergrift, Pennsylvania, steel plant. They and another co-worker were rigging the top roll to an overhead crane for repositioning when the crane moved unexpectedly. As the crane moved the 14-ton roll toward Ressani by its secured end, Carney shouted a warning to him and then approached and pushed him hard from the roll's path. Carney then turned, but before he could reach safety, the unsecured end of the roll dropped, pinning him to the floor and killing him. FILE NO: 79605

27 May 2005
MOUNT LOGAN
YUKON TERRITORY

C. H. 9146

JAMES P. HOOD, a 47-year-old helicopter pilot, rescued a hiking party that had been stranded for two days in a May 27, 2005, storm on a ridge of Mount Logan in the Yukon Territory. Erik C. Bjarnason, 40; Donald W. Jardine, 51; and Alexander C. Snigurowicz, 45, all experienced climbers, had been stranded at an altitude of about 18,000 feet. Suffering frostbite and altitude sickness and with little provision, the men radioed for help as they sought refuge in a cave they dug in the snow, their tent having blown away. Two other climbers from their party reached them after the storm abated and, setting up their tent, tended to them. Meanwhile, Hood, who was employed by the company that provided search and rescue services for a U.S. national park about 400 miles away, was informed of the situation. Agreeing to the mission, Hood and a two-man crew flew a specialized high-altitude helicopter to the scene over the course of several hours, having to refuel three times as they took a non-direct route because of inclement weather. From a staging area at an altitude of about 5,510 feet that was about 15 miles from the scene, Hood ascended alone to the climbers' location, his craft carrying minimal fuel due to weight restrictions. The diminishing light of late evening compromised his vision and depth perception in the terrain with which he was unfamiliar, as he had not flown there previously. Further, Hood was not acclimated to the thin atmosphere of the high elevation, which caused him to require supplemental oxygen and which imposed on the helicopter's performance. Unable to land at the climbers' site, Hood hovered above it as Bjarnason was helped by the others into a rescue basket suspended by a line from the helicopter. Bjarnason was then evacuated to the staging area, where Hood refueled the helicopter. He returned to the ridge and removed Jardine to the staging area in similar fashion. By then the midnight skies had darkened, Hood again took on minimal fuel and flew a third time to the scene, for Snigurowicz. After he returned Snigurowicz to the staging area, the three climbers were taken to a hospital, where they were detained for treatment of hypothermia and frostbite, two of them requiring digit amputation. FILE NO: 80138

James P. Hood

Motorist Aja D. Queen, 25, remained in the driver's seat of her car after an April 30, 2004, accident in which the vehicle left the New Kent, Virginia, highway, entered a wooded median, and caught fire in its engine area. Her daughter Jamia N. Queen, five, was in the backseat of the car, and her son Jatae K. Queen, six, was in the front seat. Motorists **ROBERT B. GOTTSCHALK**, 60, a psychiatrist, and **SETH T. STEIN**, 24, a medical supplies salesman, who had been driving behind Queen, both witnessed the accident and stopped at the scene. Gottschalk approached the burning car and, despite growing flames, leaned inside through the driver's doorway and unfastened Queen's seat belt. He then grasped Queen's arms and pulled her from the vehicle. As Queen outweighed him and was otherwise immobilized by her injuries, Gottschalk remained with her as Stein opened the rear door on the driver's side, leaned into the car, and pulled Jamia from the vehicle after first releasing her seat belt. Placing her safely away from the flames, Stein then returned, fully entered the backseat area, and freed Jatae, whose leg was caught in the wreckage. He pulled Jatae into the backseat, then out of the car. Stein then took both children back to the highway, returned to the car, and with Gottschalk took Queen to safety. Flames by then had spread throughout the inside of the vehicle and issued high above it. Queen was hospitalized for treatment of her injuries, but she was not burned and recovered. Seventeen years later, Queen, now Aja D. Anderson, contacted the Hero Fund and asked to be put in touch with Stein. "I had been trying to find them on and off for years," Anderson said. "There's not months, weeks, or days that go by where I don't think about what these men did for me, and I wanted to make sure they were okay, and I wanted them to understand how much it meant to me that they saw a burning car in the middle of the woods and came to my aid. I didn't want anything to happen to me or them without being able to say thank you." Although Stein repeatedly said he didn't feel like his actions were heroic, connecting with Anderson and her now grown children gave his rescue more meaning. "It does feel like the rescue, my actions have more purpose now," he said. FILE NO: 77667, 77668

Seventy-year-old Sigrid Szymczak-Hopson remained in her cabin in the San Gabriel Canyon of the Angeles National Forest in California on September 1, 2002, after the area had been evacuated due to forest fires in the area. Upon learning of her circumstance and knowing the path of a fire was three miles away, Sheriff's deputies **PAUL J. ARCHAMBAULT**, 43, and **JOHN AUGUSTUS ROSE II**, 32, elected to respond. With Archambault driving, the men took a sport utility vehicle on the only road into the canyon, defying both a roadblock that had been established by firefighters and warnings that the road was impassable. The first part of their 8.5-mile route was through an area over which the fire had already passed but where hot spots remained, flames flaring then receding on either side and debris littering the roadway. About a half-mile from the cabin, the road narrowed to one lane, with a 300-foot drop to the side. Flame conditions were more severe there, and dense smoke reduced visibility to only a few feet. Archambault pulled the vehicle into a parking lot near the cabin and kept it moving to avoid engine failure as Rose ran 650 feet to the cabin where he found Szymczak-Hopson. After Rose returned to the vehicle with her, Archambault pulled back onto the roadway, where conditions were deteriorating. Visibility was further limited, and intense heat made its way into the vehicle. They navigated the narrow portion of the roadway, then continued toward safety until one of the vehicle's tires flattened, about four miles from the roadblock. Another flattened shortly after, and the rest of the vehicle showed extensive fire- and debris-related damage. Firefighters responded shortly and took them to safety; neither Szymczak-Hopson nor Archambault and Rose were injured. The fire burned for 13 days across more than 20,000 acres before it was contained. In December 2016, Archambault and his wife Jacquelyn traveled to Pittsburgh to visit the Hero Fund offices. It was then he told Hero Fund staff that the 2002 rescue was "the most terrifying time of my life," but that he and Szymczak-Hopson remained in touch after the rescue.

FILE NO: 76982, 76983

C. H. 8784, 8785

COUNTY OF LOS ANGELES
CALIFOR
COUNTY OF L

Unconscious, William F. McWhorter II, 72, remained in the driver's seat of his automobile after a Los Angeles interstate highway accident in which the vehicle struck the concrete median barrier and burst into flames at its rear end on December 25, 2013. The car stopped adjacent to the barrier. Off-duty police officer **DONALD E. THOMPSON**, 54, was driving on the same highway and witnessed the accident. He stopped at the scene, jumped over the barrier, and responded to the driver's side of the car. Despite significant flames issuing 15 feet from the back of the car and spreading rapidly toward the front, Thompson opened the driver's door, with difficulty, and, using the opened door as a shield against the advancing flames, extended his upper body inside the vehicle. Heat was intense in the vicinity of the car. Searching for McWhorter's seat belt release, Thompson sustained a burn to his right hand and arm and retracted momentarily. He reached again, released the belt, and then, moving around the door, grasped McWhorter by the shirt and pulled him from the car. Two other men who had responded took McWhorter over the barrier, and one of them then pulled Thompson over as flames filled the car's interior. McWhorter required hospital treatment for his injuries, including minor burns. Thompson suffered burns, including second-degree, to his face, arms, and hand, for which he too received medical treatment. Both men recovered. Thompson was later awarded the Public Safety Officer Medal of Valor from U.S. President Barack Obama for the same rescue. Thompson has also volunteered to present the Carnegie Medal to new awardees in California. "I've been asked by a very special organization to give a very special award to a very special person," Thompson said in a 2017 presentation to **JUSTIN LEE GREENWALD**. "This award is considered this country's highest civic award for heroism." FILE NO: 86271

At night, Joel L. Merchlewitz, 39, entered the Mississippi River in La Crosse, Wisconsin, and was carried downstream by a strong current. Deputy Sheriff **JOHN P. WILLIAMS**, 41, overheard a June 25, 2011, police dispatch on the situation and responded to the riverbank. Seeing Merchlewitz disappear into the darkness, Williams removed his shoes and items of gear, donned a life vest, and dived into the water, which was deep along the bank. He swam in the direction of Merchlewitz, the current taking him about 400 feet downstream, to where he was able to hold briefly to a bridge pier. He saw Merchlewitz nearby, struggling to stay afloat, and intercepted him. As Williams held to Merchlewitz, the current carried them farther downstream, and they submerged repeatedly. Boaters aboard a private craft caught up to the men and secured them with a

C. H. 9731, 9876

(FACING PAGE) CARNEGIE MEDAL AWARDEE DONALD E. THOMPSON, RIGHT, PRESENTS THE CARNEGIE MEDAL TO JUSTIN LEE GREENWALD. GREENWALD WAS CITED BY THE HERO FUND FOR SAVING RONALD L. LALLONE FROM A NIGHTTIME FIRE IN HIS HOME ON NOVEMBER 29, 2015. THOMPSON, AN OFFICER WITH THE LOS ANGELES POLICE DEPARTMENT, WAS CITED BY THE HERO FUND IN 2014 FOR HIS CHRISTMAS DAY 2013 RESCUE OF A MAN FROM HIS BURNING CAR.

C. H. 9541

line. A fire department boat arrived shortly and took them aboard and to safety. Merchlewitz was not injured. Williams was nearly exhausted, but he recovered that night. Williams later became a volunteer presenter of the Carnegie Medal to new recipients in the Wisconsin area. "It's important to me to be able to present the Medal in person," Williams told the Commission at a board meeting in 2015. FILE NO: 84160

C. H. 9518, 9519

After a man, on July 11, 2011, entered the barroom of a Ligonier, Pennsylvania, pub and grill and had a confrontation with one of the patrons, he left the establishment but returned shortly with a semi-automatic assault rifle. About eight to ten people were in the barroom, with several more in the nearby dining room and kitchen. Among them were insurance agent **KIRK D. HALDEMAN**, 51, and his friend, **MICHAEL J. LEDGARD**, a 52-year-old contractor, who were seated at the bar. The assailant pointed the rifle at the patron he had confronted and shot him, killing him. Haldeman stood and, although he was closer to two doors leading from the barroom than he was to the gunman, ran across the room and charged the assailant. He grasped him by the arm and pushed the rifle upward. It fired again. Ledgard approached them as Haldeman forced the assailant against a wall. Reaching them, Ledgard grasped the two men and took them to the floor, the assailant losing control of the rifle. Haldeman and Ledgard secured the assailant until police arrived and arrested him. FILE NO: 84286, 84191

C. H. 9515, 9516

SueLynn Panter, 44, was jogging on a rural road in Franklin, Idaho, on September 30, 2011, when a 175-pound, three-point, mule deer started to follow her. She tried to scare it off, but it approached closer and then attacked her, taking her to the ground and pushing her into an adjacent cornfield. Over the course of several minutes, the deer mauled her, inflicting puncture wounds with its antlers. She screamed for help. Seventeen-year-old **ALEXIS RENEE VAUGHAN** and her father, **MICHAEL CRAIG VAUGHAN**, 38, an electrician, were driving nearby when Alexis saw the attack. Telling her father to stop the car, Alexis jumped from it and ran to Panter. She kicked and punched the deer to no effect. Vaughan then responded, grasped the deer by its antlers, and pulled it away from Panter, and Alexis aided Panter to the car. The deer turned on Vaughan, taking him to the ground and mauling him. Alexis returned to the cornfield with a hammer from the car and struck the deer repeatedly about its head and neck. It retreated and left the scene. Alexis aided her father to the car and drove him and Panter to the hospital, where both were treated for puncture wounds that required suturing. Alexis sustained bruising. All three recovered. FILE NO: 84483, 84413

A man armed with a revolver entered a Long Beach, California, bank on March 5, 2010, approached a teller window, and demanded money from the teller. A customer at the window, **RICHARD JOSEPH CAMP**, a 39-year-old general contractor, moved to a point about 10 feet away but remained present, as did several other customers and bank employees, as the robbery attempt ensued. When the assailant started to mount the counter, Camp rushed him from behind, grasped him, and took him to the floor. They struggled for control of the gun, which the assailant fired repeatedly, striking Camp once in his right thigh. Despite his wound, Camp continued to struggle against the assailant, disarming him and throwing the revolver aside. Another customer in the bank, **DAVID RICHMOND JONES**, 48, a carpenter, had been seated at a desk about 25 feet from the teller window. After the shots were fired, he immediately ran toward Camp, securing the weapon, and then joined in the struggle to subdue the assailant. As Jones was pinning the assailant's legs, he and Camp discovered that the assailant was armed with a second gun. Camp seized it and sent it across the floor. Police arrived shortly and arrested the assailant. Camp was treated at the hospital for his gunshot wound, which required surgery a month later. FILE NO: 83017, 82994

C. H. 9486, 9487

Robert Fiske, 66, was the lone occupant of a twin-engine airplane that lost power while in an October 5, 2009, flight. The plane crash-landed in a wooded ravine in Eden Prairie, Minnesota. Fiske was trapped inside, and flames broke out at the right side of the fuselage, near the wing. Real estate developer **ROBERT T. SCHMIDT**, 64, was in his nearby home and heard the crash. He ran to the scene, and seeing Fiske inside the plane, mounted the left wing. Schmidt tried to gain access to the smoke-filled cabin by attempting to open its canopy and breaking out a window, but he was not successful. Meanwhile, 45-year-old business executive **PAUL A. ANSOLABEHERE** had followed the stricken plane's course while traveling in the vicinity. He then ran into the ravine and joined Schmidt on the wing, where he too attempted to break into the cabin. The two men then obtained a metal bar from the plane's nearby storage compartment and with it broke through the window. They then reached inside the plane and pulled Fiske out onto the wing. Flames had grown to reach into the trees, and they breached the cabin from its right side. Schmidt and Ansolabehere lowered Fiske to the ground and, with the help of others who were responding, carried him from the ravine to safety. Fiske was hospitalized for treatment of injuries sustained in the crash and for smoke inhalation. He recovered. Schmidt had lacerations to his hands, and Ansolabehere sustained puncture wounds to a hand, minor burns to his face, and singed hair. They too recovered. FILE NO: 82626, 82916

C. H. 9418, 9419

C. H. 3796

DAVID ANDREWS, a 67-year-old farmer in Snow Hill, Alabama, kept a man from being buried alive on January 24, 1952.

John Bell, 34, was cleaning out a water well by hand. He was at the bottom of the 42-foot shaft when the wooden cribbing collapsed, burying him in sand. A fellow worker lowered on a rope was able to uncover Bell's head, but couldn't do any more. A crowd of 30 onlookers had gathered at the top, but the unstable walls dissuaded anyone else from trying to help.

Andrews, who had arrived 90 minutes after the collapse, volunteered to be lowered into the hole. Standing in a loop of rope so as not to touch the sandy walls, Andrews repeatedly filled a bucket with sand that was then hauled out. After half an hour, he had uncovered Bell's shoulders, but then further collapses buried his head under six inches of fresh sand. Andrews labored another hour, uncovering Bell to his waist, when another collapse covered him with four feet of sand.

Metal tubing was lowered, and Andrews was able to push it through the sand and position it close to Bell's head. Oxygen was pumped into the tubing, possibly saving Bell's life. Andrews labored past dark. Finally, six hours after he had started, Andrews was able to tie a rope around Bell's waist so he could be hauled out of the collapsing well. Bell was hospitalized for six days. Andrews was exhausted but recovered after resting.

FILE NO: 42490

C. H. 2679

On February 4, 1932, 29-year-old **EDWARD J. CARTAIN** saved a woman trapped in a ship heavily damaged by an explosion.

At just past midnight, Viola Rivers, 33, was sleeping in her berth aboard the tank-ship *Bidwell*, which was docked at a refinery pier in the Delaware River near Marcus Hook, Pennsylvania, when a violent explosion in one of the ship's oil bunkers tore through the vessel. The ship was rammed against the dock, and its superstructure, much of which was constructed from wooden beams, began to burn. The dock and a warehouse also caught fire. Several of the 20 to 22 people on board the ship were killed immediately.

Rivers, blown from her berth and stunned, tried to escape. Placing a life preserver on each arm, she lowered herself 20 feet down a line, then dropped another several feet into the water in one of the ship's tanks. Patches of oil burned intensely on the tank's ceiling and side beams.

Cartain, who worked at the refinery, was at home that night, but curiosity over the explosion brought him to the dockside. When someone heard Rivers's cries from under the superstructure, and her predicament was realized, Cartain decided to help.

He stripped off his pants and shirt and lowered himself down the sloping side of the ship into the oily water. Then, despite the darkness and chance of further explosions, he swam 60 feet until he reached Rivers, part of his route taking him directly under the ship's burning superstructure. Rivers had been in the water for an hour by this time and was semiconscious. Supporting the woman with one arm, Cartain was able to swim to the side of the wrecked ship by the dock, where a line was lowered and Rivers was then pulled up to safety.

Rivers suffered severe burns from the ordeal and was hospitalized for two months. A gash that he received on his right foot kept Cartain from work for six days. A month later, he developed pneumonia and was unable to work for another three weeks. FILE NO: 31919

On April 18, 1969, twelve men risked their lives to rescue a co-worker from an accident in a lead and zinc mine in Salmo, British Columbia.

At 5:30 that afternoon, the mine mucker boss, Gilbert Mosses, 53, was at the top of a loading chute when he was caught by an unexpected fall of ore and knocked into the bottom of the chute. Covered except for his head and one arm by rocks of various sizes, Mosses was severely injured but conscious.

A dozen men employed at the mine gathered at the holding bin and worked for the next several hours to reach Mosses and get him out alive. They included shift bosses **ANDREW BURGESS**, 63, and **CARL A. SHELRUD**, 38; mine manager **EDWARD A. LAWRENCE**, 33; warehouse accountant and first-aid man **JOSEPH L. HEROUX**, 33; physician **IAN F. STEWART**, 46; loader operator **DALE R. BURGESS**, 24; and miners **EDWARD M. GLADU**, 36, **BRIAN D. MARTIN**, 21, **ALPHONCE P. GROTKOWSKI**, 33, **JOHN J. VOYKIN**, 37, **WAYNE R. RITTER**, 32, and **GRAHAM D. BINGHAM**, 30.

After an opening was cut in the chute's metal bulkhead, a clearing was made in the rocks piled against it. Andrew Burgess and Shelrud then crawled inside the chute and began fitting in wooden shoring to prevent further collapses. At various times during the rescue effort, Lawrence inspected the situation inside the chute, and Heroux and Stewart crawled in to minister to Mosses. Dale Burgess, Gladu, Martin, Grotkowski, Voykin, Ritter, and Bingham took turns working inside the chute to remove the rocks from around Mosses. When rocks had to be chipped away, a drill was used. If the work loosened the shoring, it was carefully reset.

Three and a half hours after the accident, Mosses was freed. He subsequently recovered from his injuries. None of the other men was hurt during the rescue. FILE NOS: 51810, 51811, 51812, 52348, 52349, 52355, 52350, 52351, 52352, 52353, 52354, 52356

C. H. 5863, 5864, 5865, 5866, 5867, 5873, 5868, 5869, 5870, 5871, 5872, 5874

Early in the afternoon of November 13, 1909, fire erupted in the escape shaft of a coal mine in Cherry, Illinois, about 100 miles west of Chicago. Four hundred eighty-four men and boys were inside the mine, and 259 of them would die as a result of the fire. Twelve of the dead and two survivors met the qualifications for the Carnegie Medal.

In operation for about four years, the mine was considered to be a model of safety. Two weeks earlier, the electrical system had malfunctioned, and kerosene torches were being used for illumination. Unfortunately, a load of hay inside a mine car, meant for the mules that worked inside the mine, caught fire from one of the torches. Although the car and its burning contents were pushed into a sump, smoke, and then flames, rose inside the escape shaft. The air ventilation flow was stopped and then reversed so as not to feed the flames, but that resulted in smoke being pulled into the main shaft.

An evacuation was ordered; by then, only the hoisting cages in the main shaft offered a possibility of escape. Four miners at work at the time, **JOHN BUNDY**, 53, mine manager, **J. ALEXANDER NORBERG**, 38, **JOSEPH ROBEZA, JR.**, 22, and **JOHN SZABRINSKI**, 29, were joined by four colleagues who responded from their homes, **ROBERT CLARK**, 28, **ANDREW McLUCKIE**, 31, **JAMES SPEIR**, 34, and **HENRY STEWART**, 28, and three other residents of the village, **JOHN FLOOD**, 49, **DOMINICK FORMENTO**, 32, and **ISAAC LEWIS, JR.**, 34, in organizing and carrying out the evacuation from inside the mine. After others were taken to the surface in a hoisting cage, the 11 boarded it, but, because of confusion caused by two different signals sent to the hoisting cage operator, the cage remained below ground for about 10 minutes. Fire reached the main shaft. When the hoisting cage was brought to the surface, the 11 men were dead of burns.

Another man, a mine examiner and boss, **CHARLES WAITE**, 43, remained inside the mine to help evacuate miners; he was found dead five days later. A second mine examiner and boss, **GEORGE EDDY**, 48, and an assistant mine manager, **WALTER WAITE**, 41, joined a group of 19 miners whose escape was blocked. Eddy and Walter Waite directed the miners to construct barriers against the flames and smoke. For seven days, the group remained imprisoned inside the mine until rescuers reached them.

The 14 Carnegie Medals awarded are the most for rescues at a single site.

FILE NOS: 5133, 5126, 5609, 5543, 5128, 4812, 5129, 5127, 5134, 4605, 4556, 5123, 5124, 5125

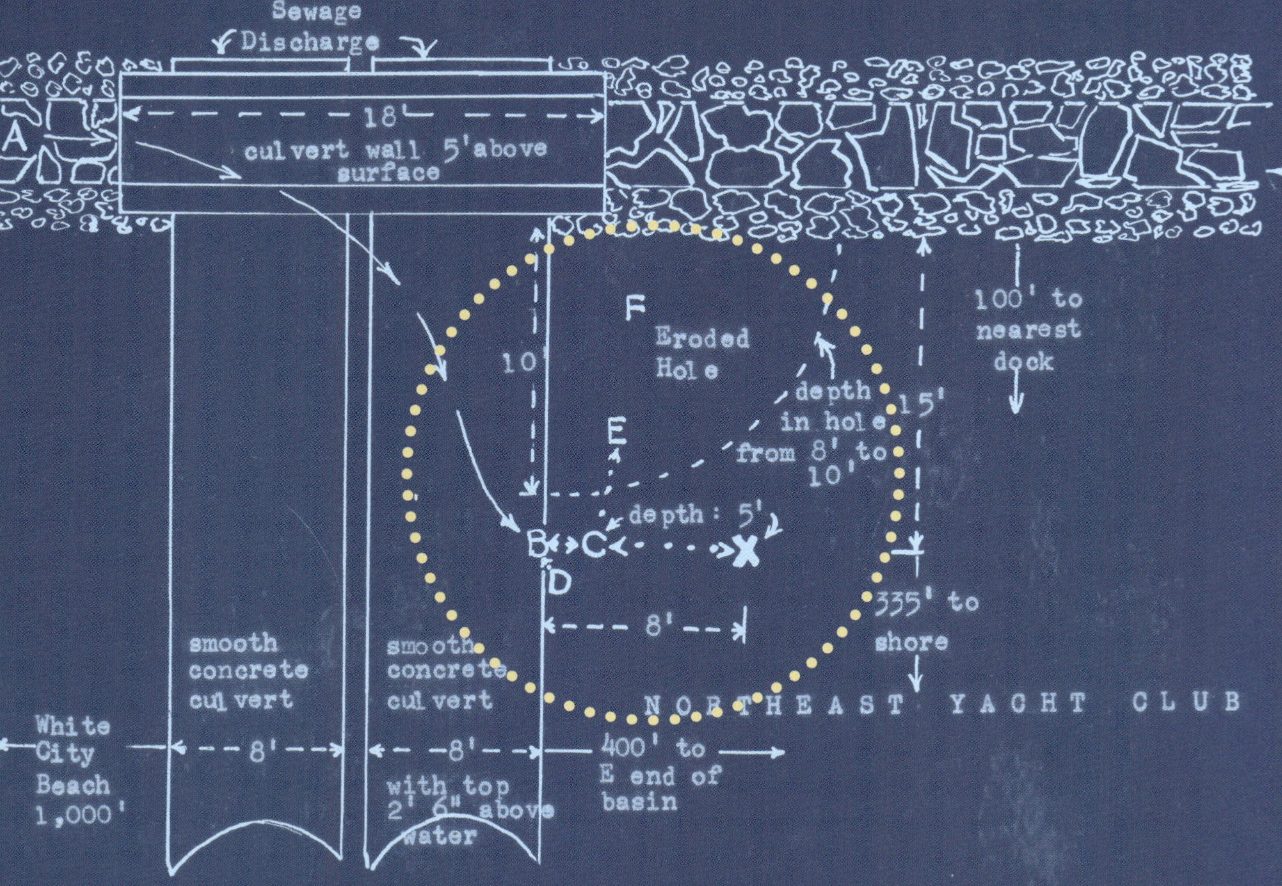

X - where Ronald J. Azzardi struggled at surface after
    falling into basin attempting to get dog at D
AB - course James A. Williams ran
BC - course Williams jumped into basin
CX - course Williams waded to Ronald
XC - course Williams waded carrying Ronald
CB - course Williams lifted Ronald to boys on culvert
DB - course Williams lifted dog to boys on culvert
CE - course Williams strode toward breakwater
E - where Williams was submerged and remained submerged
F - where body of Williams was recovered

JAMES A. WILLIAMS, a 41-year-old truck driver from Cleveland, Ohio, lost his life after saving a young boy from drowning in Lake Erie.

On May 21, 1961, Williams was fishing near a concrete culvert that protruded from a stone breakwater in the lake between White City Beach and the Northeast Yacht Club. Nine-year-old Ronald Azzardi had been on the culvert, trying to rescue a dog that had fallen into water five feet deep and was unable to get back out. Unfortunately, the boy also fell into the lake and could not climb back up onto the culvert, which rose 30 inches out of the water. Flailing to keep his head above water, Azzardi only moved away from the culvert.

Alerted to the boy's distress, Williams, himself a father of two grown children, ran to the culvert and, even though fully dressed and a poor swimmer, jumped in. He waded to the boy and lifted him onto his back. Then, with Azzardi clinging to his shoulders, Williams waded back to the culvert and lifted both the boy and the dog up to another youth who had arrived on the scene.

When both were safe, Williams began wading back toward the breakwater 15 feet away, not knowing that a hole 10 feet deep had eroded along its base. When he stepped into the hole, Williams submerged and became wedged under the culvert. Other men arrived and, using long poles, located Williams and pulled him out, but he could not be revived.

Williams was posthumously awarded a Carnegie Medal, and his widow received a monthly grant from the Commission for 35 years to help with living expenses.

"I'm not surprised he jumped in after that child," Mrs. Williams later said of her husband. "He loved children and was sorry when ours grew up. I know that if he were alive today, he'd explain jumping in by saying 'I saw a child in trouble.'" FILE NO: 45492

C. H. 4445

Eleven-year-old **KENNETH P. MAGALLANES** volunteered to be lowered 15 feet into an abandoned cesspool to save a two-year-old boy.

On February 21, 1963, young Leslie Masutani was with his father in the yard of a neighbor's house amid the sugar cane fields near Pearl City, Hawaii, when the child fell into an underground cesspool filled with three feet of muck and noxious gases but little oxygen. Masutani landed in the mat of sanitary waste and decaying vegetation and sank up to his chest.

Masutani's father ran to the cesspool's lid, but he was unable to fit through the 12-by-18-inch opening. Firemen were summoned and responded quickly, but none of them could fit through the opening either. Two air tanks were lowered into the hole to provide some ventilation.

C. H. 4653

Then Magallanes stepped forward. The schoolboy and his mother were bystanders who had come from their home nearby. With his mother's permission, Magallanes volunteered to help. Despite his initial hesitance, the fire captain agreed, fearing that further delay might be fatal to Masutani. A rope sling was tied around the young boy, and he was lowered through the tight opening.

Overcoming his nausea and fear of centipedes and scorpions, Magallanes located the child, pulled him from the muck, and wrapped his arms around him. Unfortunately, when the firemen pulled the boys up, both could not fit through the opening together. Then Masutani slipped from Magallanes's arms and fell back into the pit. After being pulled partially out to get a breath of air, Magallanes was given a second looped rope and again lowered to the bottom. This time, he got the rope around Masutani and held the child in his arms as the firemen pulled them up through the opening one at a time.

Masutani, who had spent 50 minutes in the cesspool, was badly dazed but recovered in several days. Magallanes, having been in the cesspool for nearly four minutes, was nauseated but otherwise uninjured.

FILE NO: 46402

C. H. 8026

On May 12, 1995, seven-year-old **KAYLA J. GARRIGAN** died after saving her half brother from a fire in the family's home in Manitowoc, Wisconsin.

Her father, Todd Garrigan, was at work that evening. His wife, Robin, and son Todd Jr., 6, slept in a first-floor bedroom of the two-story, wood frame building. Kayla was sleeping on a couch in the living room, while Christopher Walters, 12, was in his upstairs bedroom.

About 11 p.m., a fire broke out in the kitchen, possibly caused by one of the family's dogs turning on a burner on the stove while trying to get at some food in a pot. Mrs. Garrigan woke to the fire, and at first tried to extinguish the flames. Then she roused the two children downstairs, and called the fire department. Grabbing Todd Jr., she carried him out of the house.

Meanwhile Kayla dashed upstairs to warn Walters about the rapidly spreading fire. He met her at the bedroom doorway, and then stepped into the hallway where he could see flames at the front door. They both retreated into the bedroom. Smoke billowed into the room, and Walters opened a window. Assuming that his half sister was right behind him, he jumped out the window, spraining both ankles in the fall. But Kayla didn't follow.

The firemen who arrived shortly afterward found the young girl unconscious in a corner of the bedroom and took her to the hospital, where she died shortly afterward. Her sacrifice made Kayla the youngest recipient of the Carnegie Medal. FILE NO: 69755

On July 15, 1912, **LUTHER B. WEAVER**, part owner of a clothing cleaning and dye shop in Dallas, Texas, was fatally burned in an attempt to save an employee from fire.

George Mabern, 25, was working in the back of the two-story brick building, where a gasoline still was located in the cleaning room. An explosion of the still shook the building, and Mabern was knocked to the floor. Gasoline fumes began to spread.

When Weaver, 35, heard the explosion, he ran back to the room where Mabern lay, his arms upraised. Just as he stepped into the room, however, a second terrific explosion occurred, filling the room with a mass of flames that extended through the open door. Running through the flames, Weaver, his clothing on fire, reached Mabern and dragged him out of the room and away from the flames. Both men then fled the building to the street, where the flames on them were smothered by blankets. They were then taken to the hospital. Unfortunately, they had been too badly burned. Mabern died later that afternoon and Weaver the following day.

In addition to accepting a Carnegie Medal on behalf of her husband, Weaver's widow received a monthly grant from the Commission until her death 62 years later. FILE NO: 10516

C. H. 864

On April 11, 1978, **JOHN C. WOOD**, a 30-year-old prisoner at a state penitentiary in McAlester, Oklahoma, saved a guard from being mauled by a Doberman Pinscher.

About 2:15 that afternoon, James Martin and another man were training attack dogs on prison grounds. Wood, a former marine serving a 20- to 60-year sentence, was to act as an agitator for the dogs. He was waiting in a Jeep while Martin was working with a dog. However, when Martin stumbled and fell to the ground, the 75-pound dog leaped at him and began tearing at his head and arm.

Wood got out of the vehicle, grabbed a short length of hose, and began to beat the animal. The dog turned and tried to jump on Wood, who continued striking it with the hose. At that point, the other trainer arrived, snatched the dog's leash, and started swinging the animal in circles until it became unconscious. Martin was driven to the hospital where he received more than 200 stitches for his lacerations, but he eventually recovered.

Wood was not injured, but in addition to receiving a Carnegie Medal, for coming to Martin's aid he had his remaining sentence reduced.

FILE NO: 56256

C. H. 6359

C. H. 7061, 7062

On the morning of Friday, October 19, 1984, 50-year-old Lloyd Hansen, a senior control operator from Watsonville, California, was working at an inoperative surface condensing unit at a Pacific Gas and Electric Company fossil-fuel power plant in Moss Landing, California, adjacent to Monterey Bay.

The power plant used steam turbines to generate electricity, using the surface condenser to capture steam exhausted from the turbine and then cool it and condense it for reuse. The condenser pumped seawater transported to the plant via an underground pipe, through tubes inside a 21-foot-high, semi-circular, steel water box where the steam exhausted. The cold water cooled the steam back into liquid and collected at the bottom of the box.

The condenser was 15 feet wide at its base, tapering up. A 9-foot-wide vertical tunnel under the box contained still seawater that had sat since the broken unit was shut down 38 days earlier. As employees worked to fix the condenser, a temporary floor was installed inside the water box, leaving a three-foot-wide opening at the base of the unit to the tunnel. Workers could enter the water box through either of two small hatches.

The surface of the seawater was about 14 feet below the temporary floor, where decaying marine life floated. A dangerous concentration of dimethyl sulfide, methyl mercaptan, and hydrogen sulfide gases had built up in the tunnel, though the unit had been vented a number of times in the previous week after plant workers working to drain the tunnel detected a strong smell.

On the morning of the accident, Hansen called a 23-year-old auxiliary operator and asked him to meet him at the water box.

In the meantime, Hansen entered the water box through one of the 20- by 16-inch hatches. According to a state occupational safety and health division report, several employees saw Hansen inside the water box adjusting the submersible pump intended to drain the seawater from the tunnel.

The auxiliary operator and **REX A. LEWIS**, a 30-year-old operating foreman from Watsonville, California, approached the scene but could not find Hansen. His gloves, hard hat, and wrench lay ominously outside the hatch.

Lewis and the operator actively searched for Hansen, looking through the hatches and down through the temporary floor. The submersible pump had been placed in the water, which was creating turbulence. When it was turned off, the water calmed and Hansen could be seen floating face down on the water's surface.

Michael DeWitt Puckett, 31, a mechanic from Fresno, California, and another man responded to Lewis's and the operator's calls for help and ran to the water box.

Other co-workers rushed over with rope for Lewis and the operator to tie around themselves. Lewis and the operator entered the water box.

The operator, getting dizzy, cautioned Lewis to flee the water box, then exited to get more assistance.

From inside, Lewis instructed the men outside the box to lower him by the rope into the water tunnel so he could attempt to retrieve Hansen. Lewis reached the water's surface and placed a hand on Hansen's back to steady his descent.

Puckett then saw Lewis go limp and shouted for him to be pulled up.

The workers pulled on the rope to raise Lewis, but he became stuck on the temporary flooring inside the water box and could not be lifted higher.

Without a breathing device or rope, Puckett immediately entered the water box. Suspecting the presence of methane gas in the unit's atmosphere, he tried to breathe as little as possible as he reached toward Lewis through the opening in the floor.

Puckett grasped Lewis under his arms and pulled him up into the water box. As he lifted Lewis to one of the hatches, Puckett began feeling dizzy, and went to the other hatch to get a breath of fresh air.

Meanwhile, those outside the water box struggled to remove Lewis from the opening. Catching his breath, Puckett returned to push Lewis

Two water boxes, one being the figuring box in which Rex A. Lewis and Michael DeWitt Puckett entered to attempt to rescue their co-worker Lloyd Hansen.

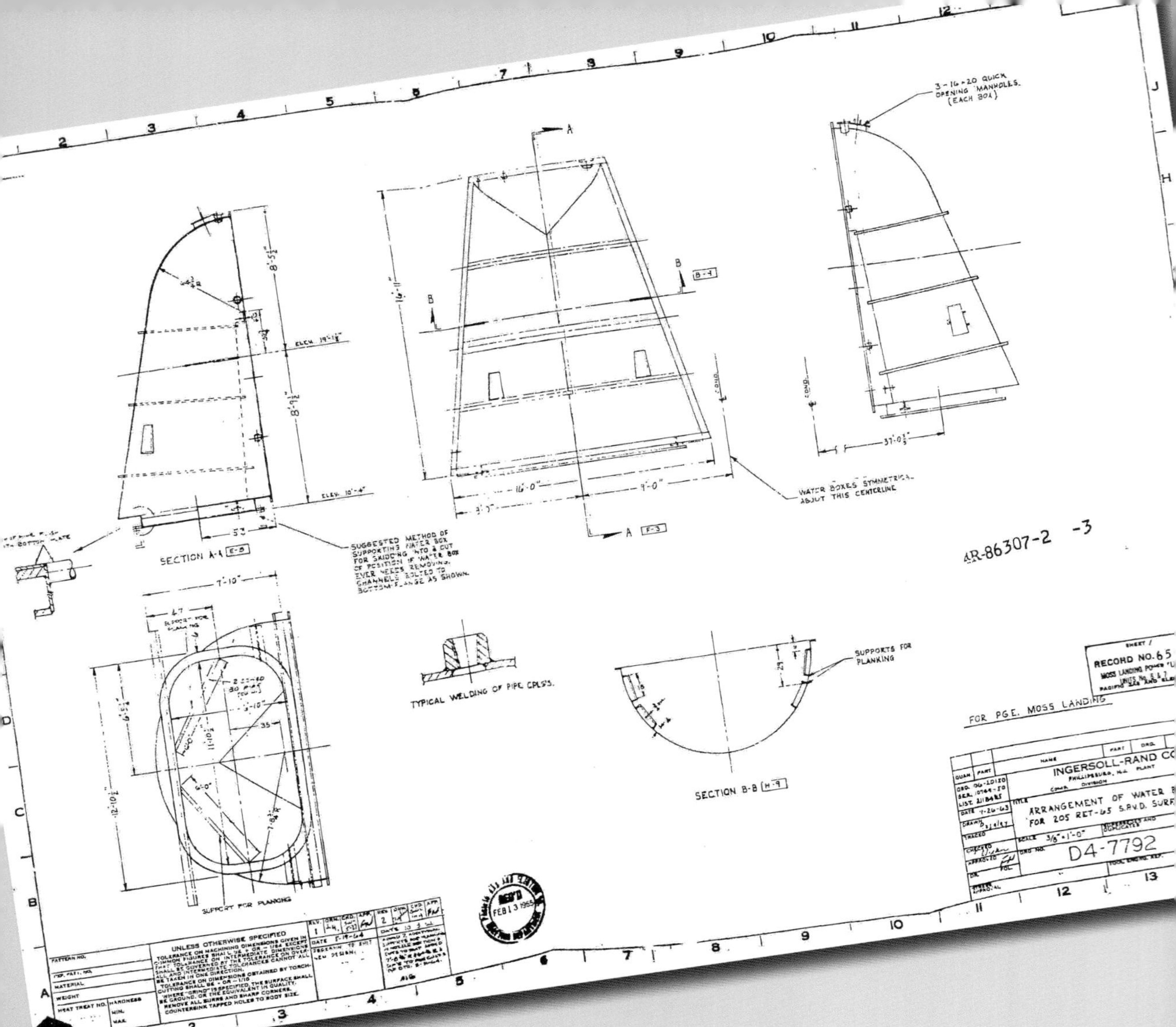

through the access point to the room outside the water tank. Lewis had stopped breathing several times and needed mouth-to-mouth resuscitation.

After Lewis had been pulled to safety and revived, Puckett left the water box to fetch a self-contained breathing apparatus that had a small oxygen tank before climbing back through the hatch and affixing the device to his face.

He clambered to secure Hansen, twice running out of oxygen and needing to get a new tank, and once entering the water. He only ceased his efforts once firefighters arrived.

It took firefighters two hours to retrieve Hansen. He was taken to a hospital and attempts were made to revive him, but they were ultimately unsuccessful.

Lewis, Puckett, and the auxiliary operator were the only three employees who had fully entered the water box to attempt a rescue, but a total of 31 employees underwent medical surveillance for exposure to the toxic gases inside the tunnel.

At the hospital, Lewis was admitted to the intensive care unit where he was treated for methane gas intoxication, lack of oxygen to the brain, and possible aspiration of water. He regained consciousness about five hours later. He was released the next day and made a full recovery.

During a conversation with Hero Fund case investigator Jeff Dooley, Lewis said that when he woke up in the hospital he thought his alarm had gone off and he was late for work.

Puckett suffered more long-term effects from his participation in the rescue effort. After receiving oxygen at the power plant, he experienced uncontrolled vomiting for six months. His doctor attributed this to Puckett inhaling one of the gases present in the water tank.

During his research, Dooley gathered eyewitness accounts of the actions of Lewis and Puckett, consulted the plant manager, reviewed a lengthy and wide-ranging company report, and accessed third-party summaries of the accident to build a solid case for awarding Puckett and Lewis for their heroic deeds.

In addition to interviewing the two rescuers, Dooley questioned two other employee eyewitnesses to the rescues.

Lewis and Puckett were awarded the Carnegie Medal on December 16, 1986, and were granted $2,500. FILE NO: 60493, 61376

26 November 1945
LAKE CHELAN
CHELAN, WASHINGTON

C. H. 3474, 3475, 3476

Margaret Rice, 15, saved a fellow student from drowning when their school bus swerved off the road during a blizzard and plunged into a deep, frigid lake. Her brother and father soon entered the scene and rescued another passenger.

On November 26, 1945, Rice was one of 20 students who, with Glenna Brown, 38, were passengers on the bus when the driver lost control on a highway that ran along Lake Chelan in central Washington. The vehicle careened over the steep bank and began to sink slowly some 20 feet out, in water 30 feet deep. Brown, Rice, and four other students managed to escape the bus. Three of the students, boys, swam to safety, but as Rice surfaced she noticed Mariette Archer, 17, floating helpless nearby. Rice swam to the bank, quickly removed her galoshes, shoes, and coat, and then swam back out to Archer. Taking hold of the unconscious girl around the neck, Rice paddled back to the steep bank and managed to lift her up onto a rock.

In the meantime, Rice's father and 17-year-old brother, who had been in a car following the bus, arrived on the scene. The brother, **Alan Herbert Rice**, entered the water and swam 40 feet out to Brown, who was unconscious and nearly submerged. With great effort, he towed her toward the bank, calling to his father for help. Although he was a poor swimmer, **Alan Randolph Rice**, 45, entered the water, swam to Brown, and aided in getting her the rest of the way in.

Fifteen students and the driver were drowned, but Archer and Brown were saved. FILE NOS: 40573, 40574, 40854

11 October 1926
HOTEL
WOODSTOCK, NEW BRUNSWICK

C. H. 2252

On October 11, 1926, **Mary Evelyn Brown**, a 15-year-old schoolgirl, risked her life attempting to prevent an "ill-natured" father from murdering his five-year-old son.

The father, a tailor in Woodstock, New Brunswick, was known to be a neighborhood bully, especially when he was drinking. That was the case when he came to a hotel, where his wife was the proprietor, about 6:30 that evening. When his wife became fearful for herself and her son, who was with her in the hotel's office, she tried to take the boy away. The father suddenly snatched the boy from his mother, dragged him from the hotel, flung him to the ground, and began attacking him with a razor.

Brown, whose home was across the street from the hotel, was washing dishes when she heard the mother scream, "He's murdering my child." Brown had often played with the boy and was familiar with the father's rages. She immediately ran out to help, thinking the father was choking the child and unaware he had a razor. Grabbing up a used, 10-pound lard bucket that had been filled with dirt, she came up behind the father, who was bending over his son. Three times she hit him on the back with the bucket, which fell from her hands on the last blow. She then kicked the father hard in the ribs once or twice, and he rolled away.

A man soon arrived and picked up the child. The young boy's throat had been slashed, and he died moments later. The father had also cut his own throat, but lingered three weeks before he died.

Although not physically injured in the rescue attempt, Brown required a few weeks to get over the emotional shock and was unable to attend school regularly for nearly two years following the incident. FILE NO: 26891

24 September 2002
APARTMENT COMPLEX
DALLAS, OREGON

On September 24, 2002, 74-year-old **MARGUERITE ZACHARY** went to the aid of a woman who had been shot multiple times by a deranged gunman.

C. H. 8739

Charlotte Woods, 59, was manager of an apartment complex in Dallas, Oregon, where Zachary, a retired nurse, lived. Just after 7 p.m., Woods was turning on the sprinkler system in the courtyard of the four-building complex when a male resident, 60, confronted her. When Woods refused to speak with him and turned her back to him, he pulled out a .40-caliber, Glock semiautomatic pistol and fired at her repeatedly.

Zachary was in her ground-floor apartment when she heard what sounded like firecrackers. Not seeing anything from her window, she stepped outside and saw Woods lying on the ground, her midsection covered in blood. While walking to the stricken woman as quickly as she could, Zachary looked up and saw the man, now on the balcony of his second-floor apartment, brandishing a gun. Overcoming her fear, Zachary continued to Woods and knelt beside her. Conscious, Woods said she couldn't feel her leg and was afraid she was going to die. The assailant then fired again, one of the shots hitting Woods in the shoulder. Zachary told Woods to lie still so the assailant would think she was dead.

For five minutes Zachary comforted Woods in the courtyard, not knowing if more shots would be fired. None was. Then several police officers arrived on the scene, summoned by a 911 call from another resident. One of the officers spotted the man and told him to drop his gun, but the man retreated into his apartment.

The officer then called to both women to crawl to safety. When Zachary answered that Woods could not move, he told her to go alone, which she did. While one officer covered the assailant's apartment, another ran out and dragged the injured woman to safety. After a five-hour siege, during which time the assailant fired several shots in his apartment, he surrendered to the police without further incident.

The man eventually pleaded guilty to assault charges and was sentenced to 13 years in prison. Despite being shot 11 times, Woods recovered after several months. Zachary was not injured. FILE NO: 76401

11 January 1907
WILDERNESS SETTLEMENT
TELMA, WASHINGTON

On January 11, 1907, **MARIE V. B. LANGDON**, a 20-year-old housewife living in a wilderness settlement in the Cascade Mountains, braved sub-zero temperatures and snow six feet deep to aid neighbors fleeing their burning cabin.

Langdon and her 25-year-old husband, Jesse, were settlers in the thickly forested area by Lake Wenatchee, several miles from the town of Telma in central Washington. The Langdons lived three-quarters of a mile from their nearest neighbors, Charles and Sophie Jacques, and their three children, Henry, 4, Gertrude, 2, and Estella, 7 months. The previous day, the two men had hiked into Telma to get supplies, but the weather prevented them from returning to their homes that night.

Early that frigid morning, Sophie Jacques had lit a fire in the stove that warmed their two-room, cedar-framed cabin. Sometime afterward, she noticed flames smoldering on the cabin wall near the stove. At first Jacques tried to extinguish the flames and then to gather up a few of the family's possessions. Unfortunately, the fire spread quickly, forcing her to flee the blazing structure with her three children, all barefoot and clad only in thin clothing.

Carrying the infant, the mother began trudging through the deep snow toward the Langdon cabin, pushing the two young children before her. After a short distance, however, Gertrude refused to go any farther, saying she was cold and tired. Removing her skirt and wrapping it around her young daughter, Jacques plunged on with her other two children.

It was 9 a.m. when Langdon heard cries for help. Rushing outside without snowshoes, she plunged through the deep, cold blanket of snow for 600 feet before encountering the now-crawling Jacques and her two children. Langdon took the infant and carried her back to the cabin, followed by Jacques. She then went back out and brought Henry to safety. Langdon built a fire and tended to the three for half an hour, then ventured into the snow again. She covered nearly three-quarters of a mile before she found Gertrude lying in the snow. The slightly built Langdon carried the limp child halfway back to her cabin before she realized Gertrude was dead. Langdon covered the child with her coat and left her in the snow, and after a hard struggle was able to make it home herself.

Though suffering from frostbite and exposure, Jacques, her son, and baby daughter all survived the incident. Langdon also required several days to recover, but otherwise suffered no long-term injuries. FILE NO: 1566

The Commission assigns to each nominated case one of 16 "types," based on the peril faced by the victim. As the table below shows, throughout the Fund's history to date a significant number of the awarded rescues took place in water or in burning buildings and vehicles. Some rescues fit no category, such as those where multiple threats are presented, or those in which the threat is unusual.

Case type:	
Attacking animal	1.7%
Human assault	5.1%
Burning building	11.0%
Burning vehicle	12.7%
Moving vehicle	7.7%
Submerging vehicle	2.2%
Drowning	35.4%
Ice	5.5%
Boat	3.2%
Electrocution	1.5%
Falling	1.1%
Exposure to elements or exertion	0.5%
Object (being struck by)	0.2%
Explosion	1.2%
Confined spaces	9.8%
"Other peril" that fits no other category	1.2%

HEROES—BY THE NUMBERS

Males performed 91 percent of the awarded rescues, females, 9 percent. The youngest rescuer was a seven-year-old girl, and the oldest was an 86-year-old woman.

LOCATIONS

The United States saw 92.4 percent of the awarded rescues, and 8.6 percent were in Canada. The states and provinces with the largest populations tend to be where the most rescues occur: Pennsylvania, 7.9 percent; California, 7.1 percent; New York, 6.6 percent; Ohio, 5.5 percent; Texas, 5 percent. The states where the fewest rescues occurred are District of Columbia and Vermont with 0.2 percent, and Wyoming with 0.3 percent. Canada's Yukon Territory and Nunavut have had 0.03 percent rescues.

Why Do They Do It?

BY SAMUEL P. OLINER
HUMBOLDT STATE UNIVERSITY

VI

ORDINARY PEOPLE,
EXTRAORDINARY ACTS OF COURAGE

We human beings can and often do extend ourselves with unfathomable degrees of caring and compassion. There are many people—ordinary folks, just going about the business of living—who risk their own lives in order to rescue others, often complete strangers, in emergency situations. I distinguish this "heroic altruism" from conventional altruism, and Carnegie heroes, the Victoria Cross or Medal of Honor winners, and rescuers in other settings that involve high risk to one's life fall into the category. Conventional altruism, which involves little or no risk to one's life, includes hospice volunteers and thousands of other volunteers who give of their time without compensation.

Upon conclusion of my interviews with Carnegie heroes, my overall findings were that they were motivated by a variety of different factors. Some expressed having compassion for the victims, many of having a sense of social responsibility toward their fellow human beings. Though all the rescue situations were dangerous, some rescuers felt they could accomplish their mission, while others felt that they could not live with themselves if they walked away from a tragedy. A few did it for religious reasons. As one rescuer said: "I am certain that God wanted me to walk by this river with my girlfriend so that I would see a couple of people drowning."

NORMOCENTRIC BEHAVIOR

Normocentric behavior, or the beliefs and values learned from parents and the community, was by far the most significant motivating factor in driving helping behavior. In 78 percent of the interviews, rescuers mentioned the importance of parental guidance and their internalization of moral norms and values. Many talked about how they had been taught at some point in their lives that people are supposed to care for one another, and they felt that being a helper is intimately connected with their own sense of who they are. This included learned values of caring and social responsibility acquired from the moral community in which they lived, and from their parents during their upbringing. They modeled moral/spiritual values conducive to forming close, caring attachments to other people. Also included in normocentric behavior is guidance by professional codes or norms and a sense of feeling that it was their responsibility to take action.

For example, a 47-year-old male truck driver who rescued a woman from her burning car following an accident stated:

> I kept thinking that the car could blow up at any second [and] she was on fire also. I was raised to help people, and that's the first thing that came to mind.

A 35-year-old construction worker who rescued two children from a burning building further illustrates the influence of parental values on his act.

> It felt like I was trying to walk through black, greasy Jell-O; it was just thick. I couldn't see anything, couldn't feel anything, and my hand landed in what I thought was an air duct … I stuck my foot in that duct so I would know where the window was, used that as my focal point, felt around the room. And I felt one kid's leg and I just grabbed the leg and just chucked him out of the window; didn't wait for anyone to catch him or anything. And I had to leave the ductwork then … crawled around the room … found the second kid, who was unconscious, and I threw him out, and then I dove out the window.

In discussing the importance of his childhood socialization—representative of the type of responses offered by other Carnegie heroes—he commented on the strong sense of duty imparted by his adoptive father, a U.S. Marine, whom he knew only for a few years while still quite young: "I was only five at the time, but he instilled in me a sense of duty and a sense of responsibility to other people. It's just something that was in my heart."

Another Carnegie hero, a 48-year-old frequent surfer and seafarer, told us how he rescued a woman from drowning in the Pacific Ocean:

> The moment I saw her … the first thought was "somebody's in trouble." There's no second thought to it. And then once I got my board and launched, it's kind of like what surfers call "total commitment," you know, total involvement. Once you take off, you paddle into a very large wave, there's no other way around it other than to go straight down and give it your full [commitment]. You can't turn around and back off … . So once I was going in the water there was no sense of my own peril. "I'm going to get her out of here. One way or another … I'm going to do it." And that's all there is to it.

When asked why he did it, he continued:

> It is my knowledge and experience with the ocean. In some ways … it's a bred-in thing because fishermen—that is something about all seafaring people—you see somebody in trouble, you do what you can … . It's kind of that unwritten code.

SOCIAL RESPONSIBILITY

Sixty-six percent of rescuers identified social responsibility as a motivating factor that influenced their decision to help a fellow human being. The stories of the following rescuers provide good examples.

A 49-year-old man risked his life to save a paralyzed woman from being hit by an oncoming train after her wheelchair became stuck in the track. He was heading alongside the track when he noticed the woman attempting to cross while the gates were being lowered for the approaching train. Seeing her shaking the wheelchair and crying out for help, he just stopped his car and jumped out. He saw the train coming; it was about 50 yards away and fast approaching:

> The train was about 20 yards away and I just grabbed her by the collar in the front and pulled her out onto me, and then she kind of fell on top of me because she was paralyzed from the waist down. Then the train was there and hit her wheelchair and drove it into my leg. And what I thought, the train had caught my leg and cut my leg off, but it was the wheelchair just hitting my leg.

When asked why many others might not risk their lives in a similar life-threatening situation, he offered:

> I think there might be some liability they're afraid of; something might happen … . Well, I don't think that's right. I think you have a certain degree of responsibility, if you see something happen like that, to try and offer some kind of help.

In another selfless rescue, a man who attempted several times to save a woman from drowning in a culvert expressed his motivation in terms of an overarching feeling of responsibility for her welfare:

> I just felt like it was my duty as a person … a matter of being a human. You've got to help somebody if they need help, if they are in trouble.

A 41-year-old man who rescued another man from drowning highlighted the responsibility that goes along with being the only person available to help:

> Seeing [him] out there … and there was no one else there. I think in some situations, people … count on the people around them … but, in fact, when I was there, it was either me or nobody.

One man demonstrated the essence of social responsibility when he explained why he saved another man from being electrocuted:

> It's like something in your mind says "Go help" …. It's like another person in me …. You know that that person is going to die or that that person needs help, and you know you've got to help them.

EMPATHY

Empathy is a salient motivating factor centered on the needs of another—on that individual's possible fate. It emerges out of a direct connection with the distressed other, or one's feeling the other's pain and not being able to live with that. Forty-two percent of the Carnegie heroes reported empathy as their motivating factor. We often use empathy interchangeably with compassion, sympathy, and pity—which are its characteristic expressions.

Reactions may be emotional or cognitive; frequently they contain elements of both. The following accounts illustrate both the cognitive and the affective traits (from our hearts *and* our heads). The driver of an 18-wheel truck told us of his very harrowing yet ultimately successful rescue of another driver. His is a story marked by a great sense of empathy for others:

> The other driver went across all three lanes, up on two wheels on one side and then two wheels on the right side, and you could tell he was out of control.... So I told my boss, who was behind about a mile or so, on the radio, I says, "Run back there, Davey, and grab the fire extinguisher." And I said, "I can see the guy hanging upside down inside the van, and it's on fire. Nobody's helping him." I said, "I'm going back, man. I'm going back to help him … ."

Running to the van, it seemed like his legs were not moving fast enough:

> I was running as fast as I possibly could, but it seemed like I was in slow motion, am I gonna make it, can I make it to get to this guy?

Then he noticed that the front of the vehicle had started dripping, melting:

> Now the truck, mind you, was upside down, or up on its side, and that would be onto the right side. That meant that the driver was up in the air in his seat and kind of suspended.... And I really don't know how the harness even works, the safety belt system works on that, but he was doubled over and I remember he had a big gash in his neck and I was concerned about that—bleeding, and he [seemed to be] unconscious … .

Inside, it didn't seem that bad, other than the smoke billowing out the windows and the victim taking fumes in. The van driver put his hand on the rescuer's shoulder and squeezed. And the hero continued:

> He said, "Please don't let me burn alive in here alone. Don't leave me to burn alive in here. I have a family." At that time I saw my whole life as a young man, even through my tour in the service. I saw my family. I could see my parents ... [and] I said, "Listen, if I can't get you out of here, I'm going to sit right

here with you and I'll hold your hand, and we'll go together." …
I didn't want to lose hope, and I guess the old boy upstairs said,
"Hey, there's the button." I hit it and he fell over my shoulder … like a bag of potatoes, perfect…. I said, "just keep your
head down, we're goin' through this thing …" But the second
we got outside, there were all kinds of people just dragging us,
pulling us away from it.

He later went on to describe the motivation for his actions:

We made it. We had just enough time and as far as me doin' it,
I just couldn't see this guy burn alive. I just didn't want to see
him burn up, because he had no reason to die, and I thought,
"Hey, I'm gonna mess somebody's plans up. You're not getting
him today. You get him, you get me. You're gonna take us both."
But I'll never forget him putting his hand on my shoulder and
when I looked at him and I could see blood on his face and
I could see tears when I said, "I won't leave you. I'll sit here with
you." I wasn't sure if he was going to let me go or not. I knew
I could get away from him and save my own self, but at that time
I just said, "Hey, you know what? You've got to die [eventually].
If it's a cause, it might as well be a damned good cause." And it
was a good call, I think, trying to help this man out…. What an
amazing man.

EFFICACY

Efficacy, which some scholars view as related to self-esteem, is
the sense that one has the power to produce effects or achieve
intended results. Throughout my research, I discerned the importance of efficacy and courage, and at 38.8 percent it was the next
most common motivational factor for Carnegie heroes. Many
times this sense of confidence was the result of prior life experiences or training, which is why it is so important to impart this to
our children and to remember it ourselves.

A belief in his abilities coupled with a strong sense of self-
reliance caused a 43-year-old Carnegie hero to crawl into a burning
house to rescue an elderly woman. When asked why he thought
some people help in these situations and others don't, he replied:

I probably thought I could do something, I thought I could
physically go in there and get her. Had I been on crutches or disabled, I probably wouldn't have even considered it. But me, the

age I was, I probably thought I could do something, I guess. Some people wouldn't dream, the house is on fire, and a common term that always bugs me is "let the authorities do it." Like, oh, that is what the fire department is for. But you know … I look at it as we have to take care of ourselves … that is my theory on this fire department stuff. I mean the fire department is going to come, but if you can pull someone out of a car or help stabilize the situation or something … people have to help each other.

INSTINCTIVE

We found that an immediate *impulsive* or instinctive response was the motivating factor over 27 percent of the time in our interviews with the heroes. Frank Farley, an educational psychologist at Temple University who has been studying heroes for the past 15 years, stated that the actions of situational heroes are frequently impulsive and that oftentimes people just act before they think.[1] Correspondingly, some of the rescuers we spoke to could not find a reason for their behavior other than stating that they just reacted to the situation without thinking.

For example, a 34-year-old woman wrestled to the ground a prisoner who was going to shoot a police officer. While the hero was standing just outside of a hospital emergency room, a female officer was escorting a prisoner out, and the restraint on the prisoner, also a female, slipped below her hip. When the officer went to pull it up, the prisoner tried to run, and as the officer tried to grab her, the prisoner hit the officer in the chest and knocked her backward and came down on top of her. The officer hit her head on the pavement. The rescuer explained further:

> I could hear her hit, and so I was just going to pull the girl off the officer, and when I got over there and started pulling on the girl, the officer starts yelling, "My gun! My gun!"… so, I am just trying to reach down there and trying to find the gun, and the girl already had it out of the holster … . So then I still couldn't feel the gun, and I am thinking, "Oh my God, she is going to blow my head off … ." Then somehow I had grabbed her wrist, and the gun sort of pointed away from us because I was still trying to bring her hand out and away from the officer so she wouldn't shoot the officer, and she fired a shot [which did not hit any of us]. Then she pointed the gun at me and ran … . I was running, but the officer's eyes caught mine and … I couldn't leave her. It

was like her eyes were screaming for help. So then I ran back
and jumped on the girl again and knocked the gun loose … and
I was able to get the gun, and the officer was able to get up to
her radio and [several officers responded].

When asked why she did what she did and why she
didn't run when she had the opportunity to, she explained it as
a "natural instinct. I knew she was going to shoot the officer.
I couldn't let this happen."

Explaining his rescue of a woman being attacked by an
assailant with a knife, one of the heroes attributed his actions to a
gut reaction:

When I did get involved, I mean, it was just a reaction. I can't
explain it, it was just response.

A 48-year-old mechanic rescued a four-year-old boy from
a burning trailer. While others looked on, this rescuer responded,
without thought to his safety, to a mother's shrieks that her babies
were inside. He smashed the door open and rushed into the
smoke and flames. Three children were in the trailer, and he was
able to pull only one of them out before the roof collapsed, killing
the other two. He said he acted on impulse alone:

I had to go in there and get them, or at least try to … . I didn't
even think about it. That's all … it was just a natural reaction.
I guess I would have done it for anyone if I saw somebody in
trouble like that.

RELIGIOUS AND SPIRITUAL BELIEFS

Over 16 percent of rescuers talked about the importance of
religion and spirituality and the belief in a divine as the source of
motivation for their compassionate acts. Some said that God told
them what they needed to do, and a few said that God or another
higher power completely took over their bodies and they essentially had no control in the matter.[2]

A 29-year-old man was driving down the street when he
saw a house on fire. He grabbed a blanket from his van and tried
first to go in through the garage, and then through the front door,
but in both places there was too much flame. He jumped a fence to
the backyard. The patio door was locked, so he grabbed the first

thing he saw—a barbecue grill. Swinging it by the legs, he broke the sliding glass door and told the people to get out. But they couldn't:

> I don't know where I got the strength from, but I did thank God that he gave me strength and the wisdom and the courage to go in there in the first place. And he gave me the wisdom to think and the strength and courage to lead them to safety … . I was going to go back into the house, but (moments later) it collapsed.

RECIPROCITY

Rescuers, like other people, have multiple values that overlap, such as caring and empathy, and any one of them might assume supremacy at any given moment. For some Carnegie heroes, norms and expectations dictate that they help others because they expect others to reciprocate when they are in need. Approximately 10 percent of those interviewed gave the reason for rescue as reciprocity.

A 21-year-old male student who rescued another man from a fiery automobile following a crash related this story: He and a friend were just about to cross the street when they heard the noise of an accelerating car approaching from down the road. The car soon slammed into the back of a car that had stopped and was waiting for the two men to cross the street. The car that was rear-ended spun around into the opposite traffic lane and left in its wake a gas trail twenty feet long. The gas ignited and the rescuer's friend froze, and then urged the rescuer away from the scene:

> I just kept thinking, What if it was me? What if I got smashed? And if nobody helped me I would just sit there and burn. I just hope and pray that if that ever happened to me, somebody would do the same thing for me.

The interviews revealed that all heroes had either a high or a moderate sense of self-esteem, social responsibility, and locus of control, the feeling that they are in charge of their lives and of the situation before them. We observed also that younger respondents and males were more likely to score as high-sensation seekers, people who may be motivated because the event is risky. Last, we noted that the majority of Carnegie heroes held either a high or a moderate sense of commonality with diverse others, meaning that they have much in common with all humankind.

Most rescuers reported that, although others stood by and did not get involved, a few onlookers did get involved later on in the sequence of rescue. A large percentage of rescuers are male, which can be explained in terms of cultural norms; even though women may be present when a tragic situation occurs, men are "expected" to get involved in rescue. However, when women are on the scene without males, they will act heroically to save lives.

Further, our interviews with the Carnegie heroes corroborate that these people are not "larger-than-life" individuals; rather, they are ordinary people who, through their socialization, have internalized a sense of responsibility and empathy for their fellow human beings. They have acquired caring norms in their lives and developed the skills that both prompt and enable them to respond in emergency situations. Their sense of self and the moral values they have acquired would not let them be bystanders. Each of us needs to learn more about compassion and caring ourselves and to teach these values to our youth.

Every person has the potential to be a rescuer, but the transformation is not one that occurs overnight. Parents and institutions have to take part in teaching and empowering the young to care. It is through a continual process of learning and practicing caring norms—internalizing the skills and values that we identified as the salient motivational factors of Carnegie Medal recipients—that one is able to respond heroically in emergency situations. It is also through this internalization that each of us has the potential for breaking through the bystander role and developing ourselves into compassionate people who help those in need.

EUROPEAN HERO FUNDS

On September 21, 1908, just over four years after the establishment of the Pittsburgh-based Hero Fund, Andrew Carnegie expanded the concept to his native land with the establishment of the Carnegie Hero Fund Trust in Dunfermline, Scotland. Carnegie's intention to export his model of honoring civilian heroes to foreign countries was revealed in a letter to Charles Taylor, first president of the Hero Fund.

"I got the idea this morning in bed listening to the organ. Why not extend Hero Fund to my Native Land Britain & Ireland. Make the Dunfermline Trust take charge of it." In a postscript he wrote, "Im [sic] very happy over this revelation this morning."

In the three years following, he established additional hero funds in France, Germany, Norway, Netherlands, Switzerland, Belgium, Italy, Sweden, and Denmark.

UNITED KINGDOM

Founded in 1908, the United Kingdom Carnegie Hero Fund Trust recognizes voluntary acts of heroism that have resulted in injury or death to the rescuer. The act must have been performed in the United Kingdom, Ireland, the Channel Islands, or the surrounding territorial waters. Those selected for recognition receive a framed certificate and citation, and their names are inscribed in the Hero Fund Roll of Honour, which is unique to the United Kingdom fund and kept in the Andrew Carnegie Birthplace Museum in Dunfermline.

The Fund also provides financial assistance, if necessary, to heroes or to the families of those who have been killed carrying out the heroic act.

FRANCE

FONDATION CARNEGIE
FRANCE

In a letter dated February 9, 1909, Carnegie offered France the gift of an initial investment of $1 million, which was intended to honor and reward those who perform acts of civilian courage, and to aid the widows and orphans of rescuers who die. French President Armand Fallières accepted the gift on July 23, 1909, and the Fondation Carnegie was established.

Medals of bronze, silver, and vermeil, as well as certificates, were awarded to those who deliberately risked their lives to save human life, and cash grants often accompanied the award. During its century of existence, the foundation made more than 12,000 awards.

The dissolution of the foundation was approved by a decree of the Ministry of the Interior on April 19, 2011, and records of its awardees are now maintained by the National Archives of France. The remaining funds of the foundation were transferred to the Franco-American Commission for Educational Exchange, Paris. The commission, which administers the Fulbright program between France and the United States, has initiated a Fulbright grant named for Andrew Carnegie and sponsors projects linking schools in both countries.

GERMANY

Founded in late 1910 after Andrew Carnegie presented his intention to Kaiser Wilhelm II. The Kaiser acclaimed the proposal as a "noble idea" and by the end of the year gave permission for the start of the Carnegie Stiftung für Lebensretter. Its first meeting was held January 20, 1911, and the fund operated until the takeover by the Nazi regime in 1934.

No activity was recorded until 2005, when a private German citizen took it upon himself to resurrect the organization. On April 15, 2006, the first meeting of the re-formed Stiftung für Lebensretter was held, but the effort was short-lived.

Established on March 21, 1911, the Carnegie Heltefond for Norge grants awards to people who, on Norwegian territory, perform voluntary acts of civilian courage to save the lives of others "in peaceful pursuit and surroundings." For a heroic act to be recognized, it must involve risk to the rescuer's life.

A board of three members who are appointed by the Ministry of Industry and Commerce governs the fund. In addition to the chair, members are the United States Ambassador to Norway and a Norwegian citizen. Financed by interest income, the fund awards bronze, silver, and gold medals, financial grants, and diplomas to those honored for their bravery. Awards are decided by judgment of the board, with reference, if possible, to reports and comments from the local police superintendent.

THE CARNEGIE
HELTEFOND
FOR NORGE
NORWAY

THE NETHERLANDS

In a letter dated March 23, 1911, to the Minister of Foreign Affairs, Carnegie expressed his pleasure that The Netherlands had agreed to establish the Stichting Carnegie Heldenfonds. He endowed the fund with a gift of $200,000, saying that he felt the amount would "meet the cost of maintaining injured heroes and their families during disability of the heroes, and the widows and children of heroes who may lose their lives . . ." The Heldenfonds awards silver and bronze medals, together with a certificate.

STICHTING CARNEGIE
HELDENFONDS
THE NETHERLANDS

SWITZERLAND

Established on April 28, 1911, shortly after the Federal Council accepted Carnegie's gift of $130,000, the Carnegie Rescuers Foundation grants awards to people who, on Swiss territory, risk their lives in peaceful endeavors to save the lives of their fellows. For an act of heroism to be recognized, the rescuer must have exposed his life or health to a real danger. Persons recognized by the Foundation receive a certificate; engraved bronze, silver, and gold medals are also awarded, as are wristwatches and monetary grants to the rescuers and their families. Young people receive a voucher for a hot-air balloon ride or a helicopter flight.

Since the establishment of the Foundation, over 8,300 people have been recognized, and more than three million Swiss

THE CARNEGIE RESCUERS
FOUNDATION
SWITZERLAND

francs in subsidies have been paid to rescuers and their families. Awards and monetary grants are announced annually.

On April 17, 1911, Carnegie informed the Belgian government of his donation of $230,000 in government bonds, the interest of which was to be used to support heroes of peace and the families of those who lost their lives as victims of their helpfulness. The Carnegie Hero Fund was adopted by royal decree on July 13, 1911.

The fund awards individuals who expose their lives to serious and threatening danger for the purpose of saving the life of another human being. An extraordinary degree of selflessness, the seriousness of the danger, and the exceptional circumstances in which the acts of heroism take place are considered. Awards

CARNEGIE HERO FUND
BELGIUM

include a medal of bronze, silver, or gold, and a diploma, and in some cases, just a diploma. Financial support is also granted to relieve the material needs of destitute families, and to help finance the studies of the heroes' children. The fund recognizes about 50 cases a year.

ITALY

In a letter dated June 17, 1911, Carnegie expressed his satisfaction that the Italian government had accepted his offer of $750,000 to establish the Fondazione Carnegie Per Gli Atti De Eroismo in Italy to undertake work similar to that of the hero fund in the United States. The fund was recognized under Italian law on September 25, 1911. In addition to awarding gold, silver, and bronze medals to heroes and heroines, the fund also makes monetary grants in exceptional cases. In recent years, the number of awards has averaged about 30 a year.

THE FONDAZIONE CARNEGIE
PER GLI ATTI DE EROISMO
ITALY

SWEDEN

The Carnegiestiftelsen was established on October 6, 1911, in response to a letter Andrew Carnegie had written to the King of Sweden at the beginning of that year offering $230,000 for a hero fund. The fund awards individuals who voluntarily, or otherwise beyond what may be deemed to be their duty, have, by some gallant action in the peaceful walks of life, risked their lives in order to save human lives in the territory of Sweden and on Swedish ships.

THE CARNEGIESTIFTELSEN
SWEDEN

For many years, the fund offered money to those who had suffered when saving or trying to save lives, and also to the families of heroes when there was a need. Currently, the social insurance system in Sweden normally helps in such situations, and, according to the statutes of the fund, it cannot offer money if the social authorities are obliged to help. Today, the award consists of a gold watch, a diploma, and a monetary grant.

DENMARK

Carnegie initiated the establishment of this fund on December 30, 1911, in a letter from him to King Frederik VIII. Royal Assent by the King affirmed the Carnegies Belønningsfond for Heltemod, endowed with $125,000 on February 24, 1912. It recognizes

CARNEGIES
BELØNNINGSFOND
FOR HELTEMOD
DENMARK

outstanding acts of selfless heroism performed in Denmark, Greenland, and the Faroe Islands, or in their territorial waters.

The award consists of a diploma and 10,000 Danish crowns, or more in special cases. In cases where the rescuers lose their lives, the fund may grant financial assistance to the surviving dependents. A medal may also be awarded in recognition of certain heroic acts. Awards are announced once a year, in December. For the past several years, the number of awards made annually has ranged from 15 to 30.

NOTES

THE DAY THE VALLEY WEPT

1 Pamphlet written shortly after the disaster to raise funds for the families of the deceased miners, whereabouts unknown.

2 F. W. Cunningham, Fourth Report of the Department of Mines of Pennsylvania, Part II "Bituminous," 1904 (Harrisburg PA: Harrisburg Publishing Co., State Printers 1905), 663.

3 H. M. Bitner, "Night of Terror at Mine," *The Pittsburg Press*, January 26, 1904, 2.

4 "Miners Entombed," *The New York Times*, January 26, 1904, 1.

5 Carnegie Hero Fund Commission Website (http://www.carnegiehero.org/history.shtml).

6 Correspondence from the Andrew Carnegie Relief Fund to George A. Bigley, chairman, Cheswick Relief Committee, February 9, 1904. Carnegie Hero Fund Commission Archives.

ANDREW CARNEGIE

1 W. J. Holland, *Twenty-five Years of the Carnegie Hero Fund Commission, 1904–1929* (Pittsburgh: Carnegie Hero Fund Commission), 7.

2 Andrew Carnegie, *Autobiography of Andrew Carnegie* (Boston: Houghton Mifflin Company, 1920), 263.

3 Letter from Andrew Carnegie to Frank M. Wilmot, November 11, 1913. Carnegie Hero Fund Commission Archives. Translation from the Online Scots Dictionary.

4 Carnegie. Andrew Carnegie came across this proverb in the newspaper the *Scottish American*, 258–259.

5 Ibid., 7.

6 Ibid., 18.

7 Ibid., 6.

8 Ibid., 24.

9 Kathlann M. Kowalski, "An Empire of Steel," *Cobblestone* (April 1999), 14.

10 Joseph Frazier Wall, *Andrew Carnegie* (New York: Oxford University Press, 1970), 224–225.

11 Burton J. Hendrick, *The Life of Andrew Carnegie* (Garden City: Doubleday, Doran & Co., Inc., 1932), 49.

12 Wall, 1034.

13 Carnegie, 3.

14 Ibid., 232.

15 Ibid., 101–102.

16 *Annual Report* 1987, Carnegie Hero Fund Trust, Abbey Park House, Dunfermline, 8.

17 "Steel King Steps Aside; 5,000,000 For Mill Men," *Pittsburgh Commercial Gazette*, 1.

18 Andrew Carnegie, *The Gospel of Wealth and Other Timely Essays* (Garden City, Doubleday, Doran & Company, Inc., 1933), 17. First printed in the *North American Review*, June and December, 1889.

19 Holland, 5.

20 "Steel King Steps Aside," 1.

21 Hendrick, 255.

22 Thomas S. Arbuthnot, *Heroes of Peace* (Pittsburgh: Carnegie Hero Fund Commission, 1935), 33.

23 Letter from Andrew Carnegie, undated. Carnegie Hero Fund Commission Archives.

24 Letter from Andrew Carnegie to Frank M. Wilmot, May 13, 1912. Carnegie Hero Fund Commission Archives.

25 Letter from Andrew Carnegie to Charles L. Taylor, June 4, 1904. Carnegie Hero Fund Commission Archives.

26 Hendrick, 350–351.

27 Wall, 894.

28 Ibid., 896.

29 Ibid., 713.

30 Ibid., 796.

THREAD FOR A WEB

1 Joseph Frazier Wall, *Andrew Carnegie* (Pittsburgh: University of Pittsburgh Press, 1989), 792.

2 In 1911, the Carnegie Relief Fund would merge into and become the nucleus of the U.S. Steel and Carnegie Pension Fund.

3 Andrew Carnegie, *Autobiography of Andrew Carnegie* (Boston: Houghton-Mifflin Company, 1920), 256–257.

4 Ibid., 266–267.

5 Andrew Carnegie, "Wealth," *The North American Review*, CXLVIII, 391 (June 1889), 662.

6 Ibid.

7 John D. Rockefeller (1839–1937), Carnegie's philanthropic "rival," gave away $540 million during his lifetime. Rockefeller Archive Center (http://www.rockefeller.edu/archive/). Several historians of philanthropy refer to the early 20th century development of "scientific giving." One important example is Judith Sealander, "Curing Evils at Their Source: The Arrival of Scientific Giving," in Lawrence J. Friedman and Mark D. McGarvie, eds., *Charity, Philanthropy, and Civility in American History* (Cambridge, UK: Cambridge University Press, 2002), 217–239.

8 John W. Jordan, editor-in-chief, *Genealogical and Personal History of Western Pennsylvania* (New York: 1915), 31.

9 In 1968, the Carnegie mansion became the Cooper-Hewitt, National Design Museum, Smithsonian Institution. The gift shop is located in Carnegie's study, where visitors can still read the original painted quotations.

10 Hartley M. Phelps, "Making Heroism Profitable," *World To-Day* (March 1910, 18), 261.

11 Frederick Lynch, DD, *Personal Recollections of Andrew Carnegie* (New York: Fleming H. Revell Company, 1920), 144. Accessed through University of Virginia Electronic Text Center.

12 Ibid.

13 John N. Ingham, "Reaching for Respectability: The Pittsburgh Elite at the Turn of the Century," in Gabriel P. Weisberg, DeCourcy E. McIntosh, Alison McQueen, eds., *Collecting in the Gilded Age: Art Patronage in Pittsburgh, 1890–1910* (Hanover: University Press of New England), 48.

14 Herbert Newton Casson, *The Romance of Steel: The Story of a Thousand Millionaires* (New York: Barnes, 1907), viii.

15 Thomas S. Arbuthnot, *Heroes of Peace* (Pittsburgh: Carnegie Hero Fund Commission, 1935), 37.

16 Carnegie, Autobiography, 267.

17 http://www.carnegieinternational.org.

18 Reed information: Mary Brignano and J. Tomlinson Fort, *Reed Smith: A Law Firm Celebrates 125 Years* (Pittsburgh, 2002).

19 Porter information: National Model Railroad Association (http://www.nmra.org/library/Porterbook.html); *Biographical Directory of the United States Congress*, 1774–Present (http://bioguide.congress.gov/scripts/biodisplay.pl?index=P000441); and Weisberg, McIntosh, McQueen, 83.

20 William Bender Wilson, *Robert Pitcairn 1836–1909: In Memoriam* (Pittsburgh, 1913), 15.

21 J. B. Calvert, "Notes on Pennsylvania Railroad Operation and Signaling" (www.du.edu/~jcalvert/railway/prr/prrsig.htm).

22 Wilson, 26.

23 Tom Rea, "William J. Holland: The Man Who Brought Dinosaurs to Pittsburgh." *Western Pennsylvania History* (Winter 2001–02, 84, 4), 28.

24 *Pittsburgh Post-Gazette* (December 14, 1932).

25 William G. Lytle, Jr., "Dr. William J. Holland, 'Young Over 70,' Looks Forward to Many Projects," *The Pittsburgh Press* (December 1, 1931).

26 Robert C. Alberts, *Pitt: The Story of the University of Pittsburgh, 1787–1987* (Pittsburgh: University of Pittsburgh Press, 1987).

27 Anderson information: Phyllis Dain in Bohdan S. Wynar, ed., *Dictionary of American Library Biography* (Littleton, CO: Libraries Unlimited, 1978), 7–11.

28 Blackburn information: *The Book of Prominent Pennsylvanians: A Standard Reference* (Pittsburgh: Leader Publishing Co., 1913), 111; *The Carnegie Magazine* (January 1932).

29 Letter from Andrew Carnegie to Charles L. Taylor, March 12, 1904.

30 *The National Cyclopedia of American Biography*, 16 (New York: James T. White & Co., 1918), 88.

31 *The National Cyclopedia of American Biography*, 20 (New York: James T. White & Co., 1929), 96–97.

32 *Pittsburgh Gazette Times* (December 7, 1916).

33 *The National Cyclopedia of American Biography*, 33 (New York: James T. White & Co., 1929), 500–501.

34 Jackson information: George Thornton Fleming, *History of Pittsburgh and Environs, from Prehistoric Days to the Beginning of the American Revolution*, 5 (New York, Chicago: The American Historical Society, Inc., 1922), 175–178; *The National Cyclopedia of American Biography*, 16, 128.

35 Scott information: *Biographical Review, Containing Life Sketches of Leading Citizens of Pittsburg [sic] and the Vicinity, Pennsylvania*, 24 (Boston: Biographical Review Publishing Co., 1897), 395; Fleming, 306; Frank C. Harper, *Pittsburgh of Today, Its Resources and People*, 2 (New York: The American Historical Society, Inc., 1931-1932), 853.

36 H. K. Webster, "Just Heroes: How the Carnegie Hero Fund Works in Practice—The Heroes

It has Rewarded—What It Means to be a Hero,"
American Illustrated Magazine LX, 5
(September 1905), 570.

37 Ibid.

38 Letter from Andrew Carnegie to Frank M.
Wilmot, April 3, 1904. Carnegie Hero Fund
Commission Archives.

39 "Certified Heroes," *The Independent*, 70
(May 11, 1911), 969.

40 Webster, 570.

41 Letter from Andrew Carnegie to Charles L.
Taylor, June 4, 1904. Carnegie Hero Fund
Commission Archives.

42 Webster, 571–572.

43 "The Roll of Heroes," *The Outlook*, 105
(November 1913), 565.

44 Cynthia Crossen, "Distinguishing a Hero from
the Merely Brave," *The Wall Street Journal*,
June 17, 1996, B8.

THE HERO HUNTERS

1 Thomas S. Arbuthnot, *Heroes of Peace*
(Pittsburgh: Carnegie Hero Fund Commission,
1935), 37.

2 Hartley M. Phelps, "Making Heroism Profitable,"
World Today, 18 (March 1910), 262.

3 Lewis Edwin Theiss, "The Sleuth and the Hero,"
Harper's Weekly, 56 (June 8, 1912), 9.

4 Theiss, 9.

5 *2307 Quarterly* (October–December, 1960).

WHY DO THEY DO IT?

1 Bob Calandra, 1999. "Why they do it." in
R. Jerome, S. Schindehette, N. Charles, and
T. Fields-Meyer, "Heroes Among Us," *People
Weekly* (November 22, 1999), 141.

2 Ibid., 141.

ACKNOWLEDGMENTS

This book is for the Carnegie heroes.

We are deeply grateful for all of them, and their loved ones, who provided information, photographs, memories, and insight.

A special thanks as well goes to the Commission board and staff, past and present, especially the late Doug Chambers, whose vision and effort gave us a wonderful centennial volume, *A Century of Heroes*, to honor and update, and Walter Rutkowski, for his significant contributions to the 2004 volume. We are grateful to Abby Brady, Elijah Lambiotte, and Colin Cavada for their contributions to this edition.

Great credit for this new compilation goes to Jewels Phraner, the Commission's Communications Director, who carried the bulk of the load in gathering and presenting new material and was the chief writer of new material.

Thanks goes to the talented Bill Garrison for generously contributing original material for this book in honor of heroes.

Continued and renewed thanks to original contributors to the centennial piece whose work is reprinted here: Mary Brignano, Carol Bleier, and Samuel P. Oliner.

And finally, a special thanks to Mark Laskow, for his long leadership and priceless insights on his 20-plus years leading the Carnegie Hero Fund Commission, and for his mentorship and friendship, equally.

Eric P. Zahren, President and Chair, Carnegie Hero Fund Commission
Editor